## Praise for *Dancing with the Dragon*

"With almost three decades of on-the-ground experience investing in China's energy sector, Patrick Jenevein provides an unvarnished, firsthand account of both the promise and pitfalls of doing business in China. He recounts his journey and his interactions with officials and business leaders with a sense of adventure, optimism, and humor. Yet ultimately, his engagement with China ends with corruption and betrayal, featuring secretly taped recordings and dramatic courtroom battles. The result is a 'much needed' and uniquely nuanced portrayal of what it means to dance with the dragon."

**— Elizabeth C. Economy, Senior Advisor (for China) to the Secretary of Commerce, and bestselling author of *The World According to China*, among others**

"In *Dancing with the Dragon*, Patrick Jenevein and Steve Fiffer present Jenevein's harrowing David v. Goliath story of partnering with then battling the Chinese state's behemoth defense contractor with equanimity and determination. Helpful to leaders around the world, the authors go on to express provocative but insightful suggestions on addressing a broad range of challenges that emanate from the Communist Party of China and doing business in China. Simply: *caveat emptor*."

**— Kenneth A. Hersh, President and CEO, George W. Bush Presidential Center and co-founder and former CEO, NGP Energy Capital Management**

"Patrick Jenevein has a story to tell. Quite a story. And he tells it in an appealing, conversational style facilitated by his excellent collaborator, Steve Fiffer. Much like a television documentary, Patrick and Steve adopt a question-and-answer interview format that works perfectly, drawing the reader into the web of manipulation, deceit, and commercial exploitation orchestrated by the Communist Party of China. Like a business version of a whodunit, Patrick's narrative will shock the average reader with its exposé of the hardball tactics his Chinese 'partners' used to undercut his budding enterprise and appropriate his company's employees, projects, and opportunities. As the *Wall Street Journal* observed, the 'legal record should serve as a warning to any American considering business with ... Chinese state-owned enterprises.'"

**— Robert W. Jordan Ambassador (Ret.), and author (with Steve Fiffer) of *Desert Diplomat: Inside Saudi Arabia Following 9/11***

"Jenevein's story reads like a thriller. Knowing he made it through the journey and prevailed, his takeaways from brawling with the Communist Party add perspectives that can and should help any US administration stand up to China."

**— Dr. Rob Spalding, Brig Gen, USAF (Ret), CEO of SEMPRE, and bestselling author of *War Without Rules: China's Playbook for Global Domination* and *Stealth War: How China Took Over While America's Elite Slept***

"In *Dancing with the Dragon*, Patrick Jenevein delivers a master class in how to use customized intelligence and the rule of law to thwart the malevolent intentions of a major PRC state-owned enterprise. This book should be required reading for business and government leaders grappling with the challenges posed by the Communist Party of China. The Communists messed with the wrong Texan!"

**— Jay T. Young, CAPT (Ret.), USNR, Intelligence, President, Dallas Committee on Foreign Relations**

# DANCING WITH THE DRAGON

## Cautionary Tales of the New China from an Old China Hand

**Patrick Jenevein**
**in conversation with Steve Fiffer**

CHRISTMAS LAKE PRESS

Published by Christmas Lake Press 2024
www.christmaslakecreative.com

ISBN 978-1-960865-22-9



Interior layout by Daiana Marchesi
Map of China by Cacahuate, amendments by Peter Fitzgerald and ClausHansen,
https://commons.wikimedia.org/wiki/File:Map_of_China_%28en%29.png

# DANCING WITH THE DRAGON

Doug Dyer, Thanks for picking up this book!

Patrick [illegible]

For victims of fear, injustice, and oppression

There is a tide in the affairs of men
Which, taken at the flood, leads on to fortune;
Omitted, all the voyage of their life
Is bound in shallows and miseries.

—WILLIAM SHAKESPEARE, *JULIUS CAESAR*

"Now look, your grace," said Sancho, "what you see over there aren't giants, but windmills, and what seem to be arms are just their sails, that go around in the wind and turn the millstone."

"Obviously," replied Don Quijote, "you don't know much about adventures."

—MIGUEL DE CERVANTES, *DON QUIJOTE* (TRANS. BURTON RAFFEL)

# Contents

# Foreword

Whether you are a businessperson, a policymaker, or a layperson interested in learning more about China, by picking up this book you have afforded yourself the unique opportunity to eavesdrop on a fascinating conversation about one brave American's interaction with the Red Dragon.

Americans are grateful for the risks and sacrifices freely given by their military brethren, who never know when their country will call upon them to serve in combat. But less visible to the public are those American citizens who engage in overseas commerce—and live with concern, exposure, and personal risk on a different kind of battlefield. *Their* engagement in principled free enterprise can contribute to greater prosperity as well as advance the interests of American core values to the benefit of free people everywhere. In many instances, such men and women are our 'commercial' ambassadors who contribute to an international framework intended to promote access to open markets, free trade, and economic stability, inspired by the 'rules-based system' as we know it, one that fashioned an engine for development, lifted generations out of poverty, and powered a dedicated focus on the improvement of the human condition. Hard bargaining on level playing fields with true commercial counterparts is how free markets should work inside this system. But when sovereign governments slip into the fray in the guise of commercial enterprises, the 'game,' 'the organizing principles of the system,' and the proverbial 'goal post,' all change. American businessmen and women are then playing on decidedly unlevel fields—and do so at commercial and personal peril. US businessmen and women can become targets for other countries' intelligence and security services. Occasionally, the consequences rise to the national level.

To survive (much less thrive) in this commercial 'combat' with foreign sovereign commercial entities, American business adventurers must use not only the traditional tools of business, but also an appreciation that their counterparties are more than just business adversaries. These valiant merchants must learn to navigate complex environments and crosscurrents of laws, cultures, personalities, and politics. Misappreciation of these elements, or missteps, or malign acts by the adversaries can wipe out the accomplishments of years of work, sometimes with a single change in foreign leadership.

The People's Republic of China offers opportunities that attract both bold entrepreneurs willing to stake their futures on their hard work and global industries seeking economies of scale for production processes.

In *Dancing with the Dragon*, Steve Fiffer teases out Patrick Jenevein's story of ambitious but disciplined efforts to build not one but two "unicorn" companies, each worth more than a billion dollars, only to lose both to the exercise of sovereign greed and flexing of sovereign might.

But the story tells much more than just that. Jenevein uses the twists and turns of his encounters with Chinese leaders to reveal lessons learned and articulate approaches that work to constrain bad faith behavior directed by the Communist Party of China.

— William J. Haynes II, General Counsel of the Department of Defense (2001-2008) and Admiral (Ret.) Patrick M. Walsh, Commander, US Pacific Fleet (2009-2012), Vice Chief of Naval Operations (2007-2009)

## Author's Note

"It's all AVIC," said the President and CEO of one of AVIC's subsidiaries, Ascendent Renewable Energy.

In this book, you will read about AVIC, AVIC HQ, AVIC IHC, AVIC IRE, CAIGA, CATIC, CATG, and other subsidiaries with reformulations of AVIC's name. Your authors do not aim to confuse. The American Arbitration Association addressed the alphabet soup, finding that the "evidence overwhelmingly shows that AVIC HQ, AVIC International, AVIC IRE, AVIC TED, and Ascendant operated as one entity..."

For people in China, the names and their variants have a rationale. "AVIC" stands for the Aviation Industry Corporation of China. The "CA" in other names stands for "China Aviation." When you read AVIC or CA, think Aviation of China or China Aviation. For Chinese, the rest of the name of an AVIC subordinate, by including the name of a municipality, province, or the nation, reflects that company's proximity to the apex of AVIC's power and headquarters in Beijing. The closer to Beijing, the more significant the subsidiary.

The Communist Party of China applies names in English to achieve its objectives. Clarity for foreigners ranks low among its priorities. Upon achieving objectives, or finding that names impede serving its needs, the CPC may rename or reconstitute an entity.

In our use of names, we abbreviate the Communist Party of China to "CPC." Many in the United States and elsewhere use CCP. Litigation against AVIC, among other lessons, teaches the value of identifying legal persons accurately. It's also easy to use the more correct "CPC" abbreviation. For more reasoning on this decision, please see Pointe Bello | Insights | To

Effectively Meet Challenges the PRC Ruling Party Poses, Learn and Use its True Name. (https://www.pointebello.com/insights/prc-ruling-partys-true-name)

Finally, many of the events and conversations described in the book took place a number of years ago. We've tried our best to relay events accurately in all respects. The CPC's own comprehensive files may hold documents that, if shared, may improve the precision of memories. In a few instances we've changed the names of certain parties.

## Acknowledgments

Yih-Min Jan initiated a venture and stuck with what became our great adventure. His balance of brilliance, shrewdness, compassion, and grace helped us make better decisions, chalk wins over the long haul, and finish with triumph.

Tony Stewart, Jim O'Bannon, Kathleen McLaurin, all from the law firm Jones Day (Nights, Weekends & Holidays), energetically, intelligently, and devotedly supported and guided our corporate efforts.

Lew LeClair for providing truly strategic thinking, planning, and following through with tactical maneuvering to establish jurisdiction and arbitrability over China's biggest defense contractor and, ultimately, corner the communist-controlled company in a California bankruptcy court; Jim Moseley for finding critical, precedential cases that nailed AVIC in Beijing for its subordinates' activities in the United States.

Scores of people—associates and friends—in the PRC whom I honor best by not mentioning their names. The political party that may make or take their livelihoods or may simply crush their lives ironically raises them up as real heroes. The Communist Party would not like my suggestions for its "Chinese Heroes Wall," because these heroes would be on it.

Scores of friends in the United States, especially in Texas, and even more particularly from our parish. Over the decades of dancing with the dragon, they ensured my crossing to safety thus far. If I could get back to them, they would make me safe. Many of them pushed me to write this book with Steve.

In addition to their myriad other roles, two authors, Bob Jordan, former US Ambassador to Saudi Arabia, and Rob Spalding, retired US Air Force Brigadier General. Ambassador Jordan, in his powerfully effective intellectual and diplomatic cadence, articulated compelling reasons for me to take up the pen—a polite way to say he gave me a strong, swift kick in the britches to get writing. General Spalding, with matched acuity and forcefulness, a wing commander's earned confidence, and a Joint Chiefs China strategist's awareness, quickly delivered the second boot.

And Steve Fiffer. The letter to Chairman Lin Zuoming at AVIC shows you what kind of writing I can do. Whatever you think of the letter, I could not have gotten any book out without Steve's framing, writing, nudging, and driving me to write, too. He made hard work delightfully fun. It still tickles me that Gale Sayers trained with Steve years ago. It tickles me more to think if I ever eat cicadas again, Steve and I will do so together.

Sally Shiels Schupp for creating the pleasingly simple yet provocatively stunning art for the book cover. Notice the dragon's toes. Only imperial dragons had five toes; lesser dragons had fewer. Sally distilled decades of discernment into a bold and beautiful visual condensation of the experiences inside the book.

Cindy Birne of Cindy Birne Public Relations for bringing energy, experience, fun, and style to the ins and outs of getting a book before readers' eyes or listeners' ears.

Christmas Lake Press, led by Thomas Fiffer (Steve's brother!), published *Dancing with the Dragon.* It pleases me deeply that Tom's team literally spans the globe. As the Communist Party of China would dictate constrictions on people around the world, internationally coordinating squads can stop it. Working from Connecticut and with brutality of kindness, Erika Rundle served as copyeditor. Her incisive criticisms showed profound respect for our time and raised the quality of our collaboration. Yes, she caught and corrected typos; more importantly, she pressed for clarity where I had internalized it. She propelled that clarity onto the page.

Though I did not get to work with her directly, Daiana Marchesi, working from Argentina, provided the interior layout. Katarina Naskovski, working from Serbia, provided the cover design. Both took time to explore iterations whose final resolutions you see.

Finally, but foreshadowing new efforts, Jim Haynes and Pat Walsh for adding dimensions of appreciation for the might of the Communist Party of China and calibrating levels of fright in what I write and what actions we may undertake going forward.

## List of Acronyms

| | |
|---|---|
| AAA | American Arbitration Association |
| AVIC | Aviation Industry Corporation of China |
| AVIC IHC | AVIC International Holding Corporation |
| AVIC IRE | AVIC International Renewable Energy |
| AVIC TED | AVIC Trade and Economic Development |
| CATIC | China National Aero Technology Import and Export Corporation |
| CFIUS | Committee on Foreign Investment in the United States |
| CIA | Central Intelligence Agency |
| CNPC | China National Petroleum Corporation |
| CPC | Communist Party of China |
| CSRC | China Securities Regulatory Commission |
| DOE | Department of Energy |
| EdF | Électricité de France |
| EPA | Environmental Protection Agency |
| EXIM | Export-Import Bank |
| FBI | Federal Bureau of Investigation |
| I&W | indications and warnings |
| IP | intellectual property |
| IPO | initial public offering |
| ISR | intelligence, surveillance, and reconnaissance |
| JPSC | Jamaica Public Service Company |
| LPG | liquified petroleum gas |
| MIGA | Multilateral Investment Guarantee Agency |
| MOU | Memorandum of Understanding |

| | |
|---|---|
| MSS | Ministry of State Security |
| OBOR | One Belt, One Road |
| OPIC | Overseas Private Investment Corporation |
| PLA | People's Liberation Army |
| PRC | People's Republic of China |
| SOEs | state-owned enterprises |
| STEM | science, technology, engineering, and math |
| SWE | Soaring Wind Energy, LLC |
| T&Cs | terms and conditions |
| USAID | United States Agency for International Development |
| WTG | wind turbine generator |
| WTO | World Trade Organization |
| XWEC | Xinjiang Wind Energy Company |

# Corporate Legend (abbreviated)

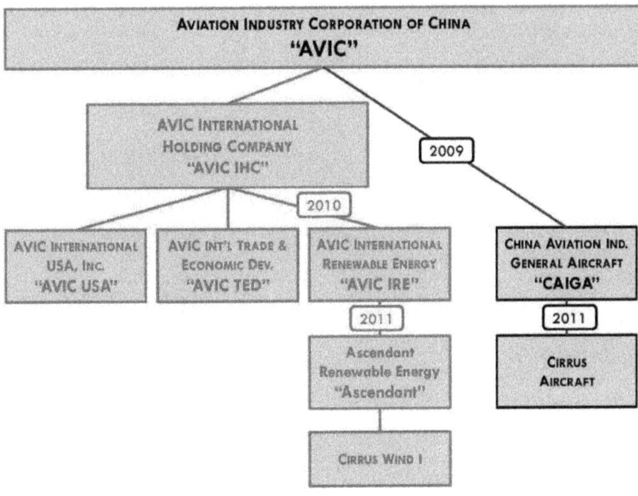

# Map of China

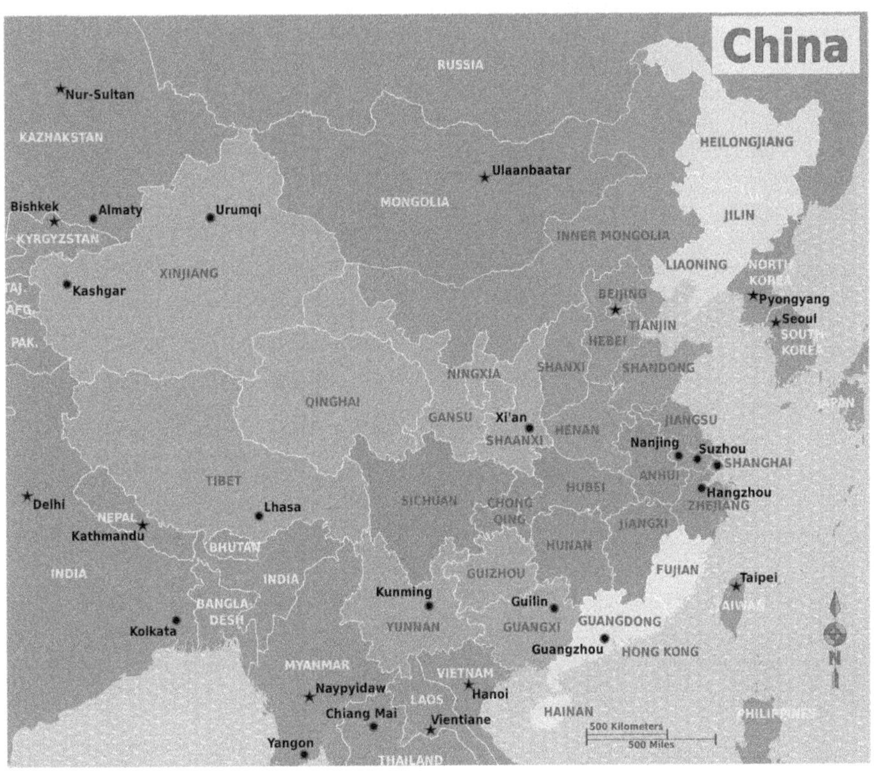
China
RUSSIA
Nur-Sultan
KAZAKHSTAN
Ulaanbaatar
HEILONGJIANG
Bishkek
Almaty
Urumqi
MONGOLIA
JILIN
KYRGYZSTAN
INNER MONGOLIA
XINJIANG
LIAONING
Kashgar
BEIJING
Pyongyang
TIANJIN
Seoul
PAK.
HEBEI
NINGXIA
SHANXI
SHANDONG
QINGHAI
GANSU
Xi'an
JIANGSU
SHAANXI
HENAN
Nanjing
Suzhou
SHANGHAI
ANHUI
TIBET
HUBEI
Hangzhou
Delhi
Lhasa
SICHUAN
ZHEJIANG
NEPAL
JIANGXI
Kathmandu
BHUTAN
HUNAN
INDIA
FUJIAN
INDIA
GUIZHOU
Taipei
Kunming
Guilin
BANGLA-DESH
GUANGDONG
Kolkata
YUNNAN
GUANGXI
Guangzhou
HONG KONG
MYANMAR
VIETNAM
Naypyidaw
Hanoi
LAOS
HAINAN
Chiang Mai
Vientiane
500 Kilometers
500 Miles
Yangon
THAILAND

# Partial List of Names and Affiliations

*Notes*:

**(1) Names of Chinese companies and people follow designations provided by AVIC.**

**(2) Family names are written in all capital letters.**

**(3) Names are listed in alphabetical order by family name.**

**The Nolan Group**

| | |
|---|---|
| Patrick JENEVEIN | Founder and CEO |

**Tang Energy Group**

| | |
|---|---|
| Ken COLLIER | Shop and Installation Superintendent |
| GAO Yang | Assistant to General Manager of Tang Energy China, later promoted to Vice Chief Representative of Tang Energy China |
| Mike GRAUL | Contract engineer |
| Yih-Min JAN | General Manager |
| Patrick JENEVEIN | CEO |

**AVIC**

| | |
|---|---|
| LIN Zuoming | Chairman |
| XU Zhanbin | Vice General Manager, also Executive Vice President |

**CATIC**

| | |
|---|---|
| LIU "Leo" Rongchun | Vice President |

**AVIC International Holding Co.** (aka AVIC **IHC**)

| | |
|---|---|
| WU Guangquan | Chairman |
| XU Hang aka "Mr. Shoe" | Assistant to the Chair |
| ZHOU Xiao Qing | Senior AVIC representative |

**AVIC INTERNATIONAL USA** (aka **AVIC USA**)

| | |
|---|---|
| ZHANG "Sherman" Xuming | President |

**AVIC IRE**

| | |
|---|---|
| LIU "Leo" Rongchun | Founder and Chairman |
| XU Hang aka "Mr. Shoe" | Vice President |

**Ascendant**

| | |
|---|---|
| Paul Thompson | CEO |
| XU Hang aka "Mr. Shoe" | Director |

**China Aviation Industry Gas Turbine Power (Group) Company**

| | |
|---|---|
| HUANG Yun | President |

**Gansu Electric Power Construction Investment & Development Corporation**

| | |
|---|---|
| LI Jianguo | General Manager-Senior Engineer |

**HT Blade**

| | |
|---|---|
| ZHANG Lin | Chairman of the Board, former Party Secretary of another AVIC company |
| ZHANG Ziguo | General Manager |

**State-owned Asset Supervision and Administration Commission**

| | |
|---|---|
| JIANG Jie-Min | Chairman, formerly: Chairman of PetroChina, Director of Qinghai Petroleum Administration Bureau |

**Soaring Wind Energy**

| | |
|---|---|
| Paul THOMPSON | General Manager |

**Xinjiang Wind Energy Company**

| | |
|---|---|
| YU Wu Ming | General Manager |
| WU Gang | Engineer |

**Goldwind**

| | |
|---|---|
| WU Gang | Founder and Chairman |

**Arbitration Panel**

| | |
|---|---|
| Steven ALDOUS | Chairman |
| Gregory SHAMOUN | |

**Attorneys for AVIC Respondents**

"Paul" MA Ming
Steve DEWOLF
Jinshu "Johnny" ZHANG
Malcolm S. MCNEIL
David G. BAYLES

**Attorneys for Claimants**

Bob JENEVEIN
Lewis T. LECLAIR

## Prologue

# How Did It Come to This?

What can I tell you about the People's Republic of China (PRC)?

As one who did business for over twenty years with the government of the PRC and the Communist Party of China (CPC) building companies in China that created jobs by bringing life-improving electricity to people; spent countless days in the cities, hinterlands, offices, and homes of the only nation that comes close to competing with the United States diplomatically, economically, militarily, and technologically; experienced personal and professional victories and defeats; briefed the Central Intelligence Agency (CIA) on what was happening on the ground there with business practices, electrical needs, energy supply issues, and more in the late 1990s and early 2000s; currently works with the US government as well as multinational corporations; and celebrated relationships with my Chinese partners but dared to take them on when they crossed lines both moral and legal, the answer is: *I can tell you a lot.*

Let's begin in the fall of 2014, in a Chinese restaurant in Los Angeles where I'm having lunch in a private room with two CPC operatives. Over my many years in the energy business in the PRC, I stayed where they stayed, ate what they ate, and drank what they drank. I swallowed my fears and ate a plateful of fried cicadas in the deserts of the Xinjiang Uyghur Autonomous Region. I closed my eyes and partook of camel's feet (yes, really!) in the shadow of the Great Wall in Gansu province. And, when being toasted or asked to toast,

I drank way too much *moutai*, a clear liquor with over 50 percent alcohol content that can bring an unsuspecting Westerner to his knees.

But as disquieting as those meals were, they pale in comparison to this lunch in my homeland. It's not the menu; the dim sum is delicious. No, what's making me ill is the conversation I'm having with Zhang Xuming and Ma Ming. Zhang, who calls himself "Sherman" Zhang when doing business in the States, is the president of the US subsidiary of the Aviation Industry Corporation of China (AVIC), the Chinese government's behemoth aerospace and defense conglomerate. Based in Los Angeles, Ma, aka "Paul Ma," is that subsidiary's lawyer. The three of us are prepared for a serious discussion involving hundreds of millions of dollars.

Some background: My Dallas-based company, Tang Energy Group, had been doing business with AVIC since 1997, when we collaborated on a gas-fired power plant in Gansu. Four years later we became partners in HT Blade, a mainland China-based manufacturer of wind turbine blades that we quickly grew to a value of $1.8 billion. Wishing to expand sales to the United States and other parts of the world and to enter the burgeoning, lucrative business of wind farming, Tang and AVIC and others had in 2008 created a joint venture—Soaring Wind Energy, LLC.

Simply put, AVIC was supposed to invest $600 million in this enterprise. This money was to be spent driving turbine blade production in the United States and developing wind farms internationally. Tang's role was to find wind farm opportunities, present them to AVIC for investment, and then oversee development of the newly purchased properties. Unfortunately, AVIC had not upheld its end of the bargain. Rather than fund Soaring Wind, it had created a rival company and funneled money into it to use our ideas and undertake our projects. My gut was burning.

Having watched Communist Party minions in action over several years, I can't say I was shocked by such behavior. The modus operandi of the PRC is to steamroll the little guy—particularly if he's a foreigner—and say, in effect: *Go ahead and sue me. Do you think your funds to pursue a lawsuit match ours to defend it? We've been around for millennia and can afford for this to play out for years. Can you?* The mindset was to conquer, not cooperate for the common good—a counterproductive, if not puzzling, philosophy that stood in contrast to the capitalist vision I embraced: *If we all work together, we'll all do well.*

Despite clear evidence that AVIC was breaching our contract, I had remained hopeful we could resolve our differences. Why? With plenty of prospects for wind farms on the horizon, I thought there was still a chance Soaring Wind could take off. These were good deals.

Sadly, my optimism proved as worthless as the venture. Our efforts were met with a great wall of silence. In June of 2014, with my own financial well-being in jeopardy and obligations to my investors, I reluctantly spearheaded a breach-of-contract lawsuit against AVIC and a number of its subsidiaries, including Sherman's domain, AVIC USA. Now, just a few months later, I've flown from my home in Dallas to Los Angeles to meet with him and Paul to see if we can resolve this matter without resorting to the costly arbitration proceeding required under our agreement.

Sherman is fiftyish. His English is good, as is his sense of humor. We have been dealing with each other for four or five years and enjoy each other's company. I consider him an honest, capable CPC functionary. If there is anyone with whom I might be able to put this dispute to rest, it's him.

I've only recently met Paul and am not sure what to expect—until he lowers his voice and says something like, *You know Patrick, AVIC has more than enough money to make this last a long time, longer than you have in your lifetime to enjoy the fruits of any victory you may win.* (I use italics here, rather than quoting verbatim, because the CPC may have a recording from that lunch, and I have no desire to engage in litigation with them ever again.)

Looking me in the eye, speaking in a flat tone, he says he knows I come from a prominent family in Dallas. He then goes into detail about my wife and three daughters in a way that raises the hairs on my neck. I've been trying to resolve a business dispute amicably, and now this representative of the government—who undoubtedly takes his marching orders from Beijing—is threatening my children and my livelihood.

I wish I could say I responded, "What do you mean by that, Paul? Are you really threatening me?" But I was stunned, reacted defensively, and refused to show that Paul's threat scared me. Later, I told my lawyers what had happened. They took it seriously but couldn't do anything about it and focused on preparing the case.

I found a more receptive audience with the Federal Bureau of Investigation (FBI). Over the years, agents would periodically get in touch with me when someone seeking a security clearance was using me as a reference, or when the bureau thought I could offer insight into a case with PRC connections. By chance, I received such a call a few weeks after the lunch in Los Angeles. After taking care of business, the agent thanked me for my input and asked if there was anything he could do for me.

*Hmm*. "Well, let me tell you a story, and then you tell me what you think I should do." Within days, the FBI assigned an agent to me. "Assigned" may not be the terminology the bureau uses, but the point is I now had a guardian angel who I could call when necessary.

A few months later, an FBI agent let me know that "if there were to be an operation planned against you, it would likely be planned out of the Chinese consulate in Houston, and it would likely involve a drug cartel from Mexico."

I just about fell out of my chair. "Well, thank you," I stammered. "You know, there's a lot of specificity in that. How worried should I be?"

"Oh, not too worried," he said. "They're busy with a lot of other people."

The specificity in the hypothetical led me to hire a Washington, DC, firm founded by former CIA officers with expertise in such matters. Among other things, they told me I should carry a pistol. *Carry a pistol as protection against a possible attack by a Mexican drug cartel engaged by the PRC?*

How did it come to this for a middle-class kid from Dallas who went straight from college to work in a local bank, accidentally fell into the energy business, and then into partnering—and now sparring—with a world superpower?

Grab a plate of fried cicadas or, if you prefer, Texas barbeque, and I'll tell you. In the pages that follow, I'll share the story of my improbable journey in a conversation between me and Steve Fiffer, a lawyer-turned-writer who has collaborated on memoirs with former Secretary of State James A. Baker III, Southern Poverty Law Center founder Morris Dees, civil rights icon C. T.

Vivian, and my fellow Dallasites Kenneth Hersh and former US Ambassador Robert W. Jordan. To prepare for hours of talks with me, he read books about the history of China, scoured thousands of pages of court proceedings, and, he tells me, even ordered entrees from the Xinjiang region from his favorite Chinese restaurant.

Our conversation deliberately leaves out many names, changes others, and begins with the Jeneveins of Versailles.

# Chapter 1

## Do Well by Doing Good

**Steve Fiffer**: I can understand how Paul Ma's words made the hairs on your neck stand up. In threatening you, he said you came from a "prominent family." When I imagine prominent Texas families, I think of political dynasties and oil barons. Which box did the Jeneveins check?

**Patrick Jenevein**: Is there some way to indicate here that I'm chuckling? I guess you could say we were the Jeneveins of Versailles, because that was the name of one of the streets in Dallas where we lived—"we" being my folks and me and my two younger brothers, Bruce and Bob. But our house wasn't a palace, and we were far from royalty.

My dad is a doctor, a pathologist, retired now. He was raised in Monroe, Louisiana, and was the first in his family to go to college. My mom didn't work for pay; she had her hands full with her three sons. Her people came from Choctaw County, Mississippi, and she grew up in New Orleans. That's where my parents met. Dad was in medical school at Louisiana State University, and Mom was an undergraduate at H. Sophie Newcomb Memorial College, the sister school to the then all-male Tulane University. They married in 1957.

Graduating in May of 1958, my father had won a medical residency with the United States Army. I was born the same month and was six weeks old when we moved to San Antonio for Dad's "tour of duty." After another stop in Lexington, Kentucky, we moved to Dallas just before I entered second grade.

We led a very middle-class life. We went on vacations when we could afford to. My brothers and I did go to overnight summer camp, but only because Mom took a job as a cook there in exchange for our tuition.

My parents stressed the importance of education and hard work. We were expected to do well in school, do our chores, and find summer jobs when possible. They knew work built our self-esteem, and were always interested in engaging with us, hearing what we thought and had to say.

**SF**: You didn't have a family crest, but there was a Jenevein motto.

**PJ**: Yes. It was drilled into me when I was young and is just as operative now, some sixty years later: *Do well by doing good.*

**SF**: I suspect that will be a recurring theme as we continue. Back to this brief chronology: In sixth grade you transferred from public school to St. Mark's, a highly regarded, all-male, private day school in Dallas. You did quite well in the classroom and as a member of the cross-country and track teams, and then went off to Davidson, a liberal arts college north of Charlotte, North Carolina. Davidson has an excellent academic reputation, but, truth be told, it's most famous as the alma mater of NBA superstar Stephen Curry. How did you end up there?

**PJ:** Ha! Not because of my three-point shooting. I'll answer your question, but first let me say a few words about St. Mark's. It was—and still is—an amazing place. I made friendships there that matter to this day. The educational opportunities were unparalleled, and there were many teachers who inspired us. I soaked it all up. I took courses in the classics, studied Greek and Latin, and fell in love with the study of history.

**SF**: Did you have any awareness of China when you were in high school? Any interest in the Far East?

**PJ**: None whatsoever. From the outside—as opposed to how I view China now—we saw two Chinas: little Formosa and big Red China. Jim Spellings—a family friend who held a big banking job in Dallas that required him to travel internationally—told me I should learn French because Europe was growing and the United Nations used French. Living in Texas and tying much of my career to China as I have, it's clear in hindsight that studying Spanish and Mandarin would have been more relevant. But who knew?

As for Davidson, truthfully, others picked it for me. Mom and Dad thought it was important that I should see the world outside of Texas, so I didn't look for a school in-state. Mike Teitelman, who was the head of middle school at St. Mark's, told Mom I should apply to Davidson. I visited the campus on a college tour out East and liked it. Then the school offered me an honor scholarship, apparently because I ran well and studied well.

**SF**: You started out pre-med.

**PJ**: Yes. I had every intention of becoming a doctor. During summers, I worked at the now demolished St. Paul Hospital in Dallas as an operating room technician. Then I witnessed the surprising death of a patient in for routine surgery. The surgeon—whom I deeply respected—was pretty much ruined emotionally and, I learned later, professionally and financially. The death pushed me to ask if I wanted to work as hard as doctors and as diligently as this guy and have an unforeseeable event like that happen—crippling confidence, destroying relationships, evaporating savings—obliterating *everything*. The answer was no. Davidson had a first-rate history department, so I majored in that.

**SF**: History seems to have animated you. Did you take away anything from your studies that has influenced how you look at the world or foreign governments or leaders over your career?

**PJ**: Two thoughts. First, one oddity sticks out consistently—though because it consistently happens, we shouldn't find it odd. It's this: People throughout the ages and across geographies expect trends to continue. History shows us that every trend hits an inflection point. Second, doing well by doing good requires understanding who you're working with. Learn their history, personally and culturally. Learning all by itself can enrich your life. More importantly, it opens pathways to possibilities. With a bit of irony, illuminating limits leads to finding openings to develop constructive relationships.

**SF**: After graduation you eschewed graduate school. Rather than the halls of ivy, you ended up in the halls of the First National Bank of Dallas. How did that happen?

**PJ**: That family friend, Jim Spellings, was a bigwig at First National Bank. During my senior year, he took me to lunch in the bank's wood-paneled executive dining room and said, "Patrick, you can learn a lot about business from banking; it's a good place for you to see what you may or may not like about banking, but you'll see a bunch of different businesses, too, and you may find one you like better."

**SF**: And you said?

**PJ**: "I don't want to get a job just because you give me a job." And he said, "Patrick, you might get a job because of who you know, but only you can keep it." I took him at his word and started two weeks after graduation.

**SF**: As I understand it, you were the youngest officer First National Bank ever had, but you concluded that to really get promoted at the bank you needed a business degree. So you enrolled in the MBA program at the University of Texas at Austin. Your plan was to go back after graduating, but that's not what happened.

**PJ**: No. Like a lot of my classmates, I considered going to an investment bank where I could make more money. I interviewed with firms in New York but decided that wasn't the life I wanted. It's an environment where they work your ass off, which I don't mind. But they're just going to wear you out. I wouldn't grow with any decision-making authority. The job would just be grinding out numbers for somebody else.

This was 1984, and the real estate market was still booming. My friend Barbara Moroney introduced me to Nova Development, the Dallas real estate company she had joined. Nova developed small office buildings far away from downtown areas, and office warehouse spaces in Dallas's northern suburbs. The company expected its leasing agents to lead negotiations and offered a path to partnership that implied glorious riches. So that's where I went.

Spoiler alert. The riches didn't happen, but even better than getting rich, that's where I met the woman who would become my wife. Kathy and I started at Nova the same day. Not only was she pretty, elegant, and happy, she carried a *don't-mess-with-me* air that I liked. We began carpooling as coworkers. When she broke up with her boyfriend, we started dating. Then we married in 1987.

**SF**: What did you take away from Nova, besides your wife?

**PJ**: As a leasing agent, you're selling, but you can't make somebody buy something they don't need. Well, maybe some people can, but that's not good for a long-term relationship. To make a lease work you have to understand tenants' needs, then use your calculator to figure out how you can make it work together. Of course, you have to understand your own company's needs, too, and you must be willing to tell your counterparty, "No, we can't do that." You have to know what positions your company must protect.

It's problem-solving with clarity and sincerity that saves everybody time and builds trust. If you don't trust each other, it's not going to work for anyone in the long run. Respecting and protecting each other's time builds trust. Differences in understanding and perspectives always arise. But if we trust each other, we'll be able to work through the differences and difficulties that long-term relationships inevitably face.

Let me jump ahead to say that doing business in China is completely different. Here in the United States, we can actually sign an agreement that expresses a long-term commitment, which our government will enforce. We can trust each other, work on our agreement, write it down, and expect that if we die somebody else can look at it and say, "This is what they meant to do, and this is what we should do from here."

In China, you can't do that. Faith in an agreement doesn't exist—or it's minimal. In statistical terms, calibrating confidence for supporting written agreements is very low.

So what do Chinese people living in the PRC have? They, too, need trust to thrive. If you don't have laws that protect people from bullies—including autocrats—like we do here, you create substitute structures that try to express and uphold long-term commitments. Because the Communist legal system fails them, the Chinese rely on the concepts of *guanxi*, or networks, and *mianzi*, or "face"—in Chinese, 关系 and 面子, respectively—to try to ensure reliably predictable outcomes.

**SF**: We're taking a little detour here from the chronology, but it's important . . . and fascinating. Can you explain *guanxi*?

**PJ**: Professional and personal networks overlap. They have to. Without what many Americans call the "rule of law," Chinese people rely on those whose behavior they can reliably predict. In our case, your personal network and mine overlap in the person of former US Ambassador Bob Jordan, who introduced us. We build on that with a high degree of comfort. We both have more confidence in each other because of that common connection. That's especially important in China because of the unreliability or absence of a legal framework for doing business.

*Guanxi* plays a significant role, but not in the way many Americans view it. You can't use *guanxi*—well, others might—like the Mafia, or the Duttons in the television show *Yellowstone*, to take out those who annoy us. In China, Tang's positive *guanxi* worked almost like a word-of-mouth marketing plan. We made sure we brought value to the people of China. Doing so made them want to connect to us, to have *guanxi* with us.

People all over the world seek to express long-term commitments. In personal, business, and government relationships, long-term predictability ensures peace and raises living standards. To express long-term commitments in the shadow of an authoritarian regime, which trumps all other contracts, is difficult. Therefore, *guanxi* becomes useful to express and bind those commitments.

**SF**: And how would you describe *mianzi*?

**PJ**: Ah, *mianzi*. Being a man who "wants a chance to give his kids a better life" (Louis Armstrong's ideo-political approach in his song "Hello Brother," which contrasts with Henry Kissinger's geo-political theory), I share identical hopes with many Chinese fathers. Still, as we assess desires to commit resources and time to work together, we look at each other and think, *What are you made of? What have you done for your kids? Could I rely on you to support my child having children with your child in order to give our grandkids a better life*? If the answer is yes, you've got "face."

**SF**: Got it. How long were you at Nova?

**PJ**: About two years. Market realities showed us we weren't leasing space as quickly as we had projected, and we weren't getting the amount of rent per square foot we had expected. So I told the partners we needed to quit *building* buildings and start *buying* buildings. Our competitors were missing projections, too.

**SF**: How'd that go over?

**PJ**: Not very well. They liked me—they offered me a partnership—but not my idea. So I put my legs and money where my mouth was and left.

**SF**: That's rather gutsy. Did you have a detailed plan?

**PJ**: Strategically, yes; tactically, no. My plan—such as it was—was to go find buildings to buy. That was easy! But the next step was much harder. Where could I find money to support my ambition?

**SF**: How many buildings did you eventually buy?

**PJ**: None! I was, as Bill King of Bill King's Brake-O told me on a random ski lift ride, "pecking shit with the chickens"—deliberately, persistently looking for opportunities. I found plenty for sale, but none with positive cash flow, and I didn't have enough money to buy something that did not generate positive cash flow.

**SF**: But then came the opportunity that set you on a different career path.

**PJ**. Right. I bumped into a property that a bank in Oklahoma owned and had to sell. Penn Square Bank had gone bust and in doing so had almost brought down the giant Continental Illinois National Bank and Trust Company in Chicago. (Quick story, I'd actually previously brushed shoulders at a happy hour in Dallas with a legendary figure from Penn Square. He was drinking beer out of a boot, and I remember thinking, *Why are you making such a show? You're going to fall off your perch—figuratively and literally—someday.*) Anyway, in its distress Continental was auctioning off four Penn Square gas wells in Live Oak County, Texas, that the Pend Oreille Oil & Gas Company operated.

In those days, I used a little HP 12C Calculator—which I still have. Between it and my Lotus 1-2-3 software program, I plotted past production, used 1-2-3's linear regression tool to project future production, scoured the *Wall Street Journal* for natural gas prices, and came up with a cash flow projection I could believe.

I showed Dad my projections, and he said, "You should show this to Johnny Davis." Mr. Davis was a petroleum engineer. So I showed him my projections and what I thought the value of the wells was. After he completed his professional analysis, he said, "You're pretty good for an amateur."

I went to the bidding hot box and won—by about $5,000. As I recall, this was something like a $325,000 transaction. I had saved about $50,000 from my own work that I was able to invest. The rest I had to borrow or beg from friends and family.

One of those friends was Mr. Horchow. That's S. Roger Horchow, then famous for his success in the luxury catalog business, and later for his Broadway productions. Years later, when I was forty, he said, "You're old enough now to call me 'Roger.'"

For some reason, Roger—almost exactly thirty years my elder—took me on as a mentee and made our friendship dear. We each had three daughters, and both of us had started logistically complex businesses with layers of complication from international engagements. For years we met regularly for lunch. He was a source of great wisdom, supportive and always truly honest, whether we were talking about the joys and challenges of marriage or the CPC.

Getting back to that first Pend Oreille deal, Roger listened to my pitch (essentially: *I'm asking you to invest in these wells with me and I think you'll make money on your investment*), looked at my projections, and said, "I'm investing in *you*, Patrick. You're young. You're just starting off. I don't know if this will work or not, but I'm betting on you." Coming from him, that was a huge boost.

**SF**: Was it a good bet?

**PJ**: On a return-on-investment basis, this was one of the best deals I've ever done—which I attribute to hard work, acting with enough fear to reduce unknown risks, and getting lucky. Also, I learned a new thrill: writing big (to me) checks to investors like Roger.

**SF**: Would you have been just as interested in an opportunity to invest in, say, apartment buildings or car dealerships or whatever? With all due respect, did you know anything about the oil and gas or energy business at that point?

**PJ**: I knew next to nothing, Steve. When I'd worked at the bank, I had called on energy companies, but that was from a finance aspect. I wasn't grounded in: *How does this thing really make money*? In the case of energy, it was the cash flow, not the industry or product that attracted me. But once I made that first investment, I did focus on building businesses in oil and gas.

**SF**: We'll get to the particulars of some of those efforts shortly, but with the Pend Oreille investment and others that followed, did you always sleep well? Putting your own money into the pot and, even more, asking friends and family to put in their money might keep a lot of people up at night. On the other hand, there are some folks who say, "If I go broke on this, I'll just pick up and go on to the next thing." Was that you?

**PJ**: Those first few deals, I made sure as best I could that if the music stopped, the bank would get paid back. I might lose all *my* money, and I didn't like that idea at all. But I believed I had to accept that exposure to be able to do well.

I always try to structure a deal so, first, it can pay back the debt and, second, it can contribute to building a business. To my investors—people like Dad or Roger—I would say, "This is how I'm structuring it. And you know I'm borrowing money to put in, and if things go wrong, we're going to sell it to the bank." And they appreciated the approach and the forthrightness.

**SF**: Not too long after Pend Oreille, you found yourself in the middle of an investment that had gone south. But it wasn't your deal.

**PJ**: Yes. *Bluebonnet.* It wasn't my business, and it was a nightmare headache. Bluebonnet was a natural gas gathering system near Texas A&M University in College Station. Dad was among the investors, with a 4.5 percent interest. He had two partners, one a geologist and one an oil and gas property operator. Both went broke.

**SF**: Okay, I did some googling, and here's what I found:

> A gathering system usually consists of multiple pipelines laid in one area that are designed to "gather" natural gas that is produced from multiple oil wells to a central point. This central point may be a compressor station, a storage facility, a processing plant, a larger transmission pipeline or a shipping point. ("Midstream 101: Gas Gathering," Williams.com, 2024)

**PJ**: Your research nails it. In this case, Bluebonnet gathered natural gas through miles and miles of pipe to a central compressor station and a natural gas processing unit. Operations require other ancillary equipment, but natural gas processing uses drops in pressure to turn heavier natural gas molecules from a gaseous state into a liquid state. Bluebonnet sold the remaining gas and the natural gas liquids to make money.

In the mid-1980s, natural gas and natural gas liquids fell in step with collapsing oil prices. Plummeting prices bankrupted Dad's partners, and exposed partners he hadn't known about. It turned out his original partners had sold part of their interest to some guys in Minneapolis, who had resold that to other friends of theirs in Minneapolis. The Minneapolis investors had lawsuits against each other that spilled into Texas.

It was a tangled-up mess. In addition to Dad's partners, some of the gas producers—and even the bank—went broke. Here was the rub: It turned out that the note with Texas American Bank included joint and several liabilities. So suddenly Dad went from a 4.5 percent investor to potentially having liability for 100 percent of the debt.

**SF**: That's scary. Where do you come in?

**PJ**:. First of all, nobody else wanted to touch this. We all knew that since Dad was a doctor who had to show up at the hospital every day to earn his income, he couldn't manage Bluebonnet. We also knew that doctors made juicy targets for creditors. He expected to honor his obligations, but those obligations had grown twentyfold! Of course, he wanted to share or reduce any such obligation as much as possible.

With the bravado of a twenty-eight-year-old male, I thought: *I can handle this. I can help my family. I've been to business school. I've been in banking. I can fix this in six months.* To be on the safe side, I told Dad it might take a year.

Steve, it took eight-and-a-half years! But here's the silver lining: Over the course of this, I negotiated and renegotiated agreements in an adverse environment; I learned natural gas gathering, natural gas compression, natural gas processing, and even natural gas-fired electricity generation. I learned it well enough that, in May 1995, the *American Oil & Gas Reporter* asked me to write a special report in its gas compression section. I don't remember how they got my name. It may have been that I'd previously written a speech for Dick Cheney to deliver to a natural gas processing association when he led Halliburton.

**SF**: Resolving Bluebonnet took eight-and-a-half years! That lining needed a lot of silver. Were you able to conduct your own business during this time? But first, how did you come to write for Cheney?

**PJ**: A friend of mine, Katherine Hoehn, worked as Cheney's chief of staff. She asked me who could write a speech for him to deliver at an energy association meeting. I offered to provide an outline that became the speech. As for conducting my own business, that was absolutely necessary, especially after I married Kathy and we started our family—three girls over the next five years. In 1986, I created a company called the Nolan Group, which continued to invest in wells and natural gas gathering and processing systems, and to look for opportunities to develop natural gas power plants.

You probably want an example. One of the two Texans who were partners with Dad in Bluebonnet had a gathering system in South Texas. He was going broke, so the Nolan Group bought that system from him. As I recall, it may have cost a few hundred thousand dollars, but it made money, cash-flowing money.

A much bigger deal materialized in 1987. Someone—it might have been me—had the idea to use Bluebonnet gas to generate and sell electricity. It's a simple vertical integration proposal. While Bluebonnet struggled buying fresh-out-of-the-ground natural gas, breaking out the natural gas liquids and selling the remaining gas and liquids separately, others were using the gas component to generate electricity. Their value-added power production earned much higher margins; Texans were buying lots of electricity. So we thought, *Why not burn Bluebonnet's gas to generate electricity and capture a bigger value-added revenue stream*?

Well, that turned out to be an idea that actually worked, albeit a little differently than we expected. We met a couple of entrepreneurs from Fort Worth who had a similar idea. They had the electricity buyer—Texas Utility Electric Company—and we had the fuel.

Texas Utility wanted a much bigger power plant—eight times bigger—than the gas from Bluebonnet could supply. Still we said, "Okay." We knew how to sell and buy natural gas and, pretty quickly, contracted to buy natural gas from Coastal Corporation. We secured $50 million from Prudential Capital and EDS Financial to build the plant and came in a few months early and about half a million bucks under budget. On June 19, 1987, we turned it on, and on October 1, 1999, we sold it.

**SF**: A big question. It's 1987, you are twenty-nine and newly married. It's not like you came from a family of Texas wildcatters or folks whose business always put them on the cusp of success or failure. You've already described your comfortable middle-class, son-of-a-doctor background. So how does someone like you move from this rather traditional existence where certainty is the norm to a world of boom or bust? I mean, I've yet to see you drink anything out a boot!

**PJ**: Dad's partners stuck him bad. He had a lot to lose. I could help. I could do good for the family. Looking back, I had no idea what I would need to learn and do, but I did know how to learn. History teaches strategy, statecraft, problem-solving, and productivity. And history supports the optimist, the bold, and the lucky. I had all three, and one thing more: my family's support—both my birth family and my family with Kathy.

**SF**: Can you talk a little more about processing and compression?

**PJ**: Sure. Working on Bluebonnet—the problem child—required understanding physical links and overlaps, from the wellhead to the electrical transmission line. We eventually got really good at processing natural gas safely, reliably, and profitably. Soon, other oil and gas operators were asking us to process natural gas for them, so we formed NG Processing Company.

Every one of NG Processing's plants relied on compressors. To liquify certain natural gas components, we relied on the cooling that happens when gas pressures drop. Because gas expands or contracts with pressure and temperature, you cannot pump it like you can pump water. To move gas, you have to create a lower pressure area for higher pressure gas to move to. Mechanical compressors move gases. So we formed NG Compression Company and would rent out or operate compressors for oil and gas operators.

All of this led to a niche opportunity. Big oil tanks have vents to allow for the release of gas into the atmosphere. The good news is that this helps avoid explosions within the tanks. The bad news is that the gas—in the form of ethane or methane—pollutes the air. In the area around Texas A&M, NG Compression started working with Hy-Bon Engineering, a company from Midland, Texas, run by Jim Woodcock. We developed compression equipment specifically for an application known as vapor recovery—gathering gas off the tops of oil tanks.

With natural gas, we were providing a very clean fuel to power generators and manufacturers. I know some people argue that we should not use any hydrocarbons at all. We could have a long conversation about that, perhaps in an epilogue. When we started vapor recovery, we were creating cleaner alternatives, and we were keeping methane and other natural gases from going into the atmosphere. So we were capturing something valuable that we could make money on, *and* we were also cleaning the environment. It was one of those situations where—get ready!—you are doing well by doing good.

**SF**: I'd like to back up for a moment. You made some pretty big career decisions very early on. What role did Kathy play in these? Was she gung ho? *Hurray, we're off on a new adventure.* Or was she like, *You know, Honey, we have a family.*

**PJ**: Kathy earned an MBA and passed the CPA exam the first time she took it. Looking back, I realize I leaned on her a whole lot more than I was aware of as we were going through it. She comes from a farming family from northeast Arkansas and has a visceral appreciation of exposure. As a farmer, you expose crops to the uncertainty of weather. You expose a lot of money to a wide range of uncertain outcomes. She grew up with that.

I was luckier than I ever could have imagined in finding her. She would ask great questions and say, "What do you think about that?" I may have stirred up opportunities, but together we made better decisions because of her discipline.

**SF**: Your entry into the compression business resulted in another major positive. It led to a lunch with Dr. Yih-Min Jan, who eventually became your business partner and the catalyst for your ventures in China.

**PJ**: Yes. Knowing of our expertise in the processing business, Jim Woodcock invited me to attend the 1994 Permian Basin International Oil Show in west Texas. A slew of booths showed off American ingenuity—the latest applications of developing science applied as innovations and advances in oil field equipment and operations.

During the show, Jim set up a lunch for us with Yih-Min Jan and a jackass CEO of an oil field services company. Yih-Min, a brilliant, then forty-four-year-old, University of Houston PhD physicist, had grown up in Taiwan and recently retired from ARCO as a principal research engineer. After leaving ARCO, he brought a company that Woodcock had sponsored to the PRC. That company used microbes—Jim called them "bugs"—to enhance oil recovery. Microbes ingest long hydrocarbon chains and egest shorter ones. That makes the column of oil in the well lighter and easier to move out of it.

I don't recall where we ate, but I do recall getting stuck with the bill. I didn't expect Jim, who was letting me bunk at the Woodcocks, to pay, nor did I expect Yih-Min to pick up the check. The CEO had the deepest pockets, but he showed no interest in even splitting the tab.

Later that day, Yih-Min, always a class act, reached me and said he wanted to buy me lunch. That in itself says something about him. We met the next day, had a wonderful and meaningful conversation, and that, as they say in the movies, was the beginning of a beautiful friendship.

**SF**: You and I have agreed that we'll end several chapters with your take on a China-related issue currently in the news. Because we talked about your youth in this chapter, let's look at young people in today's China. The *New York Times* recently reported:

> China's young people are facing record-high unemployment as the country's recovery from the pandemic is fluttering. They're struggling professionally and emotionally. Yet the Communist Party and the country's top leader, Xi Jinping, are telling them to stop thinking they are above doing manual work or moving to the countryside. They should learn to "eat bitterness," Mr. Xi instructed, using a colloquial expression that means to endure hardships.
>
> Many young Chinese aren't buying it. They argue that they studied hard to get a college or graduate school degree only to find a shrinking job market, falling pay scale and longer work hours. Now the government is telling them to put up with hardships. But for what? (Li Yuan, "China's Young People Can't Find Jobs. Xi Jinping Says to 'Eat Bitterness,'" May 30, 2023)

Your thoughts?

**PJ:** The Communist Party has wedged itself into quite a jam. Imposing its one-child policy from 1980 to 2015, the party created a coddled cadre of about 400 million people. That's about 35 percent of the PRC's population and the youngest part of it. Those children have two parents and four grandparents treating them as if they are the most special babies to have ever been born. No one until General Secretary Xi has told them to eat bitterness.

Many grew up with access to free-world ideas and opportunities. As they age into positions of power over PRC policy, they will change the world. They will outlive Xi—if he doesn't get them killed in a war first. For the peace of the world and our own prosperity, our political and commercial leaders can—in fact, they must—nurture relationships with this cadre now.

## Chapter 2

# We Don't Pay Bribes

**PJ**: In one my favorite pictures (Image 1), Yih-Min and I have just finished a long day in Taiyuan, far east of the oilfields in Xinjiang. Our measured smiles show the confidence and trust we have in each other as well as our objectives.

**SF**: Before we get to those oil fields, let's back up and talk about the development of that beautiful friendship that changed your life.

**PJ**: When I met him, Yih-Min had been working with the China National Petroleum Corporation (CNPC), enhancing oil recovery using microbes.

**SF**: Here's what my research revealed about CNPC. It was born in 1988, when the Communist government decided to disband its Ministry of Petroleum and replace it with a state-owned company to handle all petroleum activities in China. This was part of a revolutionary trend involving a number of business sectors. Governments and companies chase access to capital markets—sources of cash for their endeavors. The PRC wanted to expand its access to capital, so it started to convert government instrumentalities into apparent corporate entities.

Within five years—not too long before your first trip to the country—CNPC was operating internationally. Fast forwarding a few years, to 1999, CNPC was restructured and became the parent company of a publicly listed entity, PetroChina. I've read that in 2022, CNPC was ranked fourth in revenue by the Fortune Global 500. That's huge. Anyway, back to Yih-Min.

**PJ**: While he was out in the oil fields in China, Yih-Min had noticed that CNPC was flaring an awful lot of natural gas.

**SF**: Ah, and when he met you at the Permian Basin Show, he learned you had a business that was capturing that flared gas so instead of just going up and polluting the atmosphere, it could actually be converted to energy.

**PJ**: Exactly. NG Processing had the technology to capture natural gas, put pressure on it or cool it—or both—to liquefy parts of it that can then be shipped out. So shortly after our get-to-know-you lunch at the show, Yih-Min called and asked if he could see one of our processing plants. Not too long after that, I picked him up at four-thirty or five in the morning, and we drove down to Bryan-College Station to look at the compression and processing facility and the interconnects, where you actually push gas from a smaller pipeline into a bigger one.

We talked a lot. No doubt, Yih-Min was checking out me as much as the technology. He politely grilled me on the way I went about analyzing business opportunities, and how we made decisions for the gathering system. He wasn't just looking at the gear. He was looking at me.

**SF**: I assume you were looking at him, too. What did you learn?

**PJ**: Of course. On this trip, I learned he had grown up in Taiwan in a house with no running water. He was very smart, very polite, and very proud of his heritage. He talked about how the Chinese have contributed many ideas to society, to civilization. And then he asked me, "What has the West contributed?"

And I said, "Well, democracy was kind of an important contribution." Which I'm happy to say he agreed with!

Over time, I observed that Yih-Min was more classically Chinese than the PRC Chinese. He knew Chinese manners. He knew classical Buddhism. He knew how to write classical Chinese, as opposed to the simplified version introduced in the 1960s during Mao's Cultural Revolution, which eliminated many centuries-old traditions. Add to that the fact that he was educated to the standards of a US PhD, and it was clear why people in China looked up to him. Joining his *guanxi* could raise their *mianzi*.

Maybe most important, I'd soon see that we shared the same values—neither one of us would entertain the idea of bribery—and work ethic. He once told me that he and I together outworked twenty of our Chinese counterparts.

**SF**: Okay. Yih-Min observes that CNPC flares lots of gas, meets you, sees your capability to capture and process that gas, checks you out, and so begins a discussion about doing something together in China. Was China even on your radar at that time?

**PJ**: No. Remember, when I was growing up, it was *Red China*. Formosa, now Taiwan, was our friend; Red China was not.

That's not to say I hadn't been looking for opportunities beyond Texas. California seemed like a logical place. But California's governor, Gray Davis, had made it clear he did not want "Texas power pirates" coming in and generating electricity.

I had considered markets outside the United States, too. In 1992, I'd gone to Uzbekistan on a trip organized by the United States Agency for International Development (USAID), which wanted American energy operators to help that country grow its natural gas industry. That was the first time I started thinking that using our expertise had benefits beyond the United States. We could make it easier for people to access energy, and, at the same time, make that energy cleaner. The United States would also benefit because we'd be bringing it together with underdeveloped countries like Uzbekistan, which might have strategic significance.

**SF**: Win-win-win.

**PJ**: Ideally. Unfortunately, sometimes—if you play by the rules—you lose the short game. Our competition in Uzbekistan turned out to be French, and they had no hesitation about bribing for business. I won't do that—it's wrong, it's against the law, and corruption destroys companies, communities, even entire countries.

While in Uzbekistan, I ran into a couple of other Americans who were working for Newmont Corporation, which was mining gold. Because this was Uzbekistan, they were getting paid in cotton.

**SF**: Seriously?

**PJ**: Yes. *You give us gold, we'll give you cotton.* Except they didn't get the cotton. Some of their people watched the right amount of cotton get loaded onto a train and watched that train pull out of the station. Others from their team waited at the destination for their payment; it never showed up. Not just the load of cotton, but the whole train disappeared.

That was a cautionary tale of corruption. Early in our relationship, I told Yih-Min I wasn't interested in getting into a situation like that, or one where either of us would be expected to offer a bribe. I think most of our counterparties appreciated that we meant it when we said: "We don't pay bribes, and we have to make money." Yih-Min agreed completely.

We made sure our counterparties knew that the US Foreign Corrupt Practices Act prohibits paying bribes. We could honestly say, "Look, if I bribe you, I go to jail. I'm not even going to think about doing it. We've gotta work on a different basis. So let's concentrate on the business and not worry about how somebody can steal money from us. Let's make it work together."

Unfortunately, many countries do not restrict their businesses, or government agents for that matter, from paying bribes. Jumping ahead to our time in China, many PRC-based companies expect to receive and pay bribes. ZTE, a PRC telecom company, even had—and may still have—a "CBO," or chief bribery officer. I observed two companies from the Netherlands and one from Germany—a wind blade designer, a wind farm operator, and a wind turbine generator (WTG) manufacturer, respectively—buy business by using tactics Yih-Min and I eschewed.

They actually told us they made sure the people who were giving them contracts got red envelopes at "Spring Festival"—which Americans call Chinese New Year. Traditionally, Chinese people give cash in red envelopes to those they wish well or those who may enhance their ability to advance financially or politically. In addition to red envelopes, those three companies also provided their counterparties with fancy gifts and trips to Europe.

If I were a single-issue voter, my issue would be fighting corruption. From studying history and working internationally, I've seen that corruption—more than any other issue—erodes communities and threatens people's livelihoods and their chances of giving their kids a better life.

But back to that trip to our facilities in Bryan-College Station with Yih-Min. He opened my eyes to another foray outside the United States. I was intrigued by the fact that a place as old as China was opening up to foreign investment. This was creating frontier-like opportunities. Growing up in Texas, with a family that had emigrated from Louisiana, I was nurtured on the idea that you go where the opportunity is. *Think about it. Be careful about it. Be thoughtful about it, but go*!

**SF**: After Yih-Min opened your eyes to the possibilities of China, did you start doing any research on your own?

**PJ**: Majoring in history, I couldn't help it. I'd studied European, Egyptian, and Greek history, but I knew next to nothing about Chinese history. So the first thing I did was start reading, just to get my bearings, figure out the order of the dynasties, things like that. Remember encyclopedias before the internet? I started there: *World Book. Encyclopedia Britannica*.

Then I started to catch up on more recent dynamics. From Mao to Deng Xiaoping to Jiang Zemin. It was fascinating to learn more—past and present, turmoil and peace. The Qianlong Emperor ruled China in the 1700s, during the same time George Washington was fighting the British and pulling the

United States together. The emperor governed a population roughly the size of the US population today. To see those events side by side, to line up the dates, helped me compare and understand our counterparties in China. Studying helped me ask better questions when I was in the PRC, and helped me develop an inside-looking-out appreciation of the challenges people in China face.

That's a point worth emphasizing. Few Americans spend the time to learn about China from the inside out.

**SF**: I'm guessing no amount of study could fully prepare you for that first trip to China in 1995. You must have been very happy to have your new partner Yih-Min at your side when you landed in Beijing.

**PJ**: That would have been nice, Steve. But it wasn't the case. I flew over all by my lonesome.

**SF**: Apropos our discussion of corruption, *The Guardian* recently ran a story under the headline, "Unsafe at the top: China's anti-graft drive targets billionaires and bankers." It reads, in part:

> Since Xi came to power in 2012, one of his flagship policies has been his anti-corruption drive. Xi sees corruption as an existential threat to the CCP and has made no secret of wanting to root out "tigers" (senior corrupt officials) and "flies" (low-level cadres). In Xi's first year in power, more than 180,000 officials were disciplined, compared with about 160,000 the year before. In the next decade, 3.7 million cadres were punished by the party's anti-graft watchdog, including about 1% of national and provincial leaders.
>
> As well as helping to rid Xi of political rivals, the campaign has been popular with the Chinese public, with many people appalled by the

> accruement of riches that increasingly accompanied political office. (Amy Hawkins, April 18, 2023)

I've seen other headlines about corruption in the Chinese military, the health industry, and most recently, real estate. What's your take on the state of corruption today and the impact it has on the US government and businesses?

**PJ:** Corruption threatens governments of all types everywhere, but especially those that rely on conquest, occupation, and oppression to establish and maintain order. Those systems exempt rulers from the rules that apply to the rest of their populations.

Xi Jinping knows this—he knows that corruption may destroy the Communist Party. He knows to fear it, but also how to use it; he cuts with both edges of corruption's sword. As China scholar Ian Easton, a professor at the US Naval War College, has noted, Xi bribed a local party boss with scarce fried egg and steamed buns to worm his way into the Communist Party after ten rejections. Xi alleges corruption against his political opponents, yet uses the slosh in the vast amounts of money his signature "One Belt, One Road" strategic offensive splashes around the world—more than one trillion US dollars!—to buy the loyalty of politically powerful families. PRC talent recruitment programs extend beyond science, technology, engineering, and math (STEM) leaders in the United States to include political leaders. US law enforcement and courts must determine the extent and effect of such efforts.

By the way, the article quoted above uses the acronym "CCP." In the 1950s, a CIA analyst abbreviated "Communist Party of China" as "CCP." I use "CPC." In one meeting with a deeply involved former senior government worker, I used the acronym "CPC" and he interrupted me and said, "You know what you're talking about."

# Chapter 3

## We Need Your Passport

**SF**: You flew to Beijing by yourself?

**PJ**: Yes. Dallas to Tokyo, Tokyo to Beijing. I remember it was May 1995, because I missed my thirty-seventh birthday. Literally.

**SF**: Literally?

**PJ**: Courtesy of the international date line. I took off before my birthday, and when I finally got to my hotel room in Beijing it was already the day after. I remember Yih-Min called me after I landed, wished me a happy birthday, and said he'd see me soon. He was already in Urumqi, where I'd be heading—again on my own—the next day.

**SF**: So he hadn't left you high and dry?

**PJ**: Oh, no. Yih-Min always covered for my vulnerabilities. Actually, we do that for each other—cover for each other's weaknesses and play to each other's strengths. He was waiting for me in Xinjiang.

This first trip was wholly exploratory. We had not formalized a relationship. Just as he'd come down to see my facility in Bryan-College Station, I was going to look and see what he'd been doing. He had targeted

Xinjiang, which you may have heard of because this is where the Communists are now torturing Uyghurs, a Muslim minority. The plan was for him to take me out into the oil fields and introduce me to some of the powers that be, so we might gauge whether there were any business opportunities.

**SF**: Besides eating "Xinjiang Style Sauteed Lamb," I've done some internet research. Xinjiang comprises about one-sixth of the land mass of the PRC—620,000 square miles—but supports only a small fraction of the population—around 25 million, or less than 2 percent of the people who the CPC governs. As previously mentioned, it's in China's northwest. It borders a bunch of different countries—Mongolia, Russia, Kazakhstan, Kyrgyzstan, Tajikistan, Afghanistan, Pakistan, and India. Its capital, Urumqi, is about 1,500 miles west of Beijing.

So you land in Beijing. Then what?

**PJ**: The plane landed after dark. You can imagine how jet-lagged I was after traveling through thirteen time zones. I don't recall how I got a ride to my hotel, but I still remember driving there on an empty six-lane highway, three lanes each way, with lights. Visibility was limited because of what I initially thought was mist but turned out to be pollution.

My four-and-a-half hour flight to Urumqi left the next afternoon. Yih-Min had arranged for a very kind lady to take me around Beijing. The next morning, she and a driver showed me a little of the city before taking me to the airport.

**SF**: What was your first impression of Beijing when morning came and you could see it?

**PJ**: I'd read a lot and talked to people who'd been to China recently. Still, seeing "the Red Dragon" for the first time overwhelmed my studied approach. First off, there were bicycles everywhere, and gray everywhere—from the skies to the drab clothing. When I actually saw the people and looked into their faces, it was shocking. The differences from the United

States were obvious. People seemed oppressed. They avoided looking at foreigners. They frowned. Their chins were down, but they were working. They were busy.

**SF**: You went back many times until about 2014, when your temerity in taking on your Chinese business partners made you persona non grata. How had Beijing changed over the course of your visits?

**PJ**: Ha, "temerity"! Lewis T. LeClair, an intelligently tenacious lawyer who provided the high-level thinking in our fight against AVIC, once used that word to describe my speaking truth to CPC power. It sounded like a compliment; later, I wondered if he thought I was nuts for punching a bully—with a nation's treasury behind it! But to your question, those bicycles turned into automobiles, driving on thousands of miles of new highways—almost always clogged with traffic. Just as roads stretched farther, buildings stretched taller. On my first trips, squatty buildings dominated a dumpy skyline. Over the years, architecture became more worldly and sophisticated: the Beijing Opera House, the CCTV skyscraper. On one trip, I got to Beijing late on the first day of Spring Festival. I was so tired, I slept through mortar-loud firework explosions, but woke when one ignited the CCTV's nearby tower.

As for the people, over the years many started looking up. They lifted their chins. They opened their eyes. They looked others in the eyes. They wore more colorful clothes, too. As time went by, we knew we had been part of helping Chinese people improve their livelihoods and quality of life, and that felt good.

**SF**: And on this first trip in May of 1995, what was Urumqi like?

**PJ**: Far west of Beijing, in the foothills of the Tian Shan mountain range, on the edges of the Gobi and Taklamakan Deserts, and near the lowest dry point on earth, it was dry and dusty. Development lagged, too. The party was adding gleaming streaks of buildings along roads in the east, but, remembering shots fired between Chinese and Russian troops in the 1960s along Xinjiang's borders, Beijing hesitated to invest in areas Russians could overtake.

Back then the Han—China's ethnic majority—still paid lip service to the territory's name: "Xinjiang Uyghur Autonomous Region." Uyghurs—whom you may know are part of a Turkic ethnic group that originated in Central and East Asia—held the highest government posts, but Han Chinese held the higher CPC posts. And in the PRC, the party, not the government, controls the army.

Mao Zedong chided party cadres that because power grows out of the barrel of a gun, the party should always command the gun. The Uyghur genocide began around 2014. When I visited almost twenty years earlier, the Uyghur population, which covered the region, was vibrant and confident. Their clothing was more colorful and drapey than the Han's, who wore more western-fitting clothes, though almost always drab. Uyghur men wore symbolic religious caps. An open-air Uyghur market sold those squared, embroidered hats, as well as knives, sides of slaughtered sheep, and more.

The bright colors and exotic patterns, the smells from all the spices for sale, and the rambunctious children running around and raising shouts from their parents promised fun for every visit. At one time, I had a drawer half-full of those caps and a handful of ornate knives. They recalled histories of lives along the Silk Road trade routes.

The city itself reminded me of when I visited Uzbekistan a few years earlier. The construction styles were similar. In hotels with elevators, I would often use the stairs—sometimes for a little bit of exercise, sometimes because the elevators worked erratically. Steps were often unevenly spaced; it appeared that one group of workers completed a flight, but then got called to another job or stopped work because of a lack of materials or changing priorities. The planning wasn't what we expect from construction in the United States. It was much more haphazard, piecemeal.

Standing in line was haphazard, too. Rather than orderly English queues where people line up in sequence and respect personal space, Chinese formed palpitating globs of humanity, pressing entry points and counters from airports to train stations and restaurants.

**SF**: How was the food?

**PJ**: Great—in taste and variety. Uyghurs make a kind of pasta dish with peppers and lamb that delights a Texas tongue. On the tables, you'll find pepper and sauces and pods of garlic. It wasn't unusual to see the locals bite into the pods like apples.

And then there were the cicadas. That was on our first trip—at a dinner in the desert at a CNPC oil field headquarters. After getting over my initial shock, I thought: *I'm the guest of honor. Everyone's looking at me.* Then I thought, *Granny always said, "Take at least two bites."*

A cicada is a two-bite minimum. Biting through the outside crunch, you find what looks like mottled pale green and off-white chopped up marshmallows, and the substance feels like slightly overcooked and chopped up spaghetti. While your tongue is working through a never-before-encountered taste, your eyes see a round table full of hardened oil field workers who grew up thinking they may have to fight Americans. Like a good vaccine jab, you quickly forget the discomfort. I can't remember how it tasted, but I have no inclination to rediscover that long-lost sensation.

**SF**: Duly noted. Where did you stay?

**PJ**: Believe it or not, on my first night in Urumqi, I stayed in a Holiday Inn. I remember we had dinner there. Four tables were full, three of them with Chinese—and every one of them had a mobile phone. They were clunkier than today's cell phones, but still, none of us had one in 1995.

The accommodations were okay—much better than some of the places I later stayed, where "truth in advertising" may have suggested a few "camping skills required" signs. At some places, you were lucky if you had running water a couple of hours a day.

**SF**: What kind of exploring did you do on this exploratory trip?

**PJ**: Just to set the scene for you, the CNPC had offices in a building in downtown Urumqi and others out in the oil fields, which looked nice and impressive from afar. The facades opened past guarded gates and onto imperial staircases. Past the staircases, open doors led to stark offices. The desks were crammed together, filled with people who never seemed to look up from their work. The *lao ban's* ("big boss's") office provided room for large, dark, polished veneer desks, stuffed chairs, trinkets, and sometimes maps. By the way, according to the CPC, maps contain state secrets.

I remember making technical presentations on natural gas processing for a dozen or so Chinese engineers in rooms that had two rings of chairs—one ring at the table and a second backed up to the conference room wall. They understood the physics of processing, but they were really interested in how we took advantage of physics in our design, our welding, and our operations.

**SF**: Were they doing any of the capturing at that point themselves?

**PJ**: From what I saw, no. The CPC could deem touring a gas processing plant the equivalent of inspecting a military facility, and my hosts controlled what I saw. Like many countries, China uses natural gas to make fertilizer for farms, but it can also serve as a feedstock to make explosives. Methane—just one of the natural gases, and the simplest of all hydrocarbons—combined with nitrogen, which makes up about 80 percent of the air around us, creates a fertilizer (or explosive) feedstock we call ammonia.

In the United States, profit opportunities enticed people to capture natural gas and use it for a variety of applications, from running militaries to making running shoes. But in the 1990s, the CPC line was that natural gas was too valuable to use for anything other than a chemical feedstock This precluded using natural gas as a fuel to supply to power plants to make electricity, which had the potential to change the lives of many Chinese people who lived nights literally in the dark.

Saying that fertilizer was needed to help grow food to feed the masses may have been a silk glove to hide the mailed fist of wanting to make explosives. But whether to feed its people, fuel its military, or power other industries, the CPC lacked natural gas processing capabilities.

Because the party is still not good at generating surplus capital, it doesn't have the money that Americans have to develop technologies to take advantage of the physics to liquefy some of the natural gas. You could argue that if the CPC spent less money on the People's Liberation Army (PLA), it would have more money to develop natural gas processing.

I should point out that this lack of capital to spur innovation and growth wasn't restricted to the oil and gas business. Other industries in the PRC also lagged behind the West. This led the country to open up and seek capital and expertise from foreign investors and entrepreneurs who were willing to supply both in order to make money.

In our case, after initially insisting they only used natural gas to make fertilizer, not fuel, the CPC eventually warmed to Yih-Min's argument that using it for fuel was better than just burning it and not getting anything out of it. Once they acknowledged this, Yih-Min told them he knew just the guy who could capture and process the gas. In fact, he'd visited his facilities in Texas.

**SF**: So Yih-Min and that "guy," aka Patrick Jenevein, have these meetings in Urumqi with the CNPC engineers. Then what?

**PJ**: We met CNPC engineers in Urumqi, in Karamay, in Korla, in Hami—all over Xinjiang. We drove out to them, to look at the oil fields. Leaving Hami to return to Urumqi alone one time, I sat in the back of a Mercedes, sipping a drink, listening to Madonna. The Mercedes was a CNPC district-owned SUV, the drink was bottled water, and Madonna was almost certainly the driver's pirated tape.

Road construction ran short cuts through safety concerns. First, the PRC lacked funds, and foreign investors were building businesses in the PRC's east, not in Xinjiang. Second, the CPC still thought good roads could pave invasion pathways for Russians coming from the west. Third, the party cares little about the safety of its governed masses.

**SF**: Once you got out to the fields, what was your objective?

**PJ**: We were looking for people we could work with, and opportunities to add value. We wanted to assess support for our technologies and operations. Working with high-pressure, high-temperature engines and compressors, and very low-temperature processing equipment, requires careful and capable mechanics and technicians. Just as cars require maintenance, repairs, or overhauls, so does natural gas equipment. If we could reach a financial agreement with CNPC, we wanted our equipment to work. That required being able to work with whatever technical capabilities the CNPC had. Once we determined that, we'd be able to project what benefits we could provide—and whether we could make any money in the process (no pun intended!).

**SF**: And by "technologies," do you mean equipment that can capture the gas being flared into the atmosphere by the wells and then process it?

**PJ**: Yes, you're working from a starting collection point through compression and processing to discharge into a pipeline—or another use, like power generation. The amounts and composition of natural gas, temperatures, elevation changes, and other factors drive equipment choices and configurations.

We take natural gas samples, then input those measurements into process simulations that we use to design whole gas systems. When gas comes out of the ground, it will be some combination of methane, ethane, propane, and butane. If you don't know what that combination is, you're only guessing what you might be able to do with it. If you know what kind of pressure and what kind of gas you have, then you can calculate outcomes under those conditions and improve your designs immeasurably. And if you can design better, you're gonna have a better financial outcome.

For our first potential project to process natural gas, we answered all our questions constructively. We actually collected a volatile natural gas sample in Xinjiang and transported it to Texas, where we ran it through a composition analysis lab. Then we ran our calculations, and told them, "The vast majority of the gas coming out of the field is methane."

That was bad news. There was nothing for us to process. To liquefy methane, you have to reach −260°F. Technically, we can do that, but it's very costly—too costly to meet our objectives.

If the gas had been ethane, propane, or butane, we could have liquified it under high pressure at only −20°F, and at a reasonable cost. That 240-degree gap was a bridge too far, from a cost-benefit analysis. We told the local entrepreneur working with CNPC that the numbers just didn't work. They were surprised we declined to accept the project.

**SF**: End of story?

**PJ**: No. When turning down work or criticizing a choice, we always try to make an accompanying suggestion. For this potential project gone bust, we suggested CNPC use clean-burning methane to generate electricity. Going out in the field, we had seen plenty of natural gas-fired engines, which you can either attach to a compressor to move gas through pipelines or to an electricity generator. Just as you can attach an engine to wheels on a car or a propeller in a boat, you can attach a natural gas-fueled engine to a compressor or a generator. In effort and effect, just change out the back end.

**SF**: Actually, I knew this wasn't the end of the story. Despite your conclusion that the project initially envisioned wasn't viable, you and Yih-Min and the CNPC did see possibilities for collaboration. In a few pages, we'll get to the projects that Tang Energy Group—the company you formed with Yih-Min in 1996—actually did execute, and others it didn't, including one that led to you being transported to the remote quarters of a disgruntled Chinese general and held incommunicado.

For now, however, I'd just like to observe that, for lack of a better term, your "fluency" in describing the technologies and processes to a layperson like me is apparent. Were you as fluent in 1995 as you are now? Or did you rely on Yih-Min with his PhD in physics, his patents, and his experience working with the CNPC?

**PJ**: Back then I was much more fluent than I am now. I'd learned a lot through Bluebonnet, NG Compression, and the Texas Utility power plant. In truth, Yih-Min looked to me to lead processing discussions. I'm not an engineer, but long before this I'd figured out that if it doesn't work mechanically—physically—it ain't gonna work financially. It's kind of a simple recognition that some people never get. If your power plant doesn't run, you don't make money. On that point, my dear bride—who doesn't care about learning the mechanics of any machine—would make a better power plant manager than many of the candidates we had for the job. Why? Because she takes financial responsibility for the physical performance of her car.

Again, when we told CNPC, "We can't add value, you should just generate electricity," they couldn't believe we had declined an opportunity to take their money.

**SF**: How long were you in China before returning home?

**PJ**: Our trip to the oil fields we've been discussing wasn't our only venture outside of Urumqi. The CNPC drove us to the Tarim Basin—known in the Uyghurs' native tongue as Altishahr, which means "six cities." Tarim, pronounced "ta-lee-moo," is one of the biggest basins in China—over 340,000 square miles. Its desert could easily have swallowed six cities. Because of its oil reserves, CNPC operated a division there.

This was a about day's drive from Urumqi. Again, we had a driver. Yih-Min and I sat in the back seat. The road goes through vast stretches of desert. Though difficult for a Texan to imagine, it may be bigger than the Texas desert. The conditions are harsh—but often the conditions in Texas where we operate are harsh. So I wasn't put off by that. But then the wind came up, and Steve, the road disappeared.

**SF**: Did you stop?

**PJ**: No! We're still driving along. I'm remembering that the locals call the desert *Taklamakan*, which means "you go in and don't come out," and I'm thinking, *How is this guy staying on the road*? If you got off the road, you could be buried in sand, suffocate, and be lost to the ages. Somehow, we got where we were going.

**SF**: Am I correct that this was the second operation you visited? What was it like compared to the first one? And what was your analysis of it, compared to those other oil fields?

**PJ**: Frankly, it's hard to recall the sequencing of all my trips. Two points merit noting. First, I was learning China from the inside, picking up innumerable insights like tesserae. Second, after we sued the PRC's biggest defense contractor many years later, a hacker pilfered files from—and added files into—our saved email cache. One message sent from Tang's server strongly suggested a state actor with an informed awareness of our case had taken over our emails. So it's hard to go back and reconstruct the timeline.

This visit to the Tarim Basin was, again, just to get the lay of the land. No deal was struck, and to be honest, my longest lasting memory is of a visit to the regional museum in Urumqi to see the Tarim mummies, which date back to 2000 BCE, and are quite well known in the scientific community.

These mummies are remarkably well preserved thanks to the dryness of the desert. Many have Caucasian characteristics and present evidence of genetic ties to Europe. Amazingly, the red hair of a few is apparent. The clothing of some also remains, including conical hats thought to belong to witches! So if you're ever in the neighborhood . . .

**SF**: I'll plug the coordinates into my GPS.

**PJ**: At the museum, I wound up talking to a Frenchman who was there trying to restore the mummies and learn what he could. He speculated that some may have descended from troops who had left Alexander the Great's army, positing: "Maybe they got tired of fighting and found a place where they could marry women, settle down, and farm."

**SF**: You mentioned a driver. Was there a representative of the CPC or PRC who was assigned to you—either to make things easier or to spy on you?

**PJ**: Yes and yes. There was one guy who almost always came along with us. His apparent role was that of "business broker"; he was trying to help US companies work with PRC companies. There was certainly an intelligence component to his work, too. I'm sure he would brief his authorities on our activities. Yih-Min got to know him pretty well. And we ate dinner and lunch together. Spending a lot of time with him, we wound up talking about a lot of things. We assumed he would report our activities and conversations, and actually saw that as potentially helpful for pressing our business case to higher authorities.

**SF**: Do you think you were thoroughly vetted before you even got to China that first time?

**PJ**: It's hard to know. Drafting in behind Yih-Min's background and good work made a difference for me. He'd been there. His Chinese is impeccable, often better than theirs. He was helping them make more money. So when it came to me, they were inclined to rely on his credibility. That I came from the United States added value to growing Tang's *guanxi* and the CNPC's opportunities to accrue *mianzi*.

More importantly, at that time the PRC was looking for foreign investment and what they called "management science"—how do companies manage their businesses to create value? So when Yih-Min said, "Let's bring in this Texan," they were inclined to believe him. They also wanted Texas technology, especially geopolitically significant Texas *oil field* technology.

So before I flew over, I'm sure they'd decided the chance to acquire that technology was worth the risk. That was kind of easy. Also, in 1995, they didn't have nearly the capability they do now to vet Americans before they visit. And finally, I was never too far out of their sight or earshot once I arrived. In the PRC, prudence requires assuming you're being watched, bugged, tagged, and taped.

I remember taking a picture of an oil rig one time with a little bitty camera that used rolls of film, and then getting chastised for photographing their energy infrastructure.

**SF**: Did you ever drive anywhere yourself?

**PJ**: Oh no. I never drove in China. First, relying on a local to drive and park was simply more efficient. Second, operating a motor vehicle in a country whose laws protect the state from people instead of the other way around avoids some existential challenges. If I had hit and injured a Chinese citizen, I would have had to take care of him or her for life. And if I'd killed him or her, I would have had to pay his/her family. At the time, the going rate for killing somebody in a traffic accident was $12,000 to $14,000.

Interestingly, in 1999, after the United States bombed the Chinese Embassy in Belgrade and killed three Chinese citizens, President Clinton went to China and gave Chairman Jiang Zemin a check for $3 million—one million dollars for each Chinese life. This was brilliant politically because the going rate for killing a Chinese citizen, according to the Communist Party, was less than 1.5 percent of that. Think about it. Bill Clinton, *the President of the United States*, shows up and says Chinese lives are worth at least $1 million each—over seventy-one times more valuable than the PRC price for a human life. (A friend engaged in producing novel technological capabilities for US defense purposes uses states' pricing of lives to indicate proclivity for slaughtering masses in war.)

**SF**: We'll talk more about the embassy bombing later. You mentioned you just assumed you were always being bugged.

**PJ**: Yes. On several early trips, a younger man helped me everywhere I went. He was capable and quick. He had a card that got us through every line, or line-glob, we encountered.

Looking back, he was almost certainly with the Ministry of State Security (MSS). The irony of learning a little bit of Mandarin from MSS amuses me. I chose to regard him as my personal aide.

By the way, I hadn't requested him. He just showed up and said he was there to help me. And he did. We'd fly from Beijing to Urumqi, and he would get my luggage off the plane first and say, "I'll bring it to your room." Before you ask, yes, I know it went into a car and they inspected it and then it got to my room.

One night, when I had just arrived in Beijing from Dallas, I was dead tired and fell hard asleep in my hotel room. Loud knocking jolted me awake. Still disoriented, I looked through the peephole and saw two guys, including my so-called personal aide. I opened the door. "We need your passport," he said. *OK, just a moment.* I got my passport and gave it to them. I still don't know why they wanted it. I was too tired to ask then, or when I got it back.

**SF**: Did you take any measures to mitigate all of this? I'm romanticizing here, but did you, like, turn up the music so you could have a conversation?

**PJ**: Regardless of the specific points, like knots that hold a net together, we knew to respect the breadth, depth, and reach of the surveillance network. First, let me talk about what the Chinese (in China) do. They mitigate their exposure to the thought police by controlling even their own thinking. Ponder that. Especially with recent onslaughts against independent thought, Chinese in the PRC allow "Xi Jinping-thought" to govern their very own thinking. It's like an infection that devours self-expressive souls.

I mitigated with honesty and sincerity—fearless sincerity. My attitude was*: OK, you wanna check up on a thirtysomething white male from the United States who has a decent education and is coming over here and going to all kinds of places, including sensitive locations in western China? I understand why you might be afraid I'm a spook.*

Within the bounds of honesty, we certainly protected our own confidential information. We acted as if Chinese agents could eavesdrop on every conversation we had. Now, there were places you could go if you really had to have a conversation—not a long one, but long enough to review important positions or considerations. We did that routinely and opportunistically. Sometimes, taking a walk and ducking into a restaurant or shop or bank branch that we seldom used provided enough time to reveal confidential concerns or developments.

"Let's go for a walk," took on significance. Sometimes, we just had to wait until we were back in the United States together at a safe place. The fact that you have to do that is just part of working in China. If you don't, you're spilling your guts, you're divulging secrets.

**SF**: Can knowing they're listening ever work to your advantage? Can you pull the old misdirection play?

**PJ:** Steve, you'd work well in the PRC. It certainly can. Not only that, if a business or government wants to negotiate effectively with CPC-controlled entities, they must engage in their own chicanery. Our second pilot project offers a straightforward, simple example of a tactic we deployed in ever-more-sophisticated environments, a tactic rarely addressed—at least openly—in academia or government.

**SF**: That project proposed selling and installing a natural gas processing plant for CNPC's Karamay oil field, about four hours northwest of Urumqi. We'll go into detail about it later. For now, let's focus on ye olde misdirection play.

**PJ**: Sure. After several days of presentations, Yih-Min stayed in Karamay to complete negotiations while I returned to Texas. Shortly after I got home, Yih-Min faxed me the latest deal terms, which were severely skewed from the letter of intent that had guided our efforts.

Knowing the authorities would be monitoring our communications, I responded with a CONFIDENTIAL fax that nailed important points. First, their negotiators had done a superb job representing CNPC. Second, they had pushed Tang Energy beyond its single project profitability point, deep into our strategic investment budget for developing a long-term relationship with CNPC. Third, I lashed out at Yih-Min for giving in too much to CNPC, arguing that they had done a fine job advancing their interest forcefully. Finally, I "instructed" Yih-Min to come home at his earliest, appropriate opportunity. While we could put in a lot of time on this "lesson," let me decode the most important parts of the message.

One: Putting "CONFIDENTIAL" in bold at the top of the page assured that CNPC's Karamay office would read the message, and assured Yih-Min I knew they would do so before delivering it to him.

Two: In the fax, I twice complimented the Karamay division negotiators. I said they had superbly represented CNPC and suggested they had "forcefully" out-negotiated both Yih-Min, an American PhD, and me, our American company's CEO. The compliments were truly sincere and had two audiences: the Karamay engineers themselves and, more importantly, their CNPC bosses. The compliments gave the engineers *mianzi*, which allowed them, perhaps ironically, more room to remaneuver in final negotiations. Revealing Tang Energy's strategic position demonstrated our sincerity, calibrated the level of our effort, and expressed our long-term commitment in a way they could qualify and trust.

Finally: Counterintuitively, I empowered Yih-Min by criticizing his efforts publicly. Yes, I had marked the fax CONFIDENTIAL, but everyone left in Karamay had read it. Making the criticism personal to, but respectful of, Yih-Min showed the CNPC that he had authority, not just responsibility, but authority and power he could use according to his discretion. In Confucian contexts, that elevated Yih-Min; it gave him *mianzi*.

The instruction for Yih-Min to "come home as soon as you find it appropriate" also reinforced his authority. It set a negotiation deadline he could use but did so in a way that gave him the freedom to manipulate it. And he did. Within hours, he concluded negotiations for a profitable project.

Many of these observations will contradict the experience of others in different places. But the CPC creates a weird environment that gives individuals responsibilities yet denies them the authority to make decisions.

Confirmation of success came a few months later, when CNPC's internal newspaper revealed they had awarded a Canadian company an identical opportunity, and had already earned over 100 percent of their investment with us before the Canadian competitor had even begun operations. More importantly, CNPC invited us to participate in developing power plants in a neighboring province.

**SF**: How mischievous of you! How often were you going to China?

**PJ**: Funny you should ask. In preparing for our conversation, I found a document that noted, "For the first six months of 1997, Dr. Jan and Mr. Jenevein spent, respectively, 107 and 22 days in China. In the same time period, two mechanics and one electrical engineer, all Americans working on Tang's behalf, spent 53 days in China."

**SF**: That's a lot of frequent flier miles. Did Kathy ever accompany you?

**PJ**: Yes. She came three times, once with my parents. I recently found a letter she wrote to the Whirlygigs in 2003, when she accompanied me to a board meeting for a power plant in Dunhuang, near the western end of the Great Wall.

**SF**: Whirlygigs?

**PJ**: In our newlywed bungalow, made so by Kathy moving wardrobe, furniture, and makeup into my bachelor pad, we bought a dishwasher that rolled and hooked up to the kitchen sink. Often, it blocked the back door, which opened right onto the kitchen. Coming home from work one day, I saw two of the girls chasing each other around the dishwasher while the third, a toddler, twirled in place like a beautiful ballerina.

I kissed Kathy and said, "We've got Whirlygigs!" And so the nickname was born.

**SF**. Ah. And Kathy's letter?

**PJ**: I found one passage that really moved me. For context, I'd been going to China for about eight years at this point:

> The bottom line to this whole trip is that you should be extremely proud of your father. Where he has gone and what he has done all this time is just short of miraculous in my mind. It is hard traveling and hard communicating and understanding the culture of these people. He is a true pioneer. Sometimes pioneers don't reap the full benefits—others do later—but he is surely a pioneer. The Chinese like him and relate to him. He understands them better than most people would, mainly because he tries so hard to understand them—their language, their life, their business needs. It is about as foreign as you can get!

I know I'm departing from the timeline, but I have one other strong memory of that trip with Kathy. The chairman of the board of the Dunhuang plant was fifty-five to sixty, lean for his age, and weathered. He exhibited a card-carrying Communist's authority—with added crustiness. Yet, we had gotten to know and respect each other. I had pushed for decisions that made good sense for the company, and he knew it.

He saw that when I was outvoted, I did everything I could to make the winning decision as successful for the company as I could. I didn't take what would have been a loss of *mianzi* as a setback at all or an insult in any way. Instead, I showed him a path to transcend his own cultural limitations.

At the dinner for board members and guests, he and I got a little personal. I asked him about his family. He said he had two daughters, and I asked, "Where are they now?" He knew. So that meant he kept up with them. Then I asked him how he'd been able to keep his family together in the 1960s and '70s. I avoided the term "Cultural Revolution," but he knew what I meant. And then this tough, old, hardline Communist started to cry. I'll never know why. Maybe he had failed to keep them together. Maybe he committed atrocities to keep them together. Maybe he was thinking he had lived through hell to get to where he was today.

**SF**: For readers like me who need a little history refresher: Mao initiated the Cultural Revolution in 1966, and it lasted until his death in 1976. The cover for his effort was that "bourgeois infiltrators" were leading the CPC and PRC in a direction contrary to his vision of Communism.

Under the banner of protecting Communism, he closed schools and employed the Red Guards to put the kibosh on all things "bourgeois," and many just plain traditional Chinese habits and structures. Older people, artists, and intellectuals were primary targets. Estimates of the number of civilian deaths during the period run from the hundreds of thousands to the millions.

Back to the discussion with your friend, the chairman. Is there a difference in deciding whether to initiate a personal discussion with a person in China, as opposed to a fellow American? Were you taking a risk, crossing a line?

**PJ**: Oh, boy. Timing and balance make the difference between success and failure, even life and death, really. So, yes, I was taking a risk. First, I was young and curious. I was also sincere, and exposing my career and ability to care for my family in ways that benefitted Chinese people.

Second, in his mind, he was my Confucian superior. He was both Han Chinese and older. I was not Chinese and younger. He was also the chairman. In Confucian ideology, there are no peer-to-peer relationships. There's always a superior and a subordinate, and older is superior to younger. Male is superior to female—not in my family where brilliant, beautiful women rule the roost, but in Confucian ideology. There is a weird situation with an older sister and a younger brother because older is superior to younger, but male is supposedly superior to the female.

As my superior, the chairman had another Confucian obligation: to help his subordinate learn. So there he was, chairman, older, and Han Chinese, and here I was asking about his family surviving the Cultural Revolution. It was clear I cared.

His reaction actually captures a broader insight: When CPC leaders question their own confidence, they act more responsibly. That's because they're trying to figure it out. They're trying to gain the upper hand. So there is struggle. There is tension. But the tension is a fight inside their brains and their hearts. *How do we make this work?*

Younger and, in a way, his mentee and responsibility, I had jabbed him with a painful memory. Quickly, I reflected that history presents each of us with opportunities and challenges and with moments or even years of great sadness. He nodded appreciatively. He indicated he knew what I said was true. He was grateful that I, his student, allowed us to move on to other subjects.

**SF**: The summer of 2023 saw publication of a book pertinent to our conversation above. Per *The Christian Science Monitor*:

> In "Red Memory: The Afterlives of China's Cultural Revolution," British journalist Tania Branigan reveals the profound yet often hidden present-day reverberations of the 1966–76 Cultural Revolution. During the fanatical campaign unleashed by Mao Zedong, Red Guards persecuted and killed millions of people across China. Betrayal and mistrust divided students and teachers, neighbors, and even families.
>
> Then, in a jarring shift, China's post-Mao leaders denounced the Cultural Revolution as a "catastrophe" as they redirected the country's energies away from the pursuit of a communist Utopia and toward market-oriented economic growth. Ordinary Chinese people were allowed to speak about the ordeal, for a time. But Beijing, eager to control the historical narrative and mute criticism of Mr. Mao, gradually began to suppress all but brief mentions of the disastrous campaign. (Ann Scott Tyson, "How the Cultural Revolution shapes Chinese families decades later," August 23, 2023)

Does this ring true to you? Also, what books would you recommend to those who wish to understand the Chinese people, the Chinese government, and the Chinese business climate today?

**PJ**: Let's start with the clarion ring of truth. Yes, absolutely, this rings true. Branigan's descriptions illuminate horrors. The rise and fall of relative political power among top leaders within the CPC that instigated those horrors scares me. The internecine resilience of one man, Mao Zedong, enabled him to inject fear, wreak injustices, and oppress an entire country's population.

What, for example, is the view from inside the Communist Party? Another missing point of view concerns the events leading up to Mao's death and the party's sequence of power struggles. Mao's loyal lieutenants compelled him to end the industrial revolution years before the Cultural Revolution. Those loyal lieutenants included Zhou Enlai and Deng Xiaoping. Mao put on a happy face and ended the industrial revolution. But he held a grudge against Zhou and Deng and feared their potential to usurp his paramount leader position.

When he could, he wreaked revenge and restored his paramount perch. That he did so by unleashing the PRC's youth against Chinese traditions and, indeed, the state itself, shows the depth of his depravity. Xi Jinping displays the same brutality in persecuting minority groups like the LGBT community and the Uyghurs in Xinjiang.

Before getting to books, look for shorter pieces: David Rennie's "Chaguan" column in *The Economist*, and anything Matt Pottinger writes.

For current issues, start with Ian Easton's *The Final Struggle: Inside China's Global Strategy* (2022). Easton works from the inside out. He uses Communist Party documents to present its expected trajectory. Personal details of its leaders support why the party pushes its policies. These details also make his book fun to read.

Elizabeth Economy's half-dozen books comprehensively analyze the PRC's positions on critical issues, from environmental concerns to political charades.

Then read *Commissioner Lin and the Opium War* (1970) by Hsin-pao Chang. Events, positions, and actions from the 1800s inform the present and future. Chang brilliantly balances perspectives and exposes vulnerabilities not just for two, but for all sides that escalate tensions into war. The density of Chang's work delights readers who have wallowed in China's habituations, for whatever reasons.

For revealing Communist Party functions, read Richard McGregor's *The Party: The Secret World of China's Communist Rulers* (2010). For negotiating with Chinese diplomatic or commercial counterparties, read almost anything by Lucian Pye. Just three pages in his *Chinese Commercial Negotiating Style* (1982) address *mianzi* and *guanxi* luminously and succinctly.

## Chapter 4

# Yes, I Provided Intelligence to the CIA

**SF**: If I understand correctly, you and Yih-Min returned from that exploratory trip to Xinjiang in 1995 somewhat sanguine about the possibility of future projects in China.

**PJ**: Yes. It seemed evident that substantial PRC companies and individual Chinese wanted to work with us. Remember, *we* were the ones who said "no" to the project in Xinjiang. We thought more opportunities might present themselves, and that if the numbers were right, we should be ready to hit the ground running. So we quickly formed Tang Energy to develop natural gas-fueled electrical power projects and natural gas processing projects. We needed the second project type to make the first work and we needed several projects to build a business.

**SF**: In a 1997 business plan aimed at potential investors, you described your mission:

> Tang plans to develop and own two energy plants in China per year for the next five years. "Energy plants," as used here, describe plants that convert the components of natural gas into various energy forms including electricity, steam, clean processed gas for fuel or feedstock

> and LPG plus other bottled gases. Plants will range in size, but all should, from a development and due diligence perspective, emulate the $50 million (initial construction cost) Wichita Falls Cogeneration Plant that Tang principals helped develop ten years ago.
>
> Chinese entities will own part of the plants that Tang develops, but Tang's growth will depend on increasing its ownership in energy plants. At such time as Tang has successfully developed eight to ten plants that produce stable cash flow, Tang will take the company to the public markets in the US or China. As an alternative, Tang may pursue a merger with a financially large and strong partner.

You also explained why you thought Tang had reason to be so optimistic:

> China needs energy, especially electricity. In the Xinjiang region, where Tang concentrates its efforts, the need is extreme. However, the region has ample, if not abundant, and largely unused supplies of natural gas . . . Xinjiang's extreme need and extreme inconvenience combine to promise higher project returns than projects in the more populated eastern regions where larger developers compete.

**SF**: How did you decide upon the name Tang?

**PJ**: Yih-Min came up with it. He already had his own company, Titan. And I had NG Processing and NG Compression—both borrowed the initials N and G from the company I'd formed in 1987, the Nolan Group, and emphasized our natural gas focus. We took the T from Titan, used A for "and" then added the N and G, and bingo we had an instant energy company, if not a powdered orange drink. Historically, the name invokes one of China's most favored dynasties, the Tang Dynasty. We didn't quite aspire to "dynasty" status, but we were hoping to significantly boost the economic prosperity of the Chinese people and to be a means for better diplomatic relations between China and the United States.

I should add here, Steve, that while we saw exciting opportunities in China, Tang didn't plan to limit its operations to the PRC. The world was our oyster, and that included the United States. Texas continued to offer possibilities, and California remained on my watch list. Natural gas acts the same, depending on temperature and pressure, the world over.

In choosing the name Tang, we subtly, but consciously, incorporated another benefit. Because *tang* suggests soaring or rising in Chinese, incorporating it into the name of the joint venture complimented our partners. If we called this book *Fiffer Tang*, the title would translate to "Fiffer Rises!" As you can see in Image 3 the "G" in our logo had an arrow that was going up, or circling and then rising. So it was a very positive way to form joint ventures. It allowed our Chinese partners to subordinate our name, with inculcated Confucian humility, to an adjective that complimented them.

**SF**: In the previous chapter, we teased a story about a disgruntled Chinese general who sent his minions for you and held you incommunicado. Before we get to that, let's talk about the two successful pilot projects you became involved with almost immediately after forming Tang.

**PJ**: Right. Project one was in a place called Yakela, very near Kuqa, on the northern rim of the Tarim Basin, south and a little bit west of Urumqi, between Korla to the east and Aksu to the west. It involved building a plant to supply electricity to a carbon black plant that generated hard currency revenue for China, when China desperately needed dollars, yen, and euros.

**SF**: For energy novices like me, what is a carbon black plant? And beyond that, did China already have a lot of these? Does the United States?

**PJ**: Carbon black goes into tires for our cars and trucks, ink for our printers, even makeup and other uses. It's older than the Dead Sea Scrolls, which were written with carbon black, and as new as the newest technologies for creating capacitors. Making carbon black starts with oxidizing heavy oil, which means altering the heavy oil in a controlled burn process to make a black powdery substance.

Texas once produced 75 percent of the nation's carbon black, but environmental concerns have closed most carbon black plants in the United States. Now, rather than paying more to make carbon black production as clean as we say we would like it to be, America has outsourced the job to the PRC, which prioritizes economic power over environmental issues. At least the natural gas-fueled power provided by Tang cleaned up their process.

**SF**: As interesting as that process is, I'm just as interested in the process that led to this deal.

**PJ**: Remember on our exploratory trip we turned down an opportunity, explaining, "Your natural gas stream is mostly methane already, so we could not add value by processing it." Then we suggested CNPC use the natural gas to generate electricity.

A few months later, CNPC asked us to provide power generation equipment for them. Again, we turned them down. "We've seen the equipment you have," we explained. "You've already got Caterpillar engines with generators on the back of them. Just use those. You don't need us to do that." They couldn't believe we turned their money down a second time.

Not too long after that, we learned of the carbon plant that used CNPC gas but needed to replace 1930s vintage airplane engines to generate electricity. That plant didn't have the budget to buy new equipment to replace the old, worn-out radial piston engines and equally aged generators. But they could buy electricity.

"Ah," we said. "We understand the physical, and we understand the financial. If you have money to buy electricity, we can figure out a way to make it work. We're going to sell you electricity at a price you can afford that still generates a sufficient profit for us. Otherwise, it won't work." So we started negotiating and, after a bit, reached a deal for our first project—an electricity-generating plant fueled by natural gas. We asked Xinjiang High New Technology, an Urumqi-based company, to join us so we could have local representation.

**SF**: And who was your Chinese counterparty for buying the electricity your plant generated?

**PJ**: Good question. You're touching on a point that concerns, or should concern, anyone trying to work in the PRC. The CPC makes it difficult to identify your true counterparty. We do know the CPC effectively controls counterparties, even if they create complex ownership webs. Americans, too, use complex ownership structures. Usually, those structures support favorable financing opportunities, or protect individuals' privacy. But the party uses complexity to obfuscate the pervasiveness of its control. Americans generally equate ownership with control. But control is control. To quote Matthew Johnson, a China expert and longtime member of the National Committee on US-China Relations: "Ownership is an obsolete concept." I'm sure we'll return to this theme. It merits repetition to ensure understanding.

Initially, our Urumqi partner told us a regional government agency owned the carbon black plant and would pay for the electricity we would produce. We searched high and low to confirm this through nongovernment sources, to no avail. I finally found someone from the CIA who told me the local government did indeed own the plant. What he didn't tell me was that the CPC was a co-owner—with a 50 percent stake—and the ultimate authority regarding plant commitments. We found that out on our own.

That arrangement complicated our efforts because, as we learned later, the local government and the local CPC bosses were squabbling out of our sight, behind the "Chinese curtain," again, in the Communist Party's shadows. From our side of the curtain, we could see shadows moving and hear characters moaning. Whether they were fighting or, use your imagination for the alliteration, we couldn't tell.

**SF**: Did you tell the guy from the CIA?

**PJ**: Darn right. I was mad. Here I am, a young American with an unbridled, perhaps reverential faith in our CIA, with its mystical aura, and it's giving me faulty intelligence. *You lied to me*, I thought, but was careful not to say. Believe it or not, he said, "Hmmm, we didn't know that. What else do you know?"

"What do you mean, what else do I know?" I asked.

"What else do you know?"

**SF**: So the CIA is asking *you*, a private citizen, to provide *it* with intelligence? Was that the only time that happened? Should I have faith in the CIA? Did you?

**PJ**: A straightforward question with a complex answer. That conversation began an interweaving relationship that would develop, with ebbs and flows, over decades. I wound up gathering information and perspectives from inside the PRC—and even the CPC—that the CIA found useful. The CPC-PRC considered both the basic information as well as the esoteric insights I gathered to be state secrets. The CIA, as you would expect, has its own sources. But, over the years that I worked with CPC-controlled entities, the CPC detained—and executed—many of those informants.

I had an advantage the CIA did not. I worked for mutual benefit. I really was trying to build businesses that benefitted us *and* our Chinese counterparts. I could ask for information we truly did need to justify investments that created jobs and made profits for Chinese and Americans. When we were negotiating building a power plant for a fertilizer plant, we asked for natural gas reservoir data, a PRC state secret, because we really did need it to secure financing. The basic truth that profits sustain jobs and attract more investments protected my inquiries and behavior.

National intelligence officers expect each other, for patriotic reasons, to lie, cheat, and steal. When they go to another country, they understand what they do often violates local laws. Countries need some amount of spying on other countries. Locally illegal behaviors can tilt sovereign choices toward war or toward peace. Just as businesses seek to confirm their counterparties' intentions and capabilities, so do nations need to gauge other nations' goals, means, and intentions. Intelligence officers understand that their own governments expect them to act illegally. Their governments provide tools and cover; nevertheless, intelligence officers' truth, which is that their countries pay them to lie, cheat and steal, provides no protection from the consequences of discovery by the nations they spy on.

The PRC's intelligence services worried that business purposes camouflaged my true priorities. Fearing I might work for the CIA, they checked me out. Thoroughly. From having personal attention to my luggage—explained as showing the government's esteem for my work—to moving to the head of long lines because of my minder's red, wallet-sized ID, to waking me from a dead sleep with pounding at my hotel door to check my passport, I understood full well that the state was watching me.

Still, the truth that I sought mutual benefit drove my actions. Like armor, truth provides a layer of protection, but with vulnerabilities. If the party ever sensed that I shared information, even information gathered for commercial reasons, I knew it would retaliate. While I could only imagine the magnitude of retaliation, I knew the party would treat Yih-Min—because he's racially Chinese—more brutally than it would treat me, because I'm racially European. I certainly couldn't reveal to Yih-Min that many things—reserve estimates, topographical maps and the keys to correcting the skew in those maps, the state of maintenance and development of engines, especially jet engines, the relationships among and within the CPC, AVIC, and CNPC leaders—interested the US government. Neither could I tell my family.

So, yes, I provided intelligence to the CIA. So did others. I opened a node on its network. Some useful intelligence for the CIA comes from "knocks," or people who knock on its door. Simply debriefing people like me working in critical industries exposes none of the agency's assets to uncertain outcomes and accomplishes important objectives. I knocked on their door to learn. Unwittingly, I walked through a door that wove me into a web of information flow. I was an asset to the CIA, but definitely not the only "asset," per se.

Now, about faith in the CIA: First, I am grateful to the officers who, to protect me, classified information I brought to them. They helped keep others from piercing my armor.

Second, faith sounds like an either-or choice. I can better answer in terms that express my confidence level in CIA effectiveness. Not knowing all it does or how it does it, overall and without reservation, I hold the CIA in high regard. As with any organization, however, my confidence in individuals serving the institution ranges widely.

Over-buoyed self-confidence, and the relative infrequency of testing its major assessments, has the effect of sinking the CIA's critical judgment capabilities. Unlike commercial outfits where competitors constantly challenge each other's positions, CIA findings irregularly face public scrutiny.

Abrupt consequences help companies rethink positions and redirect resources quickly. Infrequently tested conclusions or suppositions lead to consequential failures. Intelligence organizations around the world inferred that Saddam Hussein had developed weapons of mass destruction. More recently, in June 2023, US Secretary of State Antony Blinken met with Qin Gang just days before the CPC "disappeared" him. Both events illustrate intelligence service failures. Neither had preceding tests to authenticate or contest the veracity of underlying intelligence assessments. Time compounds the inaccuracies of even small misjudgments.

Still, the agency, and others in the US intelligence community, can and do collect essential intelligence around the world. They deploy personnel internationally and use some of the world's most advanced gear to build troves of data on various subjects. We need them. Americans should, however, calibrate our expectations to the limitations that political leadership, organizational structure, and ideological working environments impose.

**SF**: Were any other US government agencies involved in, or at least aware of, your dealings? How much did the government know of what American businesses were doing in China at the time? Was it pushing US involvement? Were some major American companies already established or trying to get established at this time? Did you have to file paperwork first—either in the US or with our embassy? Get approval? Or was it more like the Wild West, and you only called the sheriff when there was trouble?

**PJ**: That's a barrelful of questions. Interrupt or redirect me as you find helpful. In the beginning, only the CIA knew what we were trying to accomplish. I doubt they reported to the Department of Commerce or State or to the US Embassy in Beijing.

As our financial opportunities began to solidify, we did talk to other US agencies that mitigated foreign political risk for investors. Both the Export-Import Bank of the United States (EXIM) and the US Overseas Private Investment Corporation (OPIC) had programs that interested us. Frankly, however, the cost of their programs, their cumbersome requirements to engage, the turtle-like pace of their responsiveness, and their own exposure to domestic political changes led us to give up on trying to work with them.

As we moved into the wind energy business, the US Department of Energy (DOE)—especially its National Renewable Energy Laboratory—started to pay attention to our work. We also interacted with the International Finance Corporation, part of the World Bank, and the Global Environment Fund.

**SF**: According to the USAGov website, EXIM "assists American businesses export[ing] their goods by providing financial assistance in the form of loans, loan guarantees and insurance. The focus of the Export-Import Bank is on assisting small businesses."[1] What exactly were you exporting at that time, and what exactly is this insurance?

**PJ**: We were exporting natural gas processing and compression equipment. Coming the other way, we were importing money. Both directions of that exchange required us to manage exposures to uncertain outcomes, or unexpected events. Regarding the gear, neither buyer nor seller wanted, for example, to lose money if the ship carrying the gear sank in an ocean. Regarding the money, we feared a Mandarin decision that denied or delayed the relay of cash from our buyer's PRC bank to our Texas bank.

Former First National Bank of Dallas officers and our controller worked tirelessly with counterparties in the PRC to generate the very first known

[1] "Export-Import Bank of the United States (EXIM)," USAGov, 2024. https://www.usa.gov/agencies/export-import-bank-of-the-united-states#

letter of credit issued by the Bank of China that a US bank confirmed. That confirmation had the effect of protecting us from any money transfer problem.

If we could show that we did what we said we would do, then we could go to the Texas bank and receive payment. The banks learned to rely on each other. With this success, we accomplished a tough task—getting one set of banks to accept another's protocols and commitments. Contrast that with US and PRC judiciaries not accepting each other's processes and judgments.

In the first power plant, we had agreed to make money by producing and selling electricity over "the long run." That meant we were exposing our investment to the uncertainty of our PRC counterparties abiding by contractual commitments over a longer term. We've seen US presidents changing their predecessor's policies. Well, it's even worse at lower levels in the PRC. As a high-ranking PRC state-owned enterprise representative once explained: "When leadership changes . . . the new leaders don't care about the previous leaders' commitments."

To reduce our exposure to vacillatory CPC behavior, we sought US-sponsored overseas investment support. OPIC—which later merged with USAID to form the US International Development Finance Corporation—would invest with us. It would earn fees for reviewing our investment, as well as a priority return on its investment. We knew what we had to do to protect our limited cash reserves, so we found OPIC's program attractive.

**SF**: How did it fall apart?

**PJ**: Anyone watching the news is probably aware that every so often, actually quite often, when the Communist Party gets its nose out of joint due to something the United States or Taiwan has done, it flexes its PLA muscles and fires missiles into the Taiwan Strait, the sea that separates Taiwan from continental Asia. These temper tantrums display their displeasure and suggest their strength. Remember August of 2022, when then-US House of Representatives Speaker Nancy Pelosi took a delegation to Taiwan?

In March of 1996, shortly before Taiwan's presidential election, China fired more missiles as a warning to Taiwanese voters. *Electing Lee Teng-hui will lead to war*. What triggered the tantrum and firing of missiles beginning in 1995 into waters surrounding Taiwan? With a visa granted by the United States, candidate Lee had gone to Cornell University, his alma mater, to give a speech.

Remember, the PRC holds that there is only one sovereign state under the name China, with the PRC serving as the sole legitimate government. Taiwan, it insists, is an inalienable part of China. The party takes offense when Taiwanese democratic gains rise in popularity with Americans. So the PLA, the CPC's military, responds. In this case, it responded by firing missiles into international shipping lanes and airspace, disrupting commercial shipping passing through two major ports. All this happened after we had struck the deal for the plant and secured a commitment for project risk insurance from the Multilateral Investment Guarantee Agency (MIGA)—which is part of the World Bank Group—but before we'd actually begun construction.

The PLA's actions drew a rather robust response from President Clinton. He sent an aircraft carrier battle group through the strait and—here's what impacted us—suspended political risk insurance policies for American projects in China.

Here's something you may not know: American taxpayers guarantee loans the World Bank makes. So, if the CPC expropriated our investment, the World Bank wouldn't lose; American taxpayers would. Not only that, but the World Bank would continue to lend vast sums to the PRC. And the imbalance doesn't stop there. The US taxpayer guarantees the World Bank's loans to the PRC at interest rates lower than the PRC can find in commercial markets.

No surprise, MIGA counts hurling missiles at another *territory*—the CPC might react irately if I said another *country*—as an act of war. The protections we sought from MIGA included financial exposure to acts of war. With a current act of war plopped in the middle of due diligence, MIGA pulled its commitment to our project.

By the way, believe it or not, the CPC learned of the US Navy action not from its PLA, but from CNN. PLA heads rolled because of that. So we weren't the only ones disappointed in the actions.

**SF**: So with the insurance pulled, what did you do regarding the Yakela carbon black plant project?

**PJ**: We halved the planned plant size and continued without political risk protection. We then completed our obligations, supplied critically needed electricity, and provided appropriate invoices for payment. And guess what? Our electricity buyer started to dodge paying us—literally!

Normally, Gao Yang—the bright, diligent, hard-working woman who ran our Urumqi office—would board a train to Korla and take a cab to Yakela. There she would present the monthly bill for electricity we produced and collect the payment. Cash in hand—really in a briefcase—she would reverse the trip and deposit the money in our account in Urumqi.

This process worked for the first few visits. Then, the carbon black plant manager would say he didn't have cash, please come back later. Gao Yang is smart and tough, and expresses her strong sense of right and wrong forcefully. The general manager began telling his workers to tell her he was traveling and would have the money when he returned.

After three months or so—and many respectful reminders of our and their obligations, and our respectful awareness of their internal tensions—we acted. We turned off the electricity, took away difficult-to-replace electronic ignition components to prevent restart, and, as a consequence, interrupted our Communist counterparties' flow of financial power—the sale of carbon black.

**SF**: Sounds rather gutsy for a company in the early stages of trying to establish a foothold in China. What was their response?

**PJ**: Within days, we collected full payment. There are at least two important, broader lessons here. First, when dealing with CPC-controlled counterparties, in order to protect your own core interests, make sure your position allows you to pivot, giving or taking away something the CPC needs. Second, use that position swiftly. Come to think of it, there's a third point: Take care to understand the range of maneuvers the CPC permits your counterparty.

The Communist Party expects to fight for everything Americans think they have settled. The general manager at Yakela likely won accolades for creating friction in our bill collection process. Our forceful demands raised his respectability as the carbon black plant's leader, and as a fighter for the Communist Party. Rising respect for him within the party showed we could deliver something else he needed—that old word again: *face*. His career would advance based on both the real and perceived success of the plant. We gave him both.

Whether negotiating commercial contracts or national agreements, figure out what your PRC counterparty needs, both institutionally and personally. In a culture that looks to one man's rule (in the PRC, almost certainly not to one woman's), look to both contractual and, especially, personal gains.

**SF**: If someone had visited this project what would they have seen?

**PJ**: Well, not much. Imagine working on the edge of a desert, with no access to a Home Depot, Walmart, or Tractor Supply store. Then think about needing a store with much bigger parts and supplies, like oil to lubricate and tools to work on big engines. Then think about all the dust and grit that blows in off a big desert. No honeymooners around, except the party-oppressed workers who couldn't afford travel.

The old power plant had three radial airplane engines. Those are engines that look like an old wagon wheel with the propeller shaft in the middle of a circle where fat pistons take the positions of slender spokes. Those engines could have come, truly, from old biplanes.

When assembled on its foundation, our roughly 40,000 pounds of equipment could have fit on a trailer, like the big rigs on US highways. On one end, a large fan blows air over a radiator for cooling. An engine sits in the middle, a big one with pistons lined up in a tight V-shape. Attached to that on the other end is a horizontally-oriented large round can that houses the generator. Off those three main components hangs various connecting and control equipment. Bolts, conduits, pipes, and wires tie it all together. Control boxes allow workers to start, stop, monitor, and calibrate operations.

**SF**: How many people did Tang employ to build and run the plant?

**PJ**: Three of our own, plus local construction crews. Ken Collier, Gao Yang, and Mike Graul pulled it all together. Ken, who died in 2014, grew up near Merkel, Texas, which is outside of Abilene. After school let out for the summer, rather than pick cotton, Ken and a buddy would take a canteen, a blanket, a .22 rifle, and box of bullets into the Texas desert. When school was due to start, they'd come back home.

Ken grew up with freedoms few of us know. He fended for himself and stood by his friends. His mind worked faster and farther ahead than most people can think. He also laid down the most beautiful welds I have ever seen. He was Tang's source of humor and invention, and a reservoir of can-do spirit.

We've talked about Gao Yang. She had graduated from Xinjiang Institute of Engineering, earned high-level responsibilities with the Urumqi Power Administration, and garnered scorn from fellow workers by winning outstanding worker awards many times. She wanted a chance to advance based on her abilities. She was honest and smart and had a belly full of fire. We worked very well together.

Mike Graul hails from the Philadelphia area. He has travelled the world installing or repairing small and medium-sized powerplants. With a rare combination of deep engineering expertise and practical accounting experience, he brought critical abilities to get gear into the PRC, get it up and running, and get money back to Texas. Mike and Ken shared an oil-field dormitory room in Yakela. I'm not sure if the floor was dirt or rug-covered dirt.

**SF**: And what about on the Chinese side? Who's running the show?

**PJ**: Always, always, always, the Communist Party is running the show. Many of our projects were big enough to matter to us and small enough to avoid constant party scrutiny. Those projects allowed us to work with top talents in the PRC. National-level projects, with big budgets, attract attention from party officials who may not have technical expertise, but seek or expect financial reward for their membership in the CPC. That was the case with the military general we'll talk about.

The general manager of a PRC-based project in, say, Xinjiang can act like a king. He can almost determine life and death for people, but then when somebody from Urumqi comes out, that guy is suddenly subordinated and quiet and listening. But as soon as the guy from Urumqi leaves, then the local guy is back up onto the top. Now, if somebody from Beijing comes, even the guy from Urumqi is subordinated.

The top engineer may or may not be a Communist Party member, but there is always somebody lurking who has a direct line to the party. This person may not be a Communist Party member yet, but he's looking to create an opportunity to become one. Because if you're a party member, you get to ask the questions. You can go more places. You can cut lines. You get to be elite. Really privileged.

Later, we started the wind blade venture under the willful ignorance of CPC affirmative approval. We gathered all the proper licenses and permits but worked with lower-level officials to start. As we built a thriving business, the big Communists circled and gnawed into the pie.

**SF**: I was curious to know how one gets to be a party member in China, and I found this in the *South China Morning Post*:

> Potential members must apply to their local party organisations, initiating a multi-year process with more than 20 steps to determine their qualification, including submitting a formal application, meeting with the local party organisers and attending party study

> sessions. (Jane Cai and Qin Chen, "Joining China's Communist Party: how and why so many people do it, 'secret' members and expulsion," May 20, 2021)

Besides the engineers and managers, what is the Chinese workforce like at these operations?

**PJ**: Gosh. Another simple question with a tough answer. Because the party regards lives similarly to the way it regards grains of sand, it put lots of people at our disposal to build what we needed. The party had invested in the luckier ones and shown them how to operate heavy machinery. The less fortunate may have had a shovel, wrench set, or sledgehammer. All lived in relative poverty. Because they know the party regards them as project fodder, some decline to understand—at least not quickly—targets and instructions. This makes building power plants take more time. It also yields more exceptions to specifications, which, in turn, spawn operating difficulties in the future.

The party tries to keep people employed, not in the sense that they're improving their livelihoods but more to keep them from doing something else that could cause trouble for the party. The CPC much prefers to keep people working out in the sun, away from good neighborhoods, so they're tired when they go home and don't have time to think about revolution.

**SF**: You sold the plant pretty quickly after it was up and running.

**PJ**: Yes. We told our electricity buyers we wanted them to do well, but we couldn't afford their interruptions to our payments. As a solution, we proposed selling the plant to them. We learned a lot from this experience. It prepared us for a much bigger power plant in Dunhuang, in Gansu province, on Xinjiang's eastern border.

**SF**: Did you have to sell that project, too?

**PJ:** Well, kind of. We suspended our investment, but we held on to our ownership position without paying for it as we had anticipated. Funky situation. The CPC changed the rules while we were building the plant. It gutted our long-term electricity sales contract by announcing that while it had approved the contract, the party reserved the right to reset the electricity price annually. This created an odd, imbalanced arrangement: Tang had to commit to a ten-year period of performance, while the CPC's annual review privilege limited its commitment to one year. Fearing a possibility like this, we had negotiated an option to withhold our investment until our joint venture completed all contracts with terms that supported project finance according to international standards. Our contractual right then posed a challenge, or created a conflict, within the PRC system.

**SF**: How so?

**PJ**: The Communist bureaucracy had approved our contract and the joint venture's creation and operation, with us as joint venture partner. When the system changed its position on one element, we exercised our contractual right under that same system to decline to invest. The Communists had approved our ownership along with our right to suspend investment under the conditions they themselves had caused. In effect, that made us an owner without investing. But our investment predicated approval for the plant, which by then was well into construction. In other words, the Communists knotted their own knickers, creating chaos.

If we had pulled out of the project altogether, our PRC partners could have lost their positions. To avoid the possibility of manifesting PRC bumbling, which would risk invalidating approvals and terminating project development and operations, we agreed to sell our interest in the future. Almost ten years later, Qinghai Petroleum Administration, a division of CNPC, bought the plant from our joint venture. Over the years, our involvement generated positive cash flows and led to deeper and broader engagements that set up lucrative businesses.

**SF**: Some years later you spoke to the Junior League of Dallas and detailed several lessons learned from the carbon black plant project, one of which was: *We have to make money if we are going to work in China*. This simple truth, consistently conveyed and defended, can batter Communist government powers.

**PJ**: We had to make money, and we wouldn't pay bribes. We demonstrated and stuck to these simple truths by declining opportunities that didn't make money and showing our Chinese counterparties the US Foreign Corrupt Practices Act. Consistently and persistently stating these simple, demonstrable first principles shielded us from unprofitable and improper CPC proposals.

The longer lasting lesson is that telling the truth to or about the CPC can change the behaviors of its representatives.

Go back to our example: Truthfully stating our intentions, clearly articulating our fundamental principles—to work for profit and without corruption—illuminated a contrast between the chronic CPC practice of using corruption to gain elevated positions and just working hard to create goods and services that improve people's lives. Our model of doing well by doing good beat their model of taking from others to endow a few with privilege.

Over the long haul, truth beats Communist bluster. (An aside: Many poor Chinese, like many disadvantaged people around the world, take long-term perspectives because they have to do so to hold on to hope, even as their political superiors take perspectives tied to their office tenures.) To maintain its privileged position, the Communist Party must claim legitimacy it lacks. Foundationally, the CPC begins with a constitution, which it dictates to the people. Its underpinning intent, its simple truth, its first principle, is to protect the party and not the people it governs. Imagine if the United States had a similar constitution that codified the right of the government to trample the rights of its people, rather than granting rights to its citizens and prohibiting the government from removing or trampling on those rights.

Over the long haul, communities and countries that protect people from bullies, including from oppressive political parties like the CPC, empower people to realize their own potentials. Also over the long haul, that individual empowerment creates economically stronger communities and countries. The strongest communities or countries enjoy material privileges, from buying power to reserve currency benefits, which feed civil choices and field mighty militaries.

US political leaders should take note. They often speak horribly of each other and build sophisticated and persistent campaigns to pound their opponents. It disappoints me that, broadly, they reserve their courage and skill only for domestic political victories and steer clear of countering the oppression the CPC employs in the PRC and exports to Hong Kong, Tibet, Xinjiang, Mongolia, Africa and, increasingly so, South America.

**SF**: Another lesson was: *Our rule-of-law heritage provides a powerful tool to expose misbehavior.*

**PJ**: Though never perfect, and though we must keep trying, we intend our laws to protect people from oppressors. Our government's legitimacy rests on this principle. In contrast, and because it deserves repeating, the CPC uses laws to protect the oppressor from people. US "soft power" springs from this fundamentally different starting point. China's system of laws intends to protect the party. In turn, the party listens to Mao and looks for its legitimacy in the barrel of a gun.

Those who understand the CPC's inversion of intent best are the ones who cannot afford to enter the PRC legal system. For them, engaging in litigation in the PRC effectively rings the bell of damnation; they have already lost a dispute.

These people and companies, honestly trying to do good work, face a system rigged against them. They understand that features of the PRC that support their positions one day may change the next—or may change in the dark of the night without notice. Foundationally, the party has already set the stage. If the stage needs resetting to avoid an undesirable outcome for the party, it either changes the rules or directs the PRC courts to rule according to its desire, regardless of the rules.

Political leaders do not have the time to survey and understand the abuses that small and medium-size enterprises suffer. When powerful foreign leaders, commercial or governmental, travel to the PRC, they witness a highly rehearsed and tightly choreographed event sequence. They meet people who dress like them, speak English with them, engage with similar manners, and use the same esoteric vocabulary.

In a nutshell: Simple truth protected us like a shield. We went to China knowing that to do well we had to do good. Doing well meant making money. Doing good is only sustained by profits for companies, and surpluses for nonprofits. Building businesses requires investment. Productive investment demands transparency and knowing the truth.

**SF**: Your second pilot project was in Karamay. Earlier we talked about your faux fax to Yih-Min, which had the intended effect of drawing the oil field into the deal. Let's examine the project itself.

**PJ**: While working on the first pilot in Yakela, we had been negotiating to process natural gas with the Karamay oil field. Karamay, which means "black oil" in Uyghur, is a city of about 400,000—though it was only 300,000 then—located four hours northwest of Urumqi.

The Karamay oil field produced a lot of oil and with that, a lot of natural gas. We could process the associated natural gas by cooling it under pressure and turning its components (like propane, butane, and pentane) into natural gas liquids, which some call LPG, or liquefied petroleum gas. As LPG, people could take it home in canisters like propane tanks for cooking, or put it in railroad car tanks or pipelines to use for fuel or chemical feedstocks to make other modern-day products.

To do this we needed a big, heavy compressor, a processing plant that cooled natural gas well below zero, and related fixtures—pipes, fittings, connectors, nuts, bolts, and more. Plus, we needed tools to put it all together.

Shrewdly, the Communist Party-controlled oil field company pitted our company against a Canadian natural gas processor. As if it were a capitalist organization, CNPC's Karamay oil field pushed both of us to sell to them at the very best price we could afford.

Halfway around the northern hemisphere from Dallas and his family, Yih-Min led negotiations for us. As noted earlier, after several days of CNPC demanding endless concessions, I feigned explosive anger in a fax to Yih-Min claiming we were already below our cost and deep into investing for the future and demanding that he leave Karamay on the next available train. Within hours, he signed a contract. Within a year, our processing plant was operating and, according to Chinese newspapers, had paid for itself while the Canadians were still constructing their plant.

**SF**: Lessons learned on this one?

**PJ**: First: Success for us had to breed success for our counterparties. Often—well, always—our counterparties needed to gain face for either of us to succeed. The fax gave our Karamay counterparts' superiors proof they had achieved tremendous concessions from foreigners. Second, rampant or pervasive Communist snooping can serve our own objectives.

**SF**: You consummated two more deals during the tail end of the nineties, which we'll discuss in the next chapter. In one of them, you may have been the only American in history—not including spies—to have scaled a fence to get *into* a closed-off Chinese compound rather than *out of it*!

**PJ**: Ha! Yes. At three in the morning, no less.

**SF**: We talked a little about the PRC and Taiwan. After Lai Ching-te was elected President of Taiwan in January of 2024, the Associated Press reported:

> A war of words erupted the day after Taiwan's presidential and parliamentary elections, with Taiwan on Sunday accusing China of making "fallacious comments" and China criticizing the United States for congratulating the winner.
>
> The verbal sparring highlighted the seemingly intractable divide over Taiwan's fate, a major flashpoint in US-China relations that risks leading to an actual war in the future.
>
> The victory of Lai Ching-te in Saturday's election was a setback for China's efforts to bring Taiwan under its control. His Democratic Progressive Party advocates maintaining the status quo, in which Taiwan governs itself but refrains from declaring formal independence—a move that could trigger a Chinese military response. China, meanwhile, calls for what it terms a "peaceful reunification," but that seems increasingly unrealistic as most Taiwanese have come to oppose becoming part of China. (Didi Tang, "The US relationship with China faces a test as Taiwan elects a new leader," January 12, 2024)

What do you think the future holds here?

**PJ**: What the United States does can skew the odds toward peace or toward war. For peace, US leaders need to give Xi Jinping "face." Vladimir Putin's troubles and Xi's needs create opportunities, though distasteful, to turn Xi Jinping away from contemplating war over Taiwan. The distasteful aspect requires finding ways to raise Xi's stature globally and, especially, within the CPC and PRC. Xi's treatment of Uyghurs, Tibetans, Hong Kongese, and, indeed, people in China and around the world disgusts me. Rhetoric and tariffs may have pressured, but have not transformed, Xi's choices. As Putin shrinks Russian capabilities, opportunities to recover formerly Chinese territory from Russia have already crossed Xi's mind. Skilled diplomacy could turn Xi's gaze from China's east to its west.

# Chapter 5

# Oh, No, No, No, You Can't Do That

**SF**: Let's start by setting the scene. It's 1997. You, Yih-Min, and an inexperienced tagalong—dubbed "Amusing Aggravation" (not his real name), or "Amag" for short—are at the airport in Urumqi, which is set in the mountains à la Denver International Airport. Along with a handful of Chinese people, you're waiting to board a China Xinjiang Airlines plane—a Canadian DHC-6 Twin Otter, a high-wing, propeller-driven aircraft that seats up to twenty. Your destination is Aksu City, population about 700,000, the seat of the Aksu Prefecture on the northern edge of the Tarim Basin, a region whose oil fields you visited on your exploratory trip in 1995. Aksu, which means "white water" in Uyghur, is about 420 air miles and 1,360 driving miles southwest of Urumqi.

How safe did you feel about this flight? Moreover, how safe did you feel flying in China?

**PJ**: Let's put aside for a moment the time a child urinated in the aisle on one of these flights, or the time a passenger on an Urumqi to Beijing flight started a fire—in the plane, in flight—to cook his lunch! There were times I did not feel safe. Up until a few years before I started going to China, its airlines had a terrible record. But the PRC regulators did a really good job of improving safety.

Overall, it was a safe place to fly, but there were times when you'd get on an old Tupolev Tu-154 or Ilyushin Il-86, and you would think, *This thing cannot have been maintained.* There were times when you wanted to get off, but you flew anyway. On this flight to Aksu City, however, I had no qualms about the Otter; it's a sturdy, reliable, safe, easy-to-maintain airplane.

**SF**: Also in the airport in Urumqi is a small Japanese group that has chosen to rent their own Otter rather than fly with you on a scheduled flight. And this is because?

**PJ**: It's because of the rampant racism in Asia. They didn't want to be with Chinese people.

**SF**: I think a lot of Americans tend to forget about the ethnic, religious, cultural, and racial differences in that corner of the world, which over the centuries have led to discrimination and war. When you were over there, what did you observe along these lines between China and other Asian nations, as well as within China itself, which has people of so many backgrounds?

**PJ**: Some examples: For breakfast on one of my early of trips, my Chinese hosts directed me to the "foreigners" dining room, while they went to their own dining room. That time, I thoroughly enjoyed the separation, as I found myself in conversation with a telecommunications expert from France. Years later, in Beijing, Yih-Min and I walked past a Japanese restaurant where a mob had broken its windows and painted crude, murderous, racial slurs on its walls. Another time, when I needed to use a fax machine in a hotel in Urumqi, I heard a familiar accent. It shocked my Chinese minders how warmly and happily a Black Texan and I shook hands and spoke of home.

But the Uyghurs suffered, and still suffer, the most persistent expressions of prejudice. Many Han Chinese do not agree with the PRC policy that institutionalizes discrimination against Uyghurs but claim they cannot change it. The fact that they benefit from this bias might contribute to their complacence.

Confucian hierarchies come into play here, too. Just as relationships among individuals fall into slots, so do relationships among races. Individuals can and certainly do escape Confucian constructs, but their hierarchy for organizing relationships remains. Not that Americans have perfected racial harmony, but our system starts with the aspiration that all people are equal before the law. American history shows we're still working on our own prejudices.

In the PRC, the Chinese start with Confucian expressions of superiority. At the western end of the Great Wall, the inscription on the gate warns travelers that once they pass through, they will see no more people. Manipulatively, the CPC, like other political parties around the world, foments prejudices of superiority for its own purposes. Consistent with ancient Chinese imperial habits, respect for others declines with geographic remoteness. This leads the CPC to rank races with, of course, the Han Chinese coming first. They are followed by other Asians, then those of European, or Eurasian, descent, followed by those of African lineage.

In the long run, this and other CPC positions, or policies, make it more difficult for CPC-governed peoples to achieve their dreams. In the United States, laws allow people from anywhere to become American. Calling oneself "American" generally means that person has, or his or her ancestors have, involuntarily or freely, emigrated from somewhere else and adopted the historically revolutionary idea that laws should protect people and not just rulers. These observations of foundational difference do not excuse Americans' treatment of indigenous peoples, which leaves a scar on US history.

An observation, Steve: The CPC puts on shows of petulance because they work. During a recent conference, Wang Yi, the PRC's top diplomat, said to other Asians, "No matter how blonde you dye your hair, or how sharp you shape your nose, you can never become a European or American, you can never become a Westerner." Well, he's wrong. Plenty of Asians have become Americans, not because they changed hair color or surgically sculpted their bodies, but because they sought and adopted protections from US law.

Wang is stuck in an imperialistic and racist paradigm. To Han Chinese in the PRC, at least other Asians are still Asian.

**SF**: What was the purpose of this trip to Aksu City?

**PJ**: To negotiate a letter of intent we had forwarded weeks earlier for building a power plant on the northern rim of the Tarim Basin. Our counterparties included the Aksu Area Kusaxin Power Company, a prefecture-level authority, and the Kuqa Fertilizer Plant of the Xinjiang Production and Construction Corps. The first represented an electricity distribution entity. The second was a command center for the PLA.

This was the project involving the PLA general we've mentioned. He was retiring and poised to become the general manager of the company that built and operated a fertilizer plant in this region. The United States has no parallel for a PRC plant or company general manager. As noted, that person—all males in my experience—wields unquestioned authority. A general manager can go to the bank and take money from the company account, or tell an employee to run across an open desert.

The PRC's State Council had approved $300 million of funding for the project. Again, the United States has no parallel. Imagine Congress and the President approving a $300 million US taxpayer investment in a project just to give a popular admiral or general a cushy, fully staffed, retirement job for life.

Ambitions for the plant size required more electricity than the area could provide. Both for grid stability and fertilizer plant electrical reliability, the plant would connect with the local transmission wires. At some point, PRC politics or regulations may have required us to include two or more additional counterparties. Our then-friend AVIC, which had a central government monopoly to participate in operating combustion turbines like the one we planned to use at the fertilizer plant, could have claimed a right to join the project. Similarly, CNPC or Sinopec may have asserted similar claims that they controlled natural gas usage in the Aksu region.

Besides identifying initial and potential counterparties in the development group—those who would spend time and money to turn dream-spinning into spinning generators—we needed to bring key contracts together to secure financing. Potential project financiers sought to evaluate land use rights, fuel purchase, electric sales, steam sales, construction, and operating contracts.

Our memorandum of understanding (MOU), an initial stage the PRC requires, established a working group to assess feasibility, which the PRC State Development Planning Commission, later rebranded as the National Development and Reform Commission, required. The working group would also prepare and synchronize contract parameters so the development group could attract project financing. Imagine a power plant that secures a long-term source of fuel by agreeing to pay certain prices for that fuel over time. To survive, it will need a corresponding, or synchronized, commitment to sell electricity.

**SF**: Would you please explain "project financing"?

**PJ**: The term "project financing" refers to a form of financing that looks only to the project for repayment and not the parties who conceived, built, or operated it. This approach gives experts at financing power plants a very strong say in what projects earn their investment. It also benefits entrepreneurs who may generate really good ideas but lack the financial resources to fund their dreams.

Just as Chinese people living in the PRC don't have laws that allow them to express long-term commitments, neither do companies operating in the PRC. The CPC, in effect and in fact, asks investors to make long-term commitments in the territories that it governs, but promises only short-term commitments in return.

**SF**: So your plane takes off, and . . . ?

**PJ**: Flying from Urumqi to Aksu takes only about an hour and a half. But the flight climbs over the Tian Shan mountains, which rise higher than the Colorado Rockies before dropping into desert lower than sea level. As the mountains fall away, turbulence rises—and one by one all the Chinese passengers became ill. The cabin aroma alone induced some vomiting. None of our crew got sick, but it was close. After the air sickness bags ran out, passengers passed the "convenience bucket," which doubled as a lavatory. Sitting by the door in the back, it was all I could do to wait for the ground crew to open it.

**SF**: So much for the glamour of doing business in the PRC! What kind of place is Aksu City?

**PJ**: With dry desert in one direction and green mountains in the other, it looks like parts of west Texas. Like similar towns in Texas, the air carries some grit. But even poor Texas towns show a lot more wealth, from rounder bellies to conveniences like air conditioning, refrigerators, and even electric lighting.

Also like west Texans, Aksu inhabitants live close to natural gas fuel supplies. But the CPC just lets the gas flare. You've heard me preach this before: Capturing that flared natural gas to generate electricity changes people's lives. Yes, someone still has to spend money on equipment, construction, and operations, but the fuel is essentially free.

An economist or environmentalist could argue that using natural gas that would have been vented to the atmosphere to fuel electricity is even better than free. Doing so turns methane emissions into carbon dioxide emissions. In fact, emissions from an advanced gas-fired combustion turbine are cleaner than the air many people in the PRC breathe.

**SF**: Where did you stay?

**PJ**: We stayed in a so-called guest house in a compound gated with a wrought iron fence, which guards locked every night. The compound was in a residential neighborhood maybe two miles down an unpaved road from the city's market district. You crossed a bridge to get there, and there was a creek on the other side.

The guest house itself was an angular ring of rooms around a courtyard. There were bars over the windows, so you couldn't get out if you wanted to. In the morning, patriotic music blared over a speaker; if you weren't awake for it at the start, you were by the second note.

On a lot of our travels in western China we had to worry about the safety of the food. Not here. There was a little breakfast area where you could get a boiled egg and steamed buns, things you knew were cooked and safe.

Water was a different matter. It ran most of the day. But hot water ran at most a couple of hours a day. The guest house had apparently been located by the creek so it could get water more easily. However, we had to be very careful about drinking it, because what was upstream didn't have the standards of hygiene we've come to enjoy.

**SF**: Who was staying in this guest house?

**PJ**: Well, Yih-Min, me, and Amag. We never really got to know who paid Amag. Traveling with us turned him downright giddy, as if he'd been trying to go on trips like ours, to meet the people we were meeting. He described himself as our consultant, but we never did pay him. We thought he talked recklessly, and after the Aksu trip, we avoided contact with him.

**SF**: Was your counterparty also staying in the compound?

**PJ**: To our surprise, our counterparty wasn't in town when we arrived. We were given an excuse for their absence and assured they'd be there the next day. That seemed okay. The next flight out of town wasn't for four days; we'd still have time to work out the agreement. But then they didn't show up the next day, or the next.

They weren't around, but the Chinese military was all over the area. Apparently, some pretty high-level exercises were going on. One morning about a dozen uniformed soldiers, several of them fairly high-ranking PLA officers, appeared. They had their own separate rooms, but we'd be in the same breakfast area in the morning, so we were very careful with our conversation.

**SF**: While you were waiting for your counterparty, were you able to go out into the field, get a lay off the land, assess where a power plant might be built?

**PJ**: No. We weren't allowed. The people overlooking us didn't want to confront the PLA on maneuvers. So we were just stuck waiting, rereading books we had, waiting for the hot water to come on.

**SF**: After three days you must have been getting pretty close to the time your flight was scheduled to leave town. And as you've said, those flights were few and far between—twice a week.

**PJ**: Thankfully our counterparty finally showed up—at around four in the afternoon of the day before we were scheduled to leave. They apologized for the delay—which they attributed to busy schedules—but we took that with a grain of salt. In 1793, Lord George Macartney, upon arriving in Chengde, waited six days to meet with the Qianglong Emperor. I mention this because Chinese officials often look back to history for examples of how to behave. So, in our case, they may very well have been playing emperor with us.

At about four thirty, I gave a little talk to the counterparty folks in "really good" English that Yih-Min translated into "really good" Chinese, as he always did. Note the compliment at the beginning; by acknowledging how busy our counterparty was, we were acknowledging their importance:

> Thank you for meeting with us. We know how busy you are. We're pleased to have the chance to work with you. You know your countryside looks a lot like parts of Texas. We know we're on our frontier with you. We know it's a frontier for you to be coming to work with us.
>
> When I grew up, we talked about China as Red China. I never expected graduating high school to be lucky enough to have an opportunity

> to talk with you today and to have the chance to build a business together. I'm really pleased with the opportunity to do that.
>
> My family has always said we need to do well by doing good, and we've got an opportunity to do that. We know it's going to be hard. But if we work well together, we will succeed. And when we succeed, yes, we'll improve the lives of everybody here and will also improve the relationship of the United States and the People's Republic of China.

Then I presented their lead guy with a little statue of a Texas cowboy riding a horse.

**SF**: Where did that idea come from?

**PJ**: I don't remember. Our ideas of appropriate and legal gifts evolved. The typical gifts for Americans to bring to the Chinese were cigarettes and whiskey. But long before, Yih-Min and I had agreed to tell our counterparties, "Cigarettes are bad for you. So we don't bring cigarettes to people we want to work with."

We still gave them alcohol, often Texas wine. We'd do that to reinforce the frontier theme; we were on the frontier of a new relationship. The cowboy statue did that, too. So we gave it to them, explaining, "The cowboy is riding the horse in the statue now. We don't know how many times he has been knocked off, and no matter how many times we get knocked off, we'll do what we can to get back in the saddle to work with you."

The gifts hit them just right. So did the speech, which was really important. Both reflected our sincere commitment. As the leader of our side and the one with the long nose and round eyes, I was the one to represent our position authoritatively to my counterpart, whose Communist Party affiliation indicated his importance.

**SF**: Did your counterparty present you with gifts on this day? For that matter, did they ever give you gifts, or was it a one-way street?

**PJ**: Not that day. But before we left, they gave us some Uyghur caps and folding pocketknives. On other occasions, our counterparties gave us local, handcrafted pieces. A jade dragon and soapstone inkwell decorated with dragons proudly take shelf and desk space even today.

**SF**: I'm curious to know how formal such an occasion is. Do you wear a coat and tie? What do the Chinese wear?

**PJ**: To every business meeting and meal, I wore a coat and tie. Usually, Chinese participants did, too. Consistently, theirs were dreary, bland, gray with a little gray-blue for color. I wore brighter ties. And boots. After getting enough grit in my shoes, I finally just wore my work boots, which kept most of the street grit out.

Even on hot travel days, I wore long sleeve shirts. One really hot day, when we stopped for lunch, I rolled up my sleeves. Our Chinese associates noticed the modest amount of hair on my arms, compared it to their hairless arms, and then to the hair on monkeys' arms.

In the late 1990s, we saw a lot of a fellow we called "Tang Laoban." I don't remember his given name, but we called him *laoban* for "big boss," though he had no ownership in or control over Tang Energy Group. One time, Tang Laoban complimented my red tie with green fountain pens on it, so I gave it to him and replaced it with an identical tie when I returned to the States. It was, and still is, my get-stuff-done tie.

A few months later, we learned he had hung himself in jail with a tie. Much later, I told that story to some former CIA officers, who started giggling. I asked, "What's so funny?" They answered, "Well, it's like giving somebody a gun and saying, 'Here, you know what to do.' But you did it with a tie!"

**SF**: That's quite a story. If you start to call me Fiffer Big Boss, I'll know to be careful. But seriously, back in Aksu what happened after your introductory remarks and presentation of gifts?

**PJ**: We began negotiating the business points of the MOU. Even though we had sent them our version weeks earlier, we had to resolve several issues. It took hours.

When we finished, we needed a clean copy of the new MOU. We asked if there was a computer somewhere so we could amend the draft we'd sent to reflect the changes that had been negotiated. That draft was in a Microsoft Word DOS file.

They directed us to the Bank of China, which not only had the tallest building in town—four stories—but the only computer that could do the job. Think about that: The local power grid company could take us to the Bank of China after hours and tell them to let us use its computers. A shadow force connects and controls a lot of activity in the PRC. *This is great,* I thought. *I'm gonna be able to quickly amend this on a word processor, and we'll be good to go.* They drove me the two miles to the bank.

**SF**: Mission accomplished?

**PJ**: Nope. The computer showed Microsoft logos as it booted up, but it must have been a pirated copy. The word processor didn't work. That meant the whole agreement—at least six pages in each language, Chinese and English—had to be typed on an electronic typewriter. Remember those? You could actually see maybe three lines at a time on a little screen. This was going to take a while.

In the meantime, our new business partners wanted to have a celebratory dinner, which is what Chinese people living under the CPC often want to do. So Amag and I took turns shuttling between the dinner—in a nearby restaurant—and the typewriter at the bank.

The dinner was just a drunk fest, which is often the case. The CPC allows few freedoms of expression. Recognizing accomplishments gives the Chinese an opportunity to let loose with the excuse that they would like to honor you by toasting you. I call it "attack drinking" or "attack toasting." Everybody around the table wants to toast the leader of the other side. It can cost you "face" if you don't participate.

**SF**: Could you keep up with them?

**PJ**: Heck, no. Especially when they were drinking *moutai,* which I prefer to call "white lightning." It's 53 percent alcohol. Can you say "moonshine"?

To avoid hangovers, I developed a whole bunch of tricks, like saying, "I'm sorry I'm only an American. I can't drink as much as fit Chinese men." Or: "My body is still on Texas time. If you're kind to me now, I'll show equal kindness when we meet in Texas." Then, there are all kinds of games you can play like saying, "I really appreciate your toast, and because so-and-so has contributed quietly, consistently, and materially to our mutual success, I would like him or her to take this toast for me." (Recognizing a woman's contribution really got to the men.)

On this night, and any other, I preferred typing to drinking. I finished up at the bank a little after midnight, my Chinese overseers looking over my shoulder. Mine, of course, was the version in English. Now someone else had to type up the Chinese version. Our Xinjiang Airlines flight was scheduled to depart around ten the next morning. To say the least, we were cutting it close.

As two o'clock approached, I pointed to myself, made a walking motion with my fingers, and said I was heading back to the compound. They got it. And they said, "Oh, no, no, no, you can't do that." Yes, I could. I went down the stairs, out the door, and started walking. I'd only gone a few yards, when an old Russian/Chinese jeep skidded to a halt beside me. *Oh no*, I thought. *I'm really in trouble.*

The driver demonstrated concern rather than anger. So I got in and he took me to the compound. Of course the gate was locked. Did I mention there was a guard house, too?

I looked around. I'm thinking, *Our plane leaves in less than eight hours.* I wanted to get a little sleep because I knew that before departing we were going to be in front of the TV cameras to announce the agreement and have another ceremonial toasting.

**SF**: Your bed is on the other side of this locked gate. So now what?

**PJ**: I looked at the fence, and I thought of my grandfather. He used to go to baseball games with what he called "spring and fall season tickets." He would *spring* to the top of the fence and *fall* over on the other side to be able to get into the games. So I put my briefcase over my shoulder, climbed up to the top of the fence, jumped over, and made a beeline for my room.

*This is great*, I thought. *I haven't been shot. I'm going to make my plane.* I cleaned up a little bit with cold, cold water and then went to bed. I didn't sleep much because I was committed to making that ten o'clock flight.

I was awake early, expecting to be picked up at about eight for the drive to the signing ceremony and then the airport. But no one showed up. Nine, nine thirty. No driver.

At ten, I was getting mopey. *I'm going to be away from my young family for at least another four days. I don't know how I'm going to get out of here. I've already finished my book. I'm out of reading material and there's nothing else for me to do here. I guess I'll reread it.*

**SF**: What was the book?

**PJ**: *Tai-Pan* by James Clavell.

**SF**: A quick check shows it's 736 pages. I guess that could have occupied a fair chunk of time over the four days until the next flight.

**PJ**: Fortunately, that became moot. A little after ten, we had our signing ceremony in front of the TV cameras, our smiles disguising how unhappy we were with having missed our flight. I figured I'd go back to my room and get some more sleep. Instead, they said, "Okay, time to go to the airport." The mayor of Aksu had sent his fancy Toyota SUV for us.

*It's ten thirty. We've already missed our flight. Why are they wasting our time? I just want to go to bed.*

We drove to the airport anyway—the SUV even had an icemaker between the front seats—and lo and behold the airplane was waiting for us. The Communist mayor of this dusty city halfway across the northern hemisphere from Dallas, 2,170 miles from Beijing, could hold up a plane just so Americans could board it.

I slid my briefcase under the seat in front of me and settled in. The engines started, a good sign; the plane taxied, accelerated, pitched up, and climbed. My seat embraced me. My eyelids grew heavy. And then a young child with split britches instead of a diaper—a common wardrobe—two rows ahead, stepped into the aisle, squatted, and urinated a river. I snatched up my briefcase, put it on my lap, and remained tensely vigilant for the rest of the flight.

**SF**: What happened after that trip with respect to the MOU? Was a power plant built?

**PJ**: Well, from a purely commercial perspective for Tang, it flopped. From a national security perspective for the United States, it did well. Our involvement disrupted a CPC strategic decision—the decision we discussed earlier, to invest $300 million in a fertilizer plant—and produced an interesting amount of intelligence for people in Washington, DC.

We didn't know it then, but the project was, or became one of, China's top ten, State Council-approved projects of 1997. The fertilizer plant needed a $30 million natural gas-fueled, electricity-generating plant. Remember, we'd built that $50 million dollar plant in Wichita Falls, so this project fit neatly into our plan to expand such success in a very foreign land.

As discussed earlier, we knew fertilizer plants used natural gas as a feedstock, and China needed fertilizer to grow crops to feed people and to make explosives for mining, construction, and military purposes. We later learned China's State Council supported the fertilizer plant for nationally strategic objectives.

Because both the fertilizer and power plant would use natural gas, we asked a specific question that reflected our own strategic concern: "If Tang builds a power plant that uses natural gas for fuel, will the natural gas reserves last long enough for both the electricity and fertilizer plants to achieve their financial goals?"

Our persistence with this deal-threatening question ended in deep winter when a green Beijing jeep—the Chinese descriptor for a Jeep Cherokee made in China— with military license plates arrived to take us to a meeting to discuss, ostensibly, free-world power plant project finance methods.

The bigger-than-average driver and his front-seat companion drove Yih-Min and me from our hotel in Urumqi to a large pipeline facility far outside of Urumqi, and then to a small, drafty, one-story, brick-and-concrete building in a remote corner of that facility. There, our even-bigger-than-average handlers directed us to a bare table and motioned for us to sit on metal folding chairs that hit our buttocks with cold, sharp discomfort. Seeing the crisply clear sky that brought the coldest air through the windows high above our heads confirmed no one would see or hear anything that happened in that building.

Several times, exploiting a foreigner's prerogative not to understand, I rose to walk and warm myself. The guard kept barking toward Yih-Min, who told me the guard wanted me to sit down and be still. Not knowing our overseers' English proficiency, I repeated that I was too cold to sit. I didn't admit I was anxiously looking for ways out.

Then, a long time later—through an entrance we had not been permitted to approach—two heavily braided officers and three AK-47 wielding soldiers entered with authority. With the soldiers standing behind them, the officers sat on a raised section of the floor and began berating us.

A quick aside: In matters like this, as in diplomacy, the seating chart matters. I'll give you a recent example. In June of 2023, US Secretary of State Antony Blinken traveled to China. Until the eleventh hour there was some question as to whether China's Chairman Xi would even meet with him. When they did finally meet, Blinken sat midway down a long table at whose head—on a higher chair—sat the chairman. In contrast, when Bill Gates met with Xi on a non-official, nongovernmental visit just a few days earlier, the US billionaire was afforded much greater respect. He and Xi were photographed next to each other in matching high-back chairs.

Anyway, as they berated us, we kept responding that to secure capital for the general's project, we needed to know the power plant we invested in wouldn't cause disruptions to the fertilizer plant. We must have employed a hundred ways to phrase that point.

The sun was setting on the short winter day when the consistently delivered simple truth—that Tang wanted to ensure both its power plant and the fertilizer plant yielded positive, financially measurable returns—protected us from accusations that we worked for foreign governments or local dissidents who sought to undermine Chinese development. That paranoia had fueled the ad hoc "meeting."

In the following years, we learned that the State Council had initially approved the fertilizer project in order to create a retirement plan for the popular general. The $300 million investment would have created an empire that ensconced him and his loyal retinue thousands of kilometers from the capital. Our question, according to our source, led the State Council to revoke its project approval. Foreigners' scrutinizing questions empowered the project's critics and/or the general's rivals and embarrassed its supporters. Two Texans had killed a PRC top-ten national project.

**SF**: I imagine you and Yih-Min talked about this afterward. What did you say?

**PJ**: For a while, we couldn't even talk. There were three reasons: I was scared speechless, we weren't sure we could count survival as assured, and we feared surveillance. Imagine the fear people living in Xinjiang feel. It oppresses you from the inside. It leads to self-censoring, not just of activities and conversations, but of thought itself.

Think about that. In the United States, individuals define or fulfill their own American dreams. In Communist China, the party defines the "Chinese dream." The paramount leader even dictates *what* Chinese dream. To this day, Yih-Min and I choose to talk about other experiences. Part of that reflects our forward-looking attitudes, but a lingering bit shows the fearsome loss of control we had over our lives in those hours and days.

**SF**: I understand the lure of a new frontier like China—particularly to a Texan—but this seems above and beyond. Why keep going in the face of danger like this? You've got a family. You've got business opportunities in your own backyard.

**PJ**: Well, lots of reasons. We learned we could poke, yet still dance, with the dragon. On subsequent projects, we looked longer and harder at our counterparties and at their relevance and proximity to the CPC. Despite one powerful PLA general's intense pique, the groundswell of energy technologies we knew were making energy access better, and the geopolitical openings to broaden our reach into China's markets, still presented historic opportunities.

As Brutus says in Shakespeare's *Julius Caesar*, "There is a tide in the affairs of men, which taken at the flood leads on to fortune; omitted, all the voyage of their life is bound in shallows and miseries."

Also, we really were cleaning up the environment. With modern technology, when you use natural gas for fuel, you have a very clean set of emissions; $CO_2$ emissions are about half as much as coal, and 30 percent less than oil. When you replace donkey dung—used, literally, for household cooking—with natural gas, you're doing a really good thing. Families no longer suffer from inhaling the burned dung, *and* you're helping them come out of poverty.

Similarly, in bringing natural gas-generated electricity to a town or region, you're changing lives dramatically. Just think about the impact electricity had in the United States when it was introduced. Just imagine a life without it.

In China, we saw firsthand that one of the primary things a family does with electricity is put a child under a light bulb with a book, and the kid starts to learn. Then, they take the revolutionary step of buying a refrigerator. That's radical because if you have a refrigerator, women—who, in the PRC, almost invariably bear responsibility for preparing meals—don't have to spend every hour of every day thinking about the next meal. Saving food from one meal to the next, or preparing two meals at once, gives women more time to do other things.

It's exciting to be on the frontier, to pioneer uncrowded opportunity, to accept risks for financial and psychic reward. So despite the trepidation induced by angry generals (and that was the only time something quite like that happened) you move westward—literally, as well as figuratively. You're always aware that the risk of being on the frontier is that an arrow or a bullet in the back may kill you. Yih-Min and I talked about the general's wrath seriously, but in the end we decided, *Yeah, that was scary, but we need each other. China needs us and we need China. We've got expertise that improves Chinese people's lives.*

**SF**: In a sense, your honesty killed that deal.

**PJ**: Yes, and better to kill it early than see it die $300 million later.

**SF**: Lessons?

**PJ**: Understand that Communist Party bluster often hides its fear. In this instance, and yet unknown to us, Angry General understood that our honesty penetrated the Communists' system of allocating capital based on cronyism. Not only had our capitalist insistence on transparency terminated approval for his pet project, it also highlighted the superiority of clarity over opacity. A corollary operational lesson: Deeply bury your own fear so you can think clearly.

The bigger, more important national-level lesson: Political motives skew enormous capital budgets to achieve very personal objectives even at the expense of an impoverished, fearful, oppressed population. Jumping forward to using insight from this lesson, China's Communists need strong American guardrails to keep them from walking off the high balcony of hubris.

**SF**: Did you let anyone in the US government know about this incident? Your CIA contact?

**PJ**: Not for a while, and for a few reasons. First, the imminent danger had passed, so we turned our attention to other issues. Second, getting back home takes a while, and you sure do not want to bring up the incident anywhere inside the PRC.

**SF**: Did Kathy or your folks ever express reservations or fears?

**PJ**: Yes. But much later; it took years for me to tell them the story I've just told you.

**SF**: We talked about nationalism and racism in Asia. Just as the Japanese and Chinese have long had their problems with one another, so, too, have the Koreans and the Japanese—driven by Japan's colonial rule from 1910 to 1945. Yet as deep as this animosity may be, the leaders of South Korea and Japan came to Camp David for a historic summit. An August 18, 2023, Reuters headline sums it up: "US, South Korea, and Japan condemn China, agree to deepen military ties." What do you make of this?

**PJ**: Oh boy. First, the Communist Party, like other old-line imperialists, respects strength. It believes the mighty take what they want and the meek suffer what they must. So, showing strength to the CPC compels its caution and consideration of other's positions. If you believe in protecting people from oppressive political parties, instead of protecting bullies from the people, you'll prefer negotiating from a position of comprehensive strength. The United States should lean into its advantage of legitimacy. Democratic systems beat authoritarian systems in this category. They also win on generating capital, or just plain cash, to invest in improving lives and capabilities. But while democratic strengths win in legitimacy and capital, we're not where we want to be militarily. The Communist Party's military, the PLA, fields the world's largest army, and its navy operates more ships than any other navy in the world. If current trends continue, the PLA's air force will soon fly more planes than any other air force.

Second, we must depend on more than just having power, which allies and partners can amplify. Remember *face*? We must find ways to compliment the party, especially its paramount leader, to advance peace, to promote prosperity, and to lift up victims of the party's fear, injustice, and oppression. As ghastly as it may seem, we must build trust, even with a genocidal regime (both the Trump and Biden administrations have described the CPC's treatment of Uyghurs as genocide) in order to bring relief to its victims and fulfill our own moral commitments. Part of getting tough about the Communist Party's impositions of fear, injustice, and oppression requires us to suspend comfort and shelve complacency now.

Third, we need to work on these objectives every day and not less frequently. Persistence compounds small wins. Accrued over time, small wins make big differences.

Fourth and last, Xi Jinping has driven China's potential enemies together rather quickly. I'm sure other Communist Party members consider this development negatively.

# Chapter 6

# Patrick Is But a Flyspeck

**SF**: About the same time you were dealing with the fertilizer fiasco, you also became involved in the first project with your future nemesis AVIC, China's biggest aviation and defense contractor.

**PJ**: Yes, but I've got to quibble over "nemesis." To me, *we* became the Communist Party's nemesis, the persistent agitator who forced the arrogant bully to squirm. One of AVIC's most prominent lawyers, Johnny Zhang, appears to agree. In an email to our attorney, he wrote, "Patrick is but a flyspeck on the Chinese radar screen, and no one in his right mind wants to see Patrick's face ever again."

That's quite an insult, or, perhaps, a compliment. I had to look it up. Flyspeck, according to Merriam-Webster, means "a speck made by fly excrement." In the end, we won. We didn't overthrow the CPC, but we nicked 'em good. Johnny, on the other hand, later separated from his law firm over alleged hanky-panky with respect to a client's fee.

Back to the project. We talked a little about it when I told the story of the party member who cried when remembering the Cultural Revolution. This was the $30 million, 42-megawatt, gas-fired electricity generation plant near the western end of the Great Wall in Dunhuang, a city of about 200,000 people in Gansu province.

Our Communist partners chose to commission the plant on October 1, 1999. Exactly fifty years to the day earlier, Chairman Mao had proclaimed the founding of the Central People's Government of the PRC. On that day in 1949, Mao, known for his long speeches, stayed sitting, building crowd tension, until he stood and said, "Today—China—Stands—Up." Then, he sat down. Tang's Chinese counterparties wanted to applaud the CPC's consolidation of power in the PRC on this anniversary.

Because we had exceeded CNPC's expectations in our pilot project in Karamay, they introduced us to many and better opportunities. "Better" often meant "bigger" because it can take the same amount of time to negotiate a pilot project as a project that helps build a business. CNPC suggested the project near Dunhuang, which is famous and especially important to Buddhists for caves that monks dug into sandstone over a thousand years ago. One of the caves contains the second biggest Buddha in the PRC.

On the eastern side of the Tarim Basin, CNPC maintains a large operation very close to Dunhuang. They told us their own oil-field town, as well as Dunhuang itself, needed more power. For context, Dunhuang is also quite near a PRC strategic rocket launch site near Jiayuguan, a bit further from its Lop Nur nuclear weapons facility, and not too far from the scores of ballistic missile silos the PLA has dug into the desert.

As soon as we proposed using a combustion turbine, another name for a jet engine, to turn an electric generator, CPC decorum threw us into AVIC's orbit. As the sole supplier of military aircraft equipment to the PLA, AVIC must participate in any project that uses jet engines. By the time the signing ceremony came around, our partners included Gansu's provincial power plant construction and development company, the municipal grid access company, CNPC, and AVIC.

Another observation, this one in hindsight: Years later, the hours our plant operated seemed to line up with rocket launches from PLA's nearby Jiuquan launch center. We wondered if the PLA rocket forces had driven approval for our plant. We did stabilize the far end of the grid that supplied electricity for rocket launches.

**SF**: Dunhuang sounds like an interesting place. From what I gather it sits on the edge of the Gobi Desert and, in addition to being famous for those caves, was also a garrison on the Silk Road and the first trading town reached by foreign merchants entering Chinese-administered territory from the west, way back when. Did you spend much time there?

**PJ**: Yes, from the coldest week in my life to some of the warmest interactions with Chinese people. Yih-Min and I arrived in Dunhuang by taking a train from Urumqi to the train station at Jiayuguan, which is near Jiuquan and the launch complex. Then, we took a four-hour car ride to meet CNPC and AVIC personnel in Dunhuang.

Meeting the six men representing our intended counterparties reflected attention and endorsements from the PRC's highest levels. (Even though Mao Zedong said women hold up half the sky, women rarely attended our meetings.) One man (Zhou Xiao Qing) had been Deng Xiaoping's adviser for jet engines and rockets. A second (Li Jianguo) led the provincial electric power construction investment and development instrumentality and had previously supported project finance conditions.

Three others (Li Wei, Liu Zhiwei, and Huang Yun) represented the up-and-coming ranks of midlevel managers. One of them retired recently as the number one liquid natural gas authority for CNPC. A second rose with AVIC's former top executive, Lin Zuoming, only to be sacked with much of that CPC member's *guanxi*. The third muddled through the political challenges safely with persistent but plodding success.

Finally, the sixth (Jiang Jie-Min) would climb to the highest levels of CNPC and leave for one of the highest levels of CPC administration, Chairman of the State-Owned Assets Supervision and Administration Commission. Jiang may have been the smartest CPC leader I ever met. He cared deeply about the Chinese people and understood the need to reform the Communist Party. Xi Jinping imprisoned him for alleged corruption. More likely, Jiang's known positions threatened Xi's political authority.

These six men exposed their futures to the most uncertain factor of success in the PRC—the vicissitudes of the CPC's paramount leader. Their careers offer a glimpse at the many possibilities when pursuing this path.

Knowing these men and their families—and others from other projects—from inside their challenge sets helps to develop an understanding of why

CPC leaders sometimes hide from, and sometimes seek, top leaders in the United States. When Fortune 100 executives or government leaders arrive in the PRC, the CPC orchestrates their entire visit. US leaders meet people who dress, act, and speak like they do, and who went to the same schools. The CPC representatives have rehearsed how to leverage US concerns into CPC gains.

Soon after we met all the parties, Yih-Min told me the working group was going to a smaller conference room to address details, and the leaders were going to visit a nearby Buddhist monastery. I said, "Great, let's get to work." He responded that, no, I was not part of the working group. I fell into the latter category, and as such, I needed to accompany Mr. Zhou, the famous AVIC leader who had advised Deng Xiaoping.

An hour later, I was bound for the monastery . . . on a camel. (Image 4) Growing up in Texas, I had learned to sit a saddle confidently and comfortably. Not so Mr. Zhou. Anxious, if not frightened, he was grabbing the pommel as his camel lurched one way and then another to reach its towering standing position. I smiled sympathetically at him.

That was a mistake. Sympathy from a younger, non-Chinese male caused the older, Chinese male to lose face. I suffered Zhou's dour look until he destroyed me—the younger player of European descent—in front of a small hoard of Han Chinese in a pool game. Then he was all smiles. Only later did I realize I had caused his loss of face in the first instance and allowed him to recover it splendidly in the latter.

Looking back, that contest—which I had not even known was playing out—established important expectations of competing constructively, fairly, and honestly to see who could contribute better to our shared ambitions. It got us off to a good start. And we would need it.

That night it snowed, and the temperature continued to drop. The hotel's heating system couldn't compete with Mother Nature. I slept in all my clothes. In the morning, I shaved and washed my hair with water so cold it should have been ice. No shower that day.

Negotiations to sign an MOU proceeded smartly. At a celebration dinner, Mr. Zhou and Mr. Jiang—Deng's rocket master and Xi's prominent victim, respectively—allowed me to drink moderately after my toast. They taught me *sui-yi*, or "take it easy," as an alternative to *gan-bei*, or "bottoms up!" Together, we prioritized working together. (Image 5)

Scheduled to leave by airplane, we were all stranded thanks to the weather. Some decided to wait for planes to reach Dunhuang. Yih-Min and I decided to go back to our Urumqi office by train and invited Mr. Zhou to join us. He did.

Along the ride, I learned Zhou had worked in the Baltimore area for a US jet engine maker. During our previous days, he had allowed interpreters to speak for him, but he spoke English just fine, though with an accent that would have made him more intelligible ordering fish and chips in Baltimore than this Texan has been. Trundling along on rails, swaying comfortably, sitting on one of the bunks like it was a couch, I asked him what he thought of the Iraq war that had begun in 1991. Zhou's grin spread ear to ear. He answered that it was great.

"Great? I asked. "How so?"

"We sold more missiles than ever before."

I still kick my thirtysomething self for not biting my tongue and waiting to hear more. But I blurted, "How did you get paid?"

Zhou's frown returned. "That was someone else's department."

**SF**: One of the lovely discoveries over the course of our conversations is that when you were in China or elsewhere you regularly wrote letters to the Whirlygigs, reporting on your day-to-day affairs, reflecting on your efforts, and simply playing dad to three girls. What moved you to memorialize these trips you were taking?

**PJ**: One time Yih-Min and I were driving in the Gobi Desert, and he said to me, "I know you love your daughters because you talk about them all the time." So I was thinking about it. I missed them, and they were growing up. I was trying to elevate their awareness. *Here I am going to China all the time, and you might want to know why.* If anything, it started a conversation, and then as they were older, I took each one of them with me alone on one trip.

**SF**: Here's a passage from one letter you wrote to the girls that taught *me* something:

> Mom gave me *The Bridge at Andau* by James Michener to read on this trip. Its strong anti-communist theme, based on the 1956 Hungarian uprising against the Soviet Union, made me very uncomfortable. China still bans, although they enforce the ban less vehemently than before, some books. Usually, I kept it in my briefcase or coat pocket where no one could see the title. When I did read it in public places, Chinese airlines and airports, I used an Entry Form to cover one page while I read the other and shielded the whole book by keeping it close to my body, and I always jostled the book. I never left the book in the open. Many died so that we can read or write whatever we like.

In a November 1997 letter, you wrote about a trip that began with a visit to Korla, the second largest city in Xinjiang Province. There, you executed a letter of intent with the county administrative district for Tang to develop a 75-megawatt gas-fired cogeneration plant that would deliver electricity and steam to industrial users. Estimated cost: $50 million. You then described your first night in Dunhuang: "I ate camel's feet and the cook knows what else."

Camel's feet? How is that prepared? What does it look like on the plate? And, of course, what does it taste like?

**PJ**: It fills a plate, looks boiled, chews tough, like it's chewing back at you, and tastes like some crude oil smells. Others, apparently, learn to appreciate the unexpected offering.

I have another Dunhuang story. One of our warmer meetings, both in terms of weather and friendship, happened years later. Plant construction was progressing when I visited. The plant manager invited me to lunch with several others. The guest of honor sits next to the host, and across the round table from the honored guest sits the second highest ranking person. Sometimes, the top two positions will be switched for tactical advantages.

Anyway, at this lunch the project manager's wife sat directly across from me. She and her husband had recently lost their son in a traffic accident, and, with Yih-Min's help, I had expressed condolences and remembered him to others in what was becoming a close-knit Dunhuang group. Because of that, I wasn't surprised or uncomfortable with her taking an esteemed seat.

Expecting her to toast me, the table quieted. Instead, to my surprise—and discomfort—she asked, "What do you think of Mao?" My mind raced to balance sincerity and sensitivity. I answered, "Mao hurt a lot of people."

Complete silence at the table. I bit my tongue. Then the table erupted with spirited commentary on Mao. To my surprise, some offered answers criticizing Mao. Most seconded my response.

There's a lesson here: Many China hands understandably see a monolithic CPC or PRC. The CPC certainly wants foreigners to see it as completely and unassailably in charge. But where "the mountains are tall and the emperor is far away" and people develop a level of trust among themselves, human nature demonstrates fractures among the governed about their governors. US leaders could rely on these fissures to advance their objectives, but few invest the years it takes to leverage Chinese differences into better outcomes for people in the PRC and around the world.

**SF**: From what I understand, it was about a year between the time the plant was commissioned and when it became operational. What exactly takes place over such a time frame?

**PJ:** In the PRC, it takes much longer to build a power plant than in the United States. To your question though, a lot happens. CNPC officials had prioritized meeting electricity demand near Dunhuang. They had picked the fuel—natural gas—which we supported for three fundamental reasons. First, as noted, a modern natural gas-fired power plant would produce emissions that were cleaner than the air many people in China breathed.

Second, the PRC holds significant gas reserves (and routinely flares lots of it). Third, combustion turbine- or jet engine-based power plants can quickly start up or shut down to respond to changing demand requirements.

Next, the proposed participants set about proving their case. To invest our own time and money, we needed to confirm electrical needs, availability of fuel (in quantity, composition, and pressure), workers to build and operate an advanced power plant, government approvals, financing, etc. And we faced mountains of paperwork: the initial, but comprehensively burdensome, feasibility study; a joint venture agreement to guide owners' authorities and behaviors; contracts to buy fuel, equipment, supplies, etc.; agreements to use land and connect to pipelines and electrical transmission or distribution lines; operating manuals for plant personnel; reports for government entities; and setting up bank accounts. All of these, and more, also had to meet international standards for project financing—that specific type of financing that gets power plants built around the world and looks only to the power plant for its returns.

A whole other set of worries whirls around transporting equipment, tools, and technicians from wherever they are to where you need them. Jet engines and generators spinning 3,000 or 3,600 revolutions per minute depend on bearings for support. Bumps along the road during shipment can flatten those bearings. Flattened bearings keep high speed equipment from operating properly; poor operating performance leads to people not getting electricity and investors losing money.

Before equipment arrives, crews test site soil to design supporting structures and prepare for pouring concrete. Before pouring concrete, other crews need to know where and how to secure bolts that will stick up through the concrete to fix equipment securely to the platforms. Waiting for templates—full foundation-size maps for bolts, anchors, pathways, etc.—can hold up pouring concrete. Supply and service chains in the PRC routinely cut corners to save money, shrugging off American directions as too fussy about details that may not matter—or can wait if they do.

A quick story frames the problem, and at least one solution. For our first power plant pilot project in Yakela, Ken Collier, who I mentioned earlier, led our installation efforts. After the PRC crew repeatedly did the opposite of what Ken directed, he slammed a four-pound hammer against a steel I beam and cussed them out good in vernacular Texan. Slow to anger, Ken found a way to communicate effectively! The startled crew started following his directions.

Back to taking care of essential bearings during transport: Planners use trains, planes, trucks, boats, maps, time schedules, etc. In the years since we built the plant in Dunhuang, the PRC has added thousands of miles of highways. Then, however, taking heavy equipment from ocean ports over 2,000 miles of rough inland roads required powerful trucks, special air-ride trailers, and frustratingly slow driving. It took the ever-diligent, always thoughtful and tenacious Mike Graul to think through limitations and sequences to line up logistics. He had to worry about the weather, too!

Tools and technologies require extra thought, as well. Some have dual uses subject to export restrictions. Looking back, it's easier to see the persistence of the Communist Party's strategic program of military-civil fusion, where military needs (or just wants) put a cloud over all civilian activity, like an enormous umbrella, to fuse commercial innovations and strengths into military usage. The CPC places the "military" in "military-civil fusion" first to emphasize its primary importance.

**SF**: It occurs to me you might have some technology or equipment in such an operation that the PLA might find worth copying. If so, how do you protect yourself?

**PJ**: Anyone working with a PRC-based entity needs to expect that the Communist system will take whatever intellectual property (IP) they expose to PRC awareness. Under Communism, even ideas belong to the CPC. Steve, if you have a good idea, but I use it before you do, the party praises me. If the party sends you and me to gather wheat and I use the only scythe available, then good for me that I harvested more wheat than you.

In Communist ideology, property—including IP—belongs to the people. Of course, it benefits the party to administer and control property on behalf of the people. In fact, one can accurately translate the CPC's name as "the people's property party."

The party's conceptual approach scoops American assumptions that ownership equates with control. Not so to the party, which divorces our notions of ownership from control, and lets control eclipse them. Americans call that theft. Communists call it efficiency.

**SF**: Can you briefly expand on the concept of ownership versus control?

**PJ**: Sure. Americans think if they own something, they can control who uses it, what it's used for, and who gets the benefit of what it produces. Investors in American companies expect boards to direct those companies' behaviors. In the PRC, regardless of ownership, the party exercises control; it can and does direct companies' business decisions, and who benefits or suffers from those decisions.

In our case, to protect IP, we started by identifying what we had to protect. Others' experiences taught us that PRC courts are unlikely to protect the value of foreigners' assets. While the CPC's judiciary makes a show of protecting patents, it's still just a well-choreographed show. Even in cases where PRC courts rule in favor of foreigners, they often award only pittances to victims, thereby lightly punishing offenders.

We chose not to rely on legal defenses, like patents, for several reasons. If we went into PRC courts, we would enter a world of hidden processes tilted toward protecting the ruling political party and backed by an entire country's treasury. Conceding that just going into PRC courts would mean we had already lost, we decided not to ever take any truly advanced technologies into the PRC.

**SF**: Then how could you perform effectively?

**PJ**: The heat exchangers in our natural gas processing plant for the Karamay oil field serve as an example. They were critically important to reliably effective operations. Drawing three concentric circles with fins attaching the outside of one to the inside of the other could provide enough design information for an engineer to understand our conceptual IP. But to construct that concept required exceptionally sophisticated welding.

For step one of our layered defense from piracy, we welded in Texas and encased the critical heat exchangers in the processing plant's "skid," or basic steel frame, between two I beams with steel plates welded on top and bottom and insulation pumped all around the gaps in the skid.

For step two, we provided installation. We declined to simply provide installation instructions. By controlling installation, we controlled training of CNPC operators and didn't reveal construction techniques and procedures.

For step three, we then operated the plant to make sure it was making money for CNPC. After turning over operations, CNPC would have had to take the plant out of service to cut into the guts to try to learn from our proprietary know-how.

CPC agents can slice through these layers. We couldn't afford a perfect, unassailable defense, but we could raise the price to pinch our IP.

We took our licks, too. Our strategy to always keep our value to our joint venturers in front of them failed as soon as Xi Jinping's administration began its false propaganda that the West was declining and the PRC was ascending inexorably.

**SF**: A thirty-million-dollar power plant seems like a pretty big deal. Yet you sold your interest to CNPC within a year or so of it becoming operational. Why?

**PJ**: We had a tough issue to address. We had arranged financing for the plant under a set of long-term laws that included, among others, two really critical contracts—a power sales contract and a fuel purchase contract. Those two contracts had to swing together. They could not seesaw against each other. If fuel purchase prices rose, electricity sales prices would have to rise. They could rise or fall together, but rising fuel prices against falling electricity prices would bankrupt the plant.

When Beijing proclaimed it had the power to determine electricity prices annually, it made divorce inevitable. As we explained to our partners, this situation was like getting married with an untenable twist. Imagine requiring a lifelong commitment from your spouse and returning a similar promise—but with an exclusive-to-you annual option to review and renew your own commitment.

Our partners understood we couldn't go forward on such a basis. But they had two problems. First, they had learned to lean on us. Second, our joint venture had received several approvals that raised their career prospects and gave them "face" with their *guanxi* networks.

The first problem swings around a fundamental difference between the PRC and the United States. Here, when we are at our best, we push authority and responsibility for decisions to individuals. Our foundational documents seek to protect individual's lives, freedoms, work, and decisions. Generally, for good and great reasons, we trust each other.

The CPC maintains a wholly different system that foundationally protects the political party and denigrates individuals. Generally, it distrusts people. Weirdly, it may assign responsibility for a decision to an individual or group, but then not allow them the authority to make the decision.

Because of this difference, my bride would make a better power plant manager than many of those in the PRC. Kathy readily admits a strong aversion to even wanting to understand engines, generators, compressors, and the like. But she takes care of the engines that propel her car around town. Unlike many PRC plant managers, she wields authority and carries responsibility for operating her car over long periods of time. Her quality of life depends on protecting her capital investments.

In the end, we essentially got all our money back, plus some fees for consulting. But we learned something even more valuable: Systemically, this showed we couldn't make money building, owning, and operating power plants in the PRC. If the government can change agreements that have been made and approved and vetted, you can't keep doing business in an environment like that. There's simply too much uncertainty.

**SF**: As noted, AVIC figures prominently in your story later on. What was your experience with it on this project?

**PJ**: Fascinating. We met and worked well with many outstanding Chinese people. We got to know them well and pursued opportunities in and outside the PRC with them. Their integrity and intelligence and commitment to doing good impressed me immediately. So did an obvious age gap. Mr. Zhou, Deng's advisor who we talked about earlier, led AVIC's team. His lieutenants, however, skipped an entire generation—the generation Mao took out with his Cultural Revolution.

**SF**: In April of 2000, a few months before another project—the Gansu power plant—became operational, you spoke to the US-China Renewable Energy Forum in Washington, DC. I'm not bringing this up because of the way you began your remarks, but I have to admit, it was charming*: Distinguished guests, ladies and gentlemen—ni min hao. Howdy all.* How much Chinese did you learn to speak over the years?

**PJ**: Oh, I learned enough to ask my way to the men's room, to take taxis to airports, to politely request *moutai*, red wine, white wine, beer, and several different dishes. I could follow some energy and finance related conversations and even read some characters, but I remain a poor student of the language.

**SF**: The real reason I bring this speech up is to demonstrate that even then your positivity about doing business with China was tempered by concerns about "cultural and institutional obstacles" to success. Here's a partial transcript of what you said:

> When a bride and groom marry, they generally start with at least two misconceptions. First, she thinks that she can change him, and second, he thinks she will never change. Similarly, Chinese-American joint ventures struggle because they begin with misconceptions.

> The two parties often assume that they share the same goals and the same approaches to reach those goals.

You then offered three lessons, among them:

> Measuring success: Our Chinese partners and Tang all want our projects to succeed. However, only Tang must measure success in strictly financial terms. Our Chinese partners measure success in political terms, first, and financial terms, second. To many Americans, this sounds absurd. Americans believe and company owners insist that companies have to meet financial goals to continue business and to maintain financing options. Our capitalistic system works this way. To get money, we have to give customers economic value for their money, and we have to demonstrate that we have done so to financing sources.
>
> Before China began its significant and fundamental economic changes, Chinese companies had to achieve a mix of political and financial goals to get money. They had to show their financing source, the government or government-controlled bank, that they provided value to the community in political terms. Imagine what America would look like if the IRS, with its politically affected understanding of business, were deciding how much money our businesses would receive.

You concluded:

> We share many problems. Each problem gives us an opportunity to work together to make our world safer for following generations. Every solution creates more opportunity to expand the good work we do.
>
> Finally, China is a strong market not because China has 1.3 billion potential consumers, but because China has national ambitions that require a strong economy. To achieve those ambitions China must change its view of capital. Remember that at the turn of this

century, America borrowed money from all over the world and used it to create the economy that won two world wars and the cold war. Imagine what China could do for its economy if it accessed world capital markets.

Are these observations still relevant?

**PJ**: Yes. The most important nation-to-nation relationship for the United States to get right is the one with the PRC. It's the most important relationship for *the world* to get right. Constructive cooperation between these two countries raised hundreds of millions of people out of poverty, required Americans to work fewer hours to buy stuff, and generally supported peace globally.

Many critics say the United States got it wrong; we engaged China too much. Well, none have done the disciplined work to weigh the gains and losses on those investments over the past four or five decades. Our financial minds perform internal rate-of-return calculations on almost every business decision. The US government should apply similar intellectual discipline to understand how US policies, intended or not, fare under scrutiny. Instead, pontificators arrogate authority to their bold pronouncements.

**SF**: When you spoke to that forum in 2000, you noted a wind energy project in Xinjiang.

**PJ**: Yes. Opportunities had begun to present themselves. That was the good news. The bad news was that world events seemed to have a nasty way of interrupting those opportunities.

## Chapter 7

# This Could Kill Me

**SF**: We began an earlier chapter with a scene in an airport. Let's do so again. It's May 7, 1999. Your plane from the Far East has just touched down in Dallas. Kathy meets you at the gate. She looks relieved.

"I didn't know where you were," she says.

" What? Why?" you ask.

"The bombing."

"What bombing?" You don't know what she's talking about.

Kathy explains: "The TV showed crowds at the Beijing airport and people throwing rocks at American buildings in Beijing. We bombed the embassy in Belgrade."

"Whose embassy?" Total confusion.

"The Chinese Embassy."

**PJ**: I went numb. Getting back to the States takes a really long day, a day with twenty-six to twenty-eight hours in it. A lot can happen in a day—sometimes good, sometimes bad. I realized immediately that this event threatened all we had been working to accomplish in the PRC. Kathy and I just hugged each other.

**SF**: Allow me to provide some context. From late March to mid-June of 1999, NATO carried out an aerial bombing campaign—dubbed Operation

Allied Force—against Yugoslavia during the Kosovo War. While you were in the air, five US Joint Direct Attack Munition guided bombs had apparently gone awry and hit the PRC's embassy in Belgrade. Three Chinese media state journalists were killed.

This quickly became an international flap. The Chinese understandably expressed outrage. There was a chill in official US-Chinese relations, and tens of thousands of protestors took to the streets, throwing bricks at the US Embassy in Beijing. President Clinton apologized, saying it was an accident and the intention was to bomb the nearby Yugoslav Federal Directorate of Supply and Procurement. The Chinese were skeptical.

Obviously you made it home. What had you been up to in China this time?

**PJ**: I promise I'll answer. But first a story about the protests, which lasted several days. When I got back to Beijing, maybe a month later, I talked with friends from Xinjiang Wind Energy Company (XWEC). When the brick throwing began, some of our Chinese colleagues went to the US Embassy in Beijing for some state fair-like fun hurling objects at officially sanctioned targets. When they arrived at the barricade, PRC police asked them if they had party permits for throwing bricks at the embassy. They did not. The police turned them away.

Think about that. Bending a bit of a Psalm, my colleagues, in a spontaneous burst of patriotism rejoicing in the Word of the CPC, found spoils in front of them—only to discover that the party had reserved that joy for others. The brick throwers actually had PRC-supplied permits for trying to damage US sovereign property. The party controls everything, including the right to throw bricks, and even individuals' spontaneity for exhibiting patriotic fervor.

We could talk more about a B-2 Stealth Bomber taking off from Whiteman Air Force Base, refueling midair, and dropping precision bombs on the embassy; the Chinese "media" personnel working for the MSS; President Clinton gobsmacking General Secretary Jiang; and the CPC's possible retaliation with a fatal result against the US citizen who helped put an "X" on the embassy, but you asked about what I was doing in the PRC then.

As noted in the previous chapter, we had signed an MOU for the Dunhuang gas-fired cogeneration power plant in 1997. During this time, Gao Yang, whom we've talked about in detail, introduced us to Wu Gang, an engineer nearing forty years old, with a fascination for wind energy. At the time, he worked for XWEC.

Fun fact: Both of these individuals would later visit our home in Dallas. Gao Yang actually stayed with us. She thought our place was a palace. It's a nice four-bedroom, three-bath house—but hardly a mansion. A few years later, Wu Gang came by for a Sunday afternoon cookout. A former teacher, he mesmerized our children with stories and questions and sincere interest in their thoughts.

I imagine we'll be talking about how Wu Gang, a card-carrying member of the CPC, morphed XWEC into a company called Goldwind, and became its CEO. In the years that followed, Goldwind—which would become a major world player in wind energy—and Tang would discuss more projects in China and the United States. That's what occasioned Wu Gang's visit to the house.

Anyway, XWEC had erected some of the first wind turbines to generate electricity in western China in the late 1980s. It had grown dramatically in the '90s, and by this time was operating and maintaining some of the newest wind turbines in the world. Wu Gang had the very practical idea to build a natural gas-fired power plant on the XWEC wind farm in Dabancheng so XWEC could reliably provide electricity to the Urumqi grid even when the wind wasn't blowing. Dabancheng, population 40,000, is about sixty miles southeast of Urumqi. Enter Tang. With our expertise in natural gas, we could build a backup system.

**SF**: What was the relation of XWEC to the PRC?

**PJ**: Imagine a four-tiered wedding cake. XWEC and many other subsidiaries of state-owned enterprises (SOEs) and bureaus of government ministries fill the broad bottom layer. XWEC reports to the Ministry of Water Resources in Xinjiang at the next higher level, and that entity reports to the Ministry of Water Resources in Beijing, which reports to the Central People's Government, often referred to as the State Council. That's the chief administrative authority of the PRC. It's chaired by the premier, who is the number two leader in the PRC, and includes the heads of each of the constituent departments. And then there's a fifth layer—the icing, the Communist Party itself—which covers and seeps into all the other layers.

**SF**: Got it. Let's return to the reason you were in China in early May at the time of the bombing.

**PJ**: In the course of our meetings with Wu Gang, and through days at the remote Dabancheng barracks where we slept, ate, and played ping-pong after supper, we learned of Wu Gang's ambitious goals to build a world-class company from the XWEC platform. He was thinking ahead.

Backing uncontrollable wind with controllable natural gas power generation was a logical solution. The logic, however, ran into the all-controlling Communist Party, which had no way to support the set of contracts that could access commercial financing to support Wu Gang's solution. Broadly, neither did the United States. Both countries, in general, leave balancing variable wind energy production with gas, coal, and nuclear energy to electricity grid managers.

Another aside: The CPC shows its desire to control even the weather by seeding rain clouds with chemicals.

Back to your question, noting the local Xinjiang challenges, we suggested a joint venture to develop a new wind farm using project finance. The joint venture aimed, first, at financing an expansion of the Dabancheng wind farm with best-of-world finance tools, and second, at positioning XWEC to launch Goldwind. The proposed structure could attract international investment through an initial public offering (IPO) and, later, international debt financing.

**SF**: Hang on. In just three years, Tang had completed—on schedule!—two successful operating projects in Xinjiang: the industrial generating plant located at the government-owned carbon black plant, and the gas-processing project with CNPC in the Karamay oil field. You'd received full payment from your Chinese counterparts and established a trusted relationship with them. You had "face" *and* credibility! As a result, you'd been invited to partner in building that big gas-fired cogeneration plant in Gansu Province, and the natural gas-powered backup to the Dabancheng wind farm.

In short, you knew natural gas energy inside out, but as far as I can tell you didn't have any experience building wind farms. What was the incentive for Tang to pivot, or at least to add wind energy to its portfolio?

**PJ**: We knew next to nothing about building wind farms, but there were several reasons to pivot. One, we determined we'd do well, make money. Two, we'd be doing good by reducing emissions into the atmosphere. And three, the Chinese system made it virtually impossible to structure finance for the natural gas backup system in Dabancheng. There was no suite of contracts that could make that work, nor would it be approved in the PRC because it was so new.

So we dropped that idea and turned our attention to entering into a joint venture with XWEC for a 22-megawatt project that would dramatically expand the existing wind farm in Dabancheng and serve 1.5 million people and local industries that had a growing demand for electricity.

**SF**: China has no shortage of fossil fuels and at this time hadn't demonstrated a healthy concern for climate change. At the same time, the country had great plans for economic expansion—at home and globally. What was its incentive for building wind farms?

**PJ**: Please don't shoot the messenger, here. CPC orthodoxy diverges from US and European orthodoxy on climate change. In conversations over the years with a broad swath of Chinese leaders, I found a wide range of expressions for one common, core belief: National security rests on energy security.

To answer the first part of your question, the PRC suffers no shortage of fossil fuels because, more and more, it imports natural gas, oil, and coal. Looking to history, the Communist Party tightly ties up long-term access to cheap energy with strategic national advantages. In one conversation, a board member of HT Blade, which made blades for wind turbines, asked me how America consistently made more energy available to more people in cleaner forms and at lower costs without a national energy supply planning committee. He couldn't believe we trusted energy markets to guide producers, inventors, and investors with an issue so important to national security.

The advantages China presses as a result of Russia's war against Ukraine demonstrate its strategic concern. Increasingly, because of the war, Russia struggles across its political, commercial, and geographical sectors. Exploiting Russia's weakened condition, the PRC updates imperial tactics and signs long-term contracts for Russian oil and gas. Call it conquest by contract. The CPC extends and secures its control over hydrocarbon resources for cut-rate and plentiful access to energy far into the future.

The CPC plays the negative side of contractual conquest, too. It suspended imports of Australian coal, lobsters, and wine when Australians offended China's Communists by asking for information on the virus causing COVID-19. Wine exports alone amounted to about $400 million annually. Mull that over: The party created an opportunity to counter their aggression, perhaps an obligation, for us to party with Australian wine.

The Communist Party also plans grand economic expansion. It does not, however, generate sufficient capital on its own to achieve those expansive goals. The party cares about climate change primarily for the conduit it provides to foreign capital. It even feigns alignment with others' climate change concerns to get to their cash. It builds wind farms to look like a respectable borrower, investee, or—in former President of the World Bank Group Bob Zoellick's phrase—"responsible stakeholder."

The PRC's actions belie their words. Its delays in connecting solar and wind power, plus its outlays for building coal and nuclear power generation facilities expose its leaders' true position on environmental resources. It constructs hydroelectric dams in places that allow it to surge or suppress water supplies to downstream neighbors. For corroboration of the CPC's concern for the world's natural resources, look at the PLA's destruction of reef habitats in the South China Sea. Its deliberate devastation should make environmentalists' blood boil. As it turned subsurface sea towers into islands topped with PLA runways, it backed ships' spinning propellers, like seagoing Cuisinarts, into living reefs, chopped them up and smothered them with sand, concrete, and asphalt.

Like its imperial predecessors who chopped down China's forests hundreds of years ago, the party takes all it can from the environment. Look, too, at how the Communist Party treats people. It pours men's souls like ready-mix concrete into the foundations that support its political power; it assesses people's lives as equivalent to the grains of sand it crushes to form substrates for microchips. It values solar panels and wind turbines not for the environment, but for their utility in exploiting free-world financing policies. The party plays to our hopes; it seduces writers, government leaders, and ambitious cleaner energy folks like me.

Oh, and the CPC also appreciates a corollary benefit of making clean energy gear: developing those skills advances military technologies. Building long blades for wind turbines, for instance, cultivates capabilities for making airplane wings. Yes, the vibrant wind energy sector attracts many Chinese who are passionate about cleaning up the PRC's environment, but the CPC looks to protect its political power first, foremost, and forever.

As we discussed earlier, Mao insisted that political power grows from the barrel of a gun. The party needed then, and needs now, lots of cash every year to please people and have enough money left over to buy lethal military gear. More and more, that gear requires advanced technologies.

**SF**: Let's go back to the money.

**PJ**: Yes. Rich investors the world over pour money into the wind industry every year. The CPC readily recognizes cash floods. It sets up companies and programs to soak in this tidal wave of money. Even Goldwind, now one of the most successful wind turbine manufacturers worldwide, got its start from a foreign grant for $3.2 million from—get ready—Denmark.

Sending money to the PRC for wind farms also pleased multilateral financing institutions like the World Bank and US and European governments. Environmental Protection Agency (EPA) and DOE grants from the United States helped establish wind energy potential in the PRC and *for* the PRC, not for Americans.

One evening in Beijing in February 2003, I suggested to Kong Chiu, an EPA official, that the US government should provide wind data it collected to US companies, not just to the PRC. I also suggested that the United States require, in exchange for US taxpayer-funded wind research, that US wind developers have a chance to bid on wind-generated electricity sales on a price-per-kilowatt-hour basis. He immediately rejected my suggestion, telling me that the EPA was not there to help US companies. Not only does this approach transfer wealth from Americans to Communists, it also deprives the US government of practical expertise that can advance US interests.

Another irony strikes me: The United States led early wind studies because, during the Cold War, the Department of Defense sought to predict "plume dispersals." It wanted to know how fallout from large explosions would spread in response to wind patterns. The US taxpayer funded the technology to predict wind patterns. Our government then used that knowledge to assess wind regimes in the PRC, yet refused to use it in ways that allowed US companies to compete to build wind farms that could put that knowledge to use.

If you doubt the CPC's commitment priorities, note that it built wind farms it wouldn't connect to the grid. Why? Because it costs just as much to connect, say, a 100-megawatt wind farm as it does a 100-megawatt fossil fuel plant. While the connection investments for both may be about the same, electricity flows through the connection to the wind farm only when the wind blows. Top-rated wind farms in the world generate power only about one-third of the time. That means the connection to the wind farm has only about one-third of the utility, or value, of the connection to the fossil fuel electricity plant. In contrast, a fossil fuel plant can operate almost 100 percent of the time. The connection investment in it works all the time. That investment helps the economy grow. The party looks at the money, not the climate.

Let's turn to technology. I know we will be discussing HT Blade in the coming chapters. Tang and AVIC subsidiaries formed this China-based joint venture in 2001. One of HT Blade's owners, Baoding Huide Wind Power Engineering Company (Huide for short) used a now dual-purposed military tank turret factory to make wind turbines. Sure, the wind turbine work sounds like turning swords into ploughshares, but, to the party and its armed wing, it sustained budgets for the tank maker, kept its people employed, and gave them access to the world's best-in-class manufacturing techniques and processes. In addition, making long blades for wind turbines supports making long wings for drones and high-altitude, long-endurance flights for intelligence, surveillance, and reconnaissance (ISR)—even armed ISR.

**SF**: Why was wind farm expansion or creation viable, as opposed to that natural gas-fired backup plant or other natural gas projects? You mentioned contractual difficulties. Was that it?

**PJ**: Both are viable, just not together as a single project for operations and financing. PRC laws or regulations do not accommodate mixing wind and fossil fuel-driven generators as a unitary power project. Neither do US laws or regulations. Project insurance, equipment guarantees, and more create opportunities for conflict. If, for example, an accident with a wind turbine caused an electrical surge that damaged a natural gas-powered generator under warranty, who would pay for the repair? If ever inclined to do so, the PRC could, by fiat, create a legal framework that supported combining electric generation methods before the United States. Just as quickly, beware, it could contravene its previous decisions.

The good news is we turned the difficulty into an opportunity to build on what we did know. Project finance and corporate finance helped us grow our businesses in Texas. XWEC immediately understood the potential benefit for its dreams, but it had no relevant finance experience. That's why Tang could help their project take flight.

Late one afternoon in Dabancheng, after frustrating hours of going over financing scenarios, I broke Chinese protocol, got up and walked around a conference table that seemed to stretch into the desert and, to their astonishment, plopped my computer in front of XWEC's General Manager, Yu Wu Ming.

XWEC's people couldn't believe I was revealing our financial model to them. Together, we went through every line of a very large spreadsheet that showed all our inputs, all our calculations, and our expectation of profits. I showed him and his team how changing variables lowered or raised profits. I showed base cases, worst cases, and best cases. I invited their observations, questions, and corrections. That one afternoon broke the ice. Ever afterward, we shared hopes, concerns, challenges, and opportunities.

**SF**: So it was these types of opportunities you were discussing in Beijing just before the Belgrade embassy bombing?

**PJ**: Yes. Entering into discussions with XWEC, we found an advisor and advocate for our wind energy business in Madame Zheng Shu Jun. In her fifties, Madame Zheng had been one of the PRC's first lawyers to work on power plant financing with lawyers from the United States and Europe.

On May 6, 1999, XWEC representatives met with us and Madame Zheng in her office in Beijing, where we discussed the estimated cost of the construction and completion of the Dabancheng project—expanding the wind farm, not the backup system. That was an estimated $22 million. We also discussed ownership percentages for XWEC (30 percent) and Tang (70 percent). Nothing was signed. I left with little time to make my flight back to the United States and no knowledge of the embassy bombing in Belgrade.

**SF**: I'm guessing that learning of the Belgrade bombing upon landing in Dallas, and then monitoring the Chinese reaction from there did not bring a smile to your face.

**PJ**: A smile? No. Not even a frown. Just an abject, numb stare. Acts of war and project finance repel one another.

**SF**: Was it an act of war or an accident?

**PJ**: Well, let's start with the publicly available information. In late March 1999, Yugoslavian armed forces shoot down a US F-117 Nighthawk stealth attack aircraft. They move pieces of the downed plane to the PRC embassy in Belgrade. In May, a B-2 Stealth Bomber takes off from Whiteman Air Force Base in Missouri and hits the part of the PRC embassy that holds the Nighthawk parts.

The United States claims this was a building identity mistake. Isn't it strange that many Americans believe the CIA can work wonders, and also believe it cannot update a map? There's even more to the story. We know the PLA wants to break US stealth technology, and we know some in the US government believe the PRC provided technical assistance to shoot down the stealthy Nighthawk.

About a year after the bombing there was a news leak—perhaps from the Clinton Administration itself—suggesting a CIA contractor named William Bennett had chosen the embassy as a target. Fast forward to 2009 when Bennett, out for a morning walk with his wife in the exurbs of Washington, DC, was attacked and brutally murdered. His wife was also attacked, but she survived.

Some China hands still speculate that this was PRC payback for Belgrade. One tightly held memorandum relates that newspapers like the *People's Daily*—a CPC official media outlet—covered the murder in a long article, since deleted from PRC websites, entitled "The mystery of the murder of the perpetrator of the bombing of the PRC embassy in

Yugoslavia." Though awkwardly translated, it leaves little room for doubt about the CPC's take on the bombing!

The restricted distribution memorandum further states that the *People's Daily* article also addressed rumors that the PRC had orchestrated the murder of the "perpetrator," asserting that the PRC would "never consider Bennett's murder as sufficient to make up for the damages, injuries and loss of life resulting from the bombing." Ouch! Four young men from the area were convicted or pled guilty to the crimes.

**SF**: So whether an accident or intentional, the bombing repelled project finance. End of story?

**PJ**: Hardly. Kathy says the bombing would have turned others away. She also finds me hardheaded. She's right on at least the first count—but look at what we knew and what we had: The PRC economy was going great guns. The wind energy area was growing even faster. Both PRC and international organizations and financers were pouring money into the sector. We were working with good—moral and competent—people in the PRC. We had earned an excellent reputation and were continuing to grow it. We had the chance to do very well by doing good. And we *were* hardheaded.

**SF**: Two weeks after the bombing, on May 21, you sent Tang's partners an update on your various completed, ongoing, and potential projects in China, including the wind farm. First of all, how was Tang structured?

**PJ**: Tang's structure changed over time as we attracted investors from other states, Europe, and China. We started Tang Energy Group, Ltd. as a Texas limited partnership with just Texas investors. Tang served as the general partner or managing member of a series of entities that investors required us to form to protect international investors from becoming US taxpayers and to optimize tax treatment from PRC authorities. I served as CEO across the entities and as the legal representative in the PRC. Yih-Min served as general manager, a title that reflected his unquestioned importance to and within the Tang companies, and to our Chinese counterparties.

**SF**: As for that May 21 update, it began: "Embassy attacks and political mistakes complicate Tang's challenge of working successfully in China. Fundamental needs, however, continue to offer Tang opportunity." Regarding Dabancheng, you wrote:

> The wind farms would generate electricity with wind only and cost approximately $40 million. In Tang's discussions with project financing sources, some prefer "green" projects and seek projects like this one. XWEC and Tang must secure project *li xiang* and power sales contracts. Upon accomplishing these goals, we should secure financing fairly quickly.

**PJ**: All projects need government approval to proceed. Bigger projects need higher levels of approval. A *li xiang* gives more than just an approval. It comes with a fancy, government red stamp that conveys an almighty power's—the CPC's—desire for the project to proceed with support all the way to success.

When I was sixteen, I wanted a license to drive a car. I passed a written test and a driving test, and then Texas handed me a license. A *li xiang* is more than that. A *li xiang* holder can carry an impressive certificate to government offices to show that *not only is our business licensed, but the Communist Party desires our success.*

Taking the *li xiang* to the appropriate electricity purchaser gave us credibility and "face" to politely ask for a power sales contract. Without having to say it, the utility knew the party had decided our project should proceed successfully. By supporting our project, all our counterparties could gain face, or elevated status within the Communist Party.

**SF**: Shortly after sending this update, you were one of the first Americans to return to China.

**PJ**: Yes, and it was quite a return! My hosts fetched me at the Urumqi airport. On the way to the hotel, they told me they hoped I didn't mind, but they had changed my reservation to another hotel. I said I didn't mind at all and asked why. They answered that, for my safety as an American, the new reservation was at a more secure hotel.

I thanked them and thought for a moment. Then asked, "What makes it safer?" They responded that the police owned it. *What*? I thought, *The police own a hotel*? I asked them if they knew what we call hotels that the police own in Texas. They did not. "Jails," I answered. We all chuckled. Still, think about it. Police forces in the PRC own or control hotels.

The next afternoon, the vice governor of Xinjiang invited me to the Xinjiang People's Hall and to dinner afterward. That's a big deal. The party hosts internationally known political and business leaders at People's Halls all around the PRC. The vice governor later enjoyed several CPC promotions. He formally lauded Tang Energy for being among the first American companies to come back after the bombing. Then, to begin dinner, he again thanked Tang for returning to Xinjiang and promised he would drink four drinks to my one the whole night to show his sincerity.

Before the end of June, just weeks after the bombing, we signed the Xinjiang Teng Feng Electric Company, Ltd. joint venture agreement. "Xinjiang" refers to the provincial-level autonomous region; "Teng" refers to Tang Energy Group and can also mean "soaring," and "Feng" means wind in Mandarin. Soon, we had arranged for $37.5 million in Chinese debt from two banks—the Industrial and Commercial Bank of China and the Agricultural Bank of China.

**SF**: In late December of 1999, you sent an "Information Memorandum" to potential investors projecting an almost 20 percent return on equity. That's pretty darn appealing.

Before we tell the rest of the story about this project, I have another basic question for you. How exactly do you build a wind farm?

**PJ**: As the project developer, we worked like a general contractor does for construction projects. You start with the land and come back to the land. You pick a site you think has lots of wind and is affordably close to an electricity transmission line. Then you start to spend money. First, you need to measure the wind at the prospective wind farm site. Often, to meet financing criteria, you need to spend more than a year assessing the wind resource.

Expanding a profitable existing wind farm saves time because you can use the wind farm's historical data. If the meteorological towers, which measure wind speeds, directions, temperatures, and a few other factors, indicate too little wind, you kiss your dream wind farm goodbye.

While assessing the wind resource, you prepare requests for quotes from engineers, wind turbine manufacturers, and construction companies with the equipment and crews to build foundations and lift towers that reach a football field high into the sky—crews who can put nacelles that weigh about the same as an M1 Abrams tank on top of towers blowing in the wind.

Nacelles (Image 6) cover and hold the generator, its connection to the blades, electrical control equipment, and winches or other mechanisms to hoist tools and parts. Ultimately, construction crews use huge cranes to raise towers and heave nacelles and their components to the top. Then, combining aerobatic artistry and brute lifting force, they hoist three huge blades designed to catch the wind and connect them to the gearbox axle protruding from the nacelle.

Before they can even think about starting, though, engineers need soil samples to design foundations. A foundation for a wind turbine on a beach, which is all sand, differs greatly from foundations built on bedrock.

You also conduct negotiations with electricity buyers and carriers. Sometimes, but not always, these may be the same entities; sometimes, the electricity purchaser owns the transmission lines that carry the electricity from the wind farm all the way to users.

Almost simultaneously, you initiate discussions with funders—lenders, equity investors, and, to the extent applicable for a particular project, tax- or policy-motivated investors. All the while, you're making sure you avoid environmental degradations, and gathering the many required permits to build your dream wind farm.

When these sundry factors and more come together, you get the money to start construction and go back to the land. There, you pick specific wind turbine foundation sites. And that's where you run into the PLA—the military. Micrositing requires topographic maps to determine localized wind currents. The PLA treats topographic maps of the PRC as state secrets. So, first level, you have identified a topic the PRC considers classified.

Because you have walked the land for your dream wind farm with the topographic maps, you know the published maps do not match real-world topography. You learn that the PLA skews topographic maps so foreigners—whether army personnel or wind farm developers—cannot make sense of them. Because frustration has boiled over and expressed itself effectively to your PRC counterparties, they have provided the key to de-skew the maps so you can get on with picking foundation sites. That key keenly interests our intelligence community.

Once you build a wind farm, you don't need much around it from an administrative standpoint. You might want a storage shed or an office that's kind of close for monitoring operations, but you can observe and control most of a wind farm's operations from very far away.

**SF**: Sadly, sourcing project finance to expand the Dabancheng wind farm eventually failed. We'll tell that story in the next chapter, along with yet another business pivot—this one quite successful. But let's end this chapter on a high note. Tell me about climbing wind turbines.

**PJ**: Well, in addition to spending my time in banks, law offices, and on airplanes, I also crawled up wind turbine towers—all the way to the top. Understanding how these behemoths operate is essential. If operations fail, financial returns fail.

As you climb the long, long ladder inside the tower to the nacelle at the top, the play in sway gets wider and wider. Climbing my first tower with Wu Gang at Dabancheng, I lost count of the rungs. Looking down at one point enforced his admonition, "Don't look down. Keep looking up."

Looking down, you could see the range of the swing. Your brain tells you that a mark on the floor more than a football field's length below should be staying still. Your stomach flips trying to agree. I suspect you've seen wind turbines when driving in the United States The towers I was climbing in China twenty-five years ago weren't as tall as those, but they were still quite big. My friend, if you are one who gets seasick, stay on the ground!

**SF**: We talked about how the PRC controlled the brick-throwing protests directed at the American embassy after the bombing in Belgrade in 1999. Does such control still exist? "Strikes and protests increased sharply in 2023," *Nikkei Asia* recently reported, adding:

> A flurry of worker protest videos have surfaced on Douyin, the Chinese version of TikTok, in recent months as slowing demand and supply chain shifts heap pressure on the country's factories.
>
> Earlier this year, a user named Jingjing's Memory posted a video of factory workers standing in front of the gate of Huijuchang Textile in the city of Jiangyin. Text overlaid on the footage reads, "The place I worked at for over 20 years went out of business, now I have no social security and no money." (Marrian Zhou, "Factory strikes flare up in China as economic woes deepen," August 28, 2023)

What should we make of this with respect to China's domestic situation, and are there repercussions for America as well?

**PJ**: I don't know that specific story. I can tell you that the PRC's *hukou* system of residency registration limits legal migration within China. Brute economic forces, however, push employers to hire migrant workers whose own basic needs drive them to seek employment beyond their home area registration. Your *hukou* ties your pension, health care, and access to schools for your children to your registered residency. As companies close, pension liabilities shift to provincial governments, but only for those who worked in the province. As workers age, both unfunded pension liabilities and ineligible participants rise. The scale of the potential resulting financial challenges exceeds the PRC's current financial stress from its overleveraged real estate sector.

Your shrewd question about repercussions reveals your own long-term perspective. Depending on how the CPC handles the imbalance of liabilities to assets reserved to discharge those liabilities, the latent lethality of ramifications for Chinese pensioners could devour world economic security. While this may sound hyperbolic, remember the PRC's economy ranks number two globally. Its implosion would rock the world. Growing international prosperity lifts Americans. More specifically, but just touching the surface, Americans depend deeply on Chinese-made antibiotics and other healthcare products—even simple saline bags and IV tubes, which maintain many Americans' lives. China produces appliances, from computers to refrigerators to our newly indispensable smart phones, at prices that save us hours of work every year. Our oceangoing assets depend on shipyards in China. Our military sources critical components from China. Many of our pension funds invest in PRC-based stocks and bonds. Very quickly, financial difficulties in the PRC could torture American lives.

# Chapter 8

# Why Would You Do This, Patrick?

**SF**: Here's an excerpt from something you wrote to the Whirlygigs in January of 2001:

> What a difference persistence makes. Last summer, when we went to Colorado, I wondered if I had done right for our family by working in China. I know the problems, difficulties and challenges, and, now, believe that our tenacity may pay us well. NUON and Électricité de France, separately, may reward us—Tang, that is—for our efforts and the successes that we have created. But first, a little bit about the trip . . .

Why the doubts?

**PJ**: Growing a new business anywhere is tough. Doing it thousands of miles from home makes it tougher. When the nations that host your home and business throw bombs and bombast at one another, the catalyst for creating jobs—capital flows—generally slows and stops altogether for some uses.

The lead-up to—and fallout from—the Belgrade embassy bombing in May of 1999 may interest historians and diplomats for a long time. But our competitive business environment gave us a short time to make investments work. Awareness of capital interruption and a closing window of opportunity caused deep concern about failure.

Over the next eighteen months, try as we may—and we tried hard—we simply couldn't nail down project financing for the Dabancheng wind farm. Investors in America, England, France, Germany, Hong Kong, the Netherlands, the PRC, and Turkey loved our work but feared Communist Party vacillations that could wreck potential returns.

Then, as if to confirm foreign investors' fears, the PRC banks that had committed $37.5 million in loans pulled out. I remember well the sickening feeling, like a gut punch that drops you to the dirt, when I got this news. Sure, we had to inform our existing partners of a potentially lethal threat to our business plan. But we would never get back the years we invested in trying to make our wind energy business work.

I remember walking out of my hotel room to go to a meeting. As I moved down the dark, drab hallway, it felt like everything was collapsing on me. My heart sank. Here we had invested all this time, all this money. We'd built all these relationships, and it seemed pretty clear it wasn't going to work. I'd wasted my family's money. I hadn't done well for my wife and my daughters.

In that gloom, I recalled a conversation I'd had some years earlier with Jimmy Bass, a friend from high school in Dallas. In between treks all over and to the highest points in the world, Jimmy had graduated from Yale undergrad and Stanford law and joined Gibson, Dunn & Crutcher, an internationally prestigious law firm. When he was serving as the firm's managing partner in Hong Kong, he asked me, "Why would you do that, Patrick? Why wouldn't you stay in north Texas where you can grow 18 percent a year in the real estate business?"

And now here I was with a business that, rather than growing at 18 percent, looked like it was falling apart. His question haunted me.

**SF**: Did you have an answer?

**PJ**: Not exactly. One of my selling points to the Chinese was: "We're used to working on frontiers. I'm from Texas, and a lot of western China looks like a lot of western Texas. And energy is important to people in China, just like it's important to people in Texas."

What we were doing in China, and hoping to do more of, was improving people's lives, raising people's livelihoods. We were working on a frontier that mattered. Not to denigrate north Texas real estate, but a lot of people can do that. I was drawn to the challenge of doing something new, something bigger, something that was potentially very profitable, and certainly good for the people to whom we were bringing energy.

But was it good for Kathy and the Whirlygigs? When I had this really down moment in the hotel hallway in Beijing, I thought, *You know, maybe Jimmy was right. Maybe for my family's sake I should have dodged this ego-feeding, driving force of, "We're gonna do good things for the world and make money doing it."*

While slogging down the hall toward some meeting whose purpose I no longer remember, I thought of an old Episcopal prayer about not being overcome by adversity. I cataloged the fundamental facts: The PRC needs more electricity, Chinese people need cleaner air to breathe, capital seeks good wind regimes worldwide to sponsor, and capital success builds political power for the party. And then I decided, *We'll find a way to make this work.* I said to myself, *Suck it up. You're here and, yes, maybe this is the darkest moment in the storm, but at least it can't get worse.*

**SF**: It's not difficult to understand your "What am I doing in China?" moment in Beijing. But truth be told, you'd accomplished quite a bit in a relatively short time.

**PJ**: Well, you're kind. In my head, I knew that—which is probably why I snapped out of my funk pretty quickly. That and the Episcopal prayer.

Talking about Texas attitudes went further with Communists than quoting the Book of Common Prayer, so I used some of those phrases in the meeting that day: *Buck up; pull yourself up by your bootstraps; if a horse throws you, dust yourself off and get back on. If you drill a dry hole, show me where you are going to drill next? What matters is what you do next. Learn from disappointments and move on. Look back to learn, but fight forward.*

**SF**: So on this trip, which is the subject of the letter to the Whirlygigs, you were fighting forward.

**PJ**: Yes.

**SF**: And it appears you were somewhat sanguine, suggesting that persistence seemed to be paying off and that you might reap rewards. Who were NUON and Électricité de France (EdF), and what were you hoping to gain from them?

**PJ**: NUON is a Netherlands-based company created in the mid-1990s when a number of regional and local energy companies merged with Amsterdam's energy utility. NUON had sponsored wind farms near Shantou, in southeast mainland China, and was reportedly looking to invest in more wind farms in the PRC. Working with XWEC, we had completed all preconstruction work for the Dabancheng wind farm. We just needed an investor.

EdF is a multinational electric utility company owned by the French state. Simply put, as I wrote to the Whirlygigs: "EdF needs Tang for the work it does, and Tang needs to improve its access to financial resources. Tang needs French EdF because American-Chinese political tensions threaten Tang's ability to make money." The same was true with NUON; we offered a ready-to-go wind farm in the PRC's frontier market, and the company offered the possibility of financial resources.

**SF**: By the time of the January 2001 trip that was the subject of your letter, you'd been talking with NUON for several months.

**PF**: Correct. Tang had first introduced the Teng Feng Dabancheng wind farm project to NUON nine months earlier. On this 2001 trip to the Netherlands, we executed a cooperation agreement with the company. This and a confidentiality agreement allowed us to share proprietary data, information, and business plans. The agreement represented NUON's pledge that it wouldn't take our work to develop a wind farm without our participation.

**SF**: And EdF?

**PJ**: While in the Netherlands, we received the welcome news that EdF executives would like to meet with us. We quickly booked tickets and took the train to Paris.

**SF**: Unfortunately, within a few weeks you were lamenting "news of loss" to the Whirlygigs in a letter you wrote as you winged your way home from yet another trip to China, specifically Beijing, Shantou, and Urumqi.

**PJ**: We had definitely taken some hits, but, to be fair, I did tell the girls I was taking the news "with equanimity."

**SF**: True. I think the best way to describe these hits is to quote directly from that letter:

> 17 February, 2001, started with breakfast with Yih-Min and news that a second and new Chinese company wanted to enter our wind farm joint venture. Their entry threatens our position. After not sleeping particularly well, and coping without dental floss, that news hit me pretty hard . . .
>
> I mulled it over all day, stewed in it, even as we toured NUON's wind farm on Nan'ao, ate lunch, and returned.

**SF**: Why was news of another Chinese company wanting to be involved so discomfiting?

**PJ**: There were two broad areas of concern. First, the greater one: Adding PRC companies not only adds work to document agreements, but also adds complexity to respecting the hierarchies of multiple Chinese companies.

That increases opportunities for disagreement and takes time. Time is a most valuable asset.

The lesser, but very practical, concern was protecting our value from theft by additional PRC companies. The CPC encourages—indeed sponsors—raiding and plundering of foreign assets. Intellectual capital/property and what the CPC calls "management science"—how to make a business work—were all targets for CPC raiders.

The party usurps patriotism for the country with patriotic dedication to its political party. When we were developing wind farms, stealing ideas or opportunities showed patriotic fervor for the party. Nowadays, CPC laws even codify requirements that the Chinese reveal foreigners' assets, plans, and activities for national security. Even Chinese believe these laws have gone too far. Yet the party keeps them on the books.

**SF**: Okay, continuing with the letter: Correct me if I'm wrong, but I think your pride took another hit a few weeks later on yet another trip to China. You wrote the following to the Whirlygigs:

> On Wednesday (March 7), we met with Xinjiang Hui Tong Company that wants to take part of the wind to electricity project. They want to change our joint venture contract and gave us a list that began, " . . . represents a contradiction of logic . . . " Well, that sounds like they were saying, " . . . you can't think straight . . . " or " . . . you're pretty stupid . . . "
>
> I could have said, "You're absolutely right, but the joint contract comes from your country's law." It does, and Chinese law protects politicians' power before it facilitates economic growth. But, I did not have a dog in that fight and kept my good arguments to myself. Nevertheless, I think less of Hui Tong for their comment.
>
> On Thursday 8 March, in Urumqi, I met with Mr. Tsing at his home. Gao Yang, Li Li and Mr. Yang and I went. I wanted to talk to him because his position as Director of Water Conservancy in Xinjiang gives him

authority over Xinjiang Wind Energy Company and, reportedly, some authority over Xinjiang Hui Tong Company that wants to take part of wind to electricity project. Mr. Tsing, a Hui minority, married another minority, a Uyghur. They share Islam as their religion. Many Chinese practice no religion—another communist legacy.

We met Mr. Tsing at his home, a rather modest apartment by our standards, because his family was celebrating a Muslim holy period—for 3 days, I think. They would have charmed your mom with their gracious generosity. The dining room table was filled with homemade food—pastries, fruit, chocolates, lamb and more.

He poured tea for us and he broke out a 16-year-old bottle of *baizhou* that he had bought eight years ago. His wife (I'm not sure that you call her Mrs. Tsing because Chinese women keep their family's name), cooked homemade dumplings, stuffed lamb, and turnips (I think). When I thanked "Mrs. Tsing," Li Li translated into Chinese, then Mr. Tsing translated into Uyghur. She must have appreciated my appreciation because she gave me a dress that she made for you all.

9 March 2001: Gao Yang called just before I put down a book to check into my flight to San Francisco. She had "news" that changed what we accomplished last night. I think that Mr. Tsing told me the truth last night when I proposed reducing Tang's interest from 70 to 60 percent in the wind project to allow another Chinese party to join the project.

Gao Yang said that Mr. Yu, the General Manager of Xinjiang Wind Energy, said that Mr. Tsing was wrong. Somebody could be misinterpreting or misrepresenting here, or "facts" (or positions) have changed. All these changes frustrate and drain energy. I suspect that somebody from the Chinese company that wants to join the project talked to some other politician who changed the "facts" again.

**SF**: While the May 7, 1999, bombing of the Chinese embassy was a watershed moment, it seems like a drop in the bucket compared to the events of early April 2001. Before we get to those events, can you tell me where things stood with your various projects on March 31, 2001, including the status of your relationships with NUON, EdF, and XWEC/Hui Tong?

**PJ**: Gosh, it's a whole lot clearer in hindsight. NUON was working to cut us out completely, and EdF was looking to expand its intelligence-gathering capabilities. XWEC was working the most honestly and diligently, trying to expand the Dabancheng wind farm and establish precedents that would allow it to grow, first within the PRC and, eventually, beyond the PRC. We treated Hui Tong respectfully but avoided contracting with them.

**SF**: Now let's turn to the unfortunate events of April Fool's Day, 2001. That's when a US Navy intelligence aircraft and a Chinese interceptor jet collided in midair about seventy miles from China's Hainan Island province. The Chinese pilot was presumed dead, and the US plane had to make an emergency landing on the island while the PLA withheld landing permission.

In the PRC, the PLA controls virtually all airspace. This provided the excuse for the PRC to detain and interrogate the US crew of twenty-four. Of course, this all caused an international stir, threatened relations between the two countries, and raised serious obstacles to joint ventures like the ones you pursued. You were in China at the time, yes?

**PJ**: Yes. We were in the midst of meetings with AVIC. At this time we had a very positive relationship stemming from our partnership on the Dunhuang power plant. The meetings were to discuss building more wind farms in China.

Here's the scene: I'm in my hotel room in Beijing brushing my teeth before going downstairs for breakfast when CNN, suggesting US blame, reports that a US war plane has turned into the path of and collided with a Chinese fighter. Stunned, toothbrush frozen in my mouth mid-stroke, I see the TV go blank. Flipping to other channels proves it's working, but CNN remains blank.

Rushing downstairs to the lobby, I find the *People's Daily*, which confirms CNN's report. Interestingly, CNN suggested the US plane was to blame, while the *People's Daily* reported objectively that two military aircraft had collided, midair, near Hainan Island, not casting blame anywhere. Say I to myself: *We're not gonna have a good day today*.

We had our meeting and, frankly, started drinking beer at lunch because everybody knew we were in for a period of turmoil that was going to wreck our business plan. I remember one of the AVIC leaders saying, "I hope the party doesn't overplay its hand." He was right to wonder. In this case, CPC General Secretary Jiang Zemin handled the potentially massively disruptive event coolly. But think about it: A high-ranking AVIC leader and Communist Party member was talking to me about divisions within the party.

**SF**: This event hastened what I guess we could call your second great pivot, which we'll talk about in the next chapter.

**PJ**: Sounds good. But before we move on, I'd like to note another conversation Jimmy Bass and I had about doing business in China. I had asked him: "How do you figure out what people and companies you can trust in the PRC?" And he had responded: "It takes decades to figure that out." I've done a lot of thinking about that.

**SF**: And?

**PJ**: Trust spans a spectrum that includes distrust, mistrust, and no trust. Our own life experiences could probably add to that short list. With the Communist Party, I learned to always trust them in one way—and only in that one way.

This is something anyone thinking about doing business in China should understand: If you know what the party thinks will grow or preserve its power, you can predict its behavior with extraordinary confidence. Working with individual Chinese people is a different story. It took a while, but I got to know many Chinese people who I could trust to do the right thing, even if they found it difficult or unpleasant.

There's a bigger point here. The Communist Party sows distrust and mistrust among the people it governs. It's horrible. The party intentionally ensures neighbors fear each other. While all political parties may exacerbate mistrust for ephemeral gain, people all over create better lives for themselves when they can trust their fellow citizens. Chinese people live knowing the CPC will change even its constitution, if its perception of an improved outcome for itself changes. The only stability the party provides people is its monopoly on power, which, you'll remember, Mao Zedong says comes from the barrel of a gun.

This drags me back to the fundamental difference between Communism and a rule-of-law system. Communists use laws to keep people from impairing a political party's privileges. At their best, democracies fundamentally intend and create laws to protect people from oppression, political or otherwise.

Think about it. Without laws that protect people from bullies, people in the PRC do not have a system that allows them to express long-term commitment to one another in a way the state supports, so they do it in a very different way from Americans: by marrying into each other's families, celebrating Spring Festival together, building up each other's *guanxi* networks, or building up each other's "face." They have to do all these other things to ensure reliable expectations of behavior over the long run. That's partly why "face" is so important in China; if you offend me, my network will cut you down. The most elegant response to loss of face from one Chinese person to another is to fatally wound the person who caused the loss of face without them even knowing it happened—much less who did it.

People in the PRC do not live under a government that systematically protects the ingenuity of the individual. A quick story shows the contrast: Years ago, observing another's hair-trigger sensitivity to imagined offensives, our youngest simply remarked, "Get over it." Her preteen comment reflects that she trusts a taken-for-granted system that protects her individual gifts and allows her to subordinate personal affronts to developing unique talents.

Contrast her attitude with recent PRC complaints that another country has "hurt the feelings" of the Chinese people. People living in the PRC don't have the opportunity to say, "Get over it." When the government you live under protects little that belongs to you, and can take even that away at any moment, protecting "face" becomes paramount.

Oppressing the wonderful people who the CPC governs turns our credo *do well by doing good* upside down. The party is willing to crush individuality so it can do well for itself. As it does so, it tells Chinese people they are special because they subordinate their individual aspirations to the will of the party.

In democracies with theistic heritages, individuals may choose to subordinate their individuality to the divine, but they have the choice. Extrapolating observations of individuals, you can see why the United States, with a population about one fourth the size of the PRC, generates more innovation in the arts and sciences than the PRC.

**SF**: In one of your letters to the Whirlygigs you mentioned that many Chinese people practice no religion. Here's an excerpt from a recent Pew Research report:

> Based on formal religious identity, China is the least religious country in the world (among all places where survey data is available). Just one-in-ten Chinese adults self-identify with a religion, according to the 2018 Chinese General Social Survey. China also has the largest *count* of people—about 1 billion adults—who claim no formal religious affiliation.
>
> Since such a small share of Chinese adults identify with a religion, it may not be surprising that few say religion matters a lot to them.

> Just 3% of Chinese adults said religion is "very important" in their lives in the 2017–2022 wave of the World Values Survey.
>
> Yet religion still permeates the everyday lives of many Chinese people who do not claim a religion. Among the total population, a minority says they believe in religious figures and supernatural forces. But most Chinese people engage in practices premised on belief in unseen forces and spirits.
>
> Chinese people, in other words, are more religious in their *practices* than in their identities or beliefs. (Conrad Hackett, "Is China a religious country or not? It's a tricky question to answer," August 30, 2023)

Your observations and thoughts?

**PJ**: It's difficult for us to imagine the self-censorship that fear breeds. China's Communist rulers, historically, advocate atheism. Its power to take everything away from anyone under its governance without notice drives fear so deeply into one's soul that self-censorship works with constant vigilance at unconscious or subconscious levels.

Still, many Chinese people seek to approach the divine. Several times when Yih-Min would visit a Buddhist shrine or temple, the Chinese people who accompanied us would look to him to see how to act reverentially, respectfully. Afterward, we would privately discuss the effects of prayer and paths to approach the divine.

The party's position shows some signs of changing. Mao Zedong tried to remove God as a competitor to party power. That has not worked so well. As the party perceives piety as a path to power, it seeks to control piousness itself.

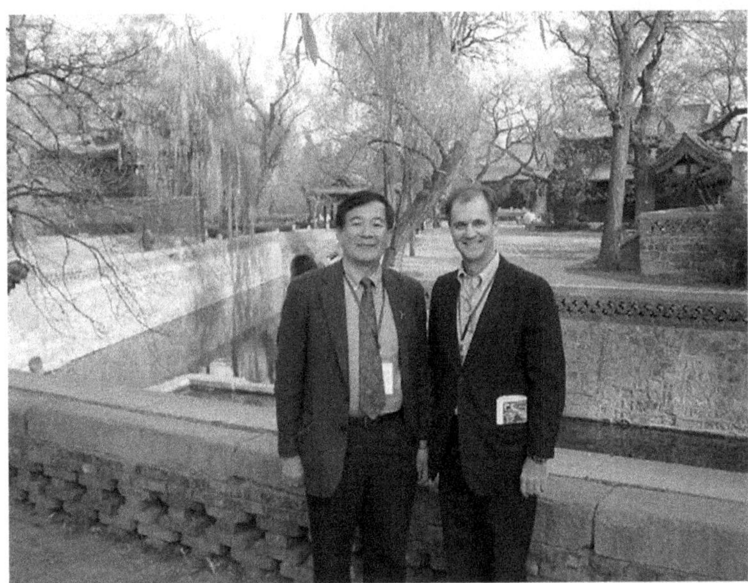

Image 1: Proud partners Yih-Min Jan and Patrick Jenevein, fortunate to share work worth doing. Taiyuan, China, circa 2003.

Image 2: Map of the People's Republic of China, from a 2008 Tang Energy Group financing presentation.

TANG
ENERGY

Image 3: The Tang Energy logo, created circa 2004. The stylized letter G suggests "going up" or "soaring" (*tang* in Chinese).

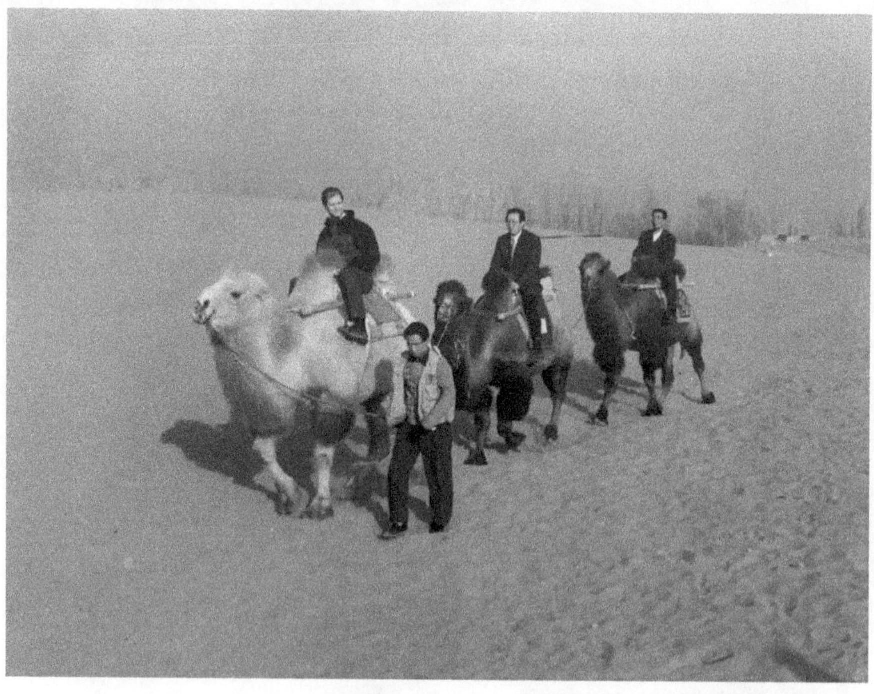

Image 4: Jenevein comfortably riding lead camel to a Buddhist monastery in the Dunhuang desert, while behind him Mr. Zhou of AVIC white-knuckles the pommel. Another AVIC official brings up the rear. Circa 1997.

Image 5: Jenevein, Jiang Jie-Min (who rose to lead the PRC's State-owned Asset Supervision and Administration Commission before his capabilities and integrity spooked Xi Jinping into "disappearing" him), and Mr. Zhou (who advised Deng Xiaoping and retired from AVIC peacefully), toasting the promise of the Dunhuang joint venture. Dunhuang, China, 1997.

Image 6: Emblazoned on the nacelle of a wind turbine generator, BHD stands for "Baoding Hui De," an AVIC subordinate and one of HT Blade's owners. BHD promotional brochure.

Image 7a: Completed blades in HT Blade's first factory yard in Baoding, China. Note the shaded bicycle parking to the left. Baoding, China, September 2003.

Image 7b: Factory workers using the "hand layup" method to produce one half of a wind blade, which is then mated with a mirrored half to form a whole blade. Today, wind blades exceed the length of a football field. Baoding, China, December 2003.

Image 8: One of Jenevein's "go to jail" cards: Huang Yun (a carefully successful AVIC executive), Jenevein, and Mr. Wang, who retired shortly after the photo was taken, only to start a competing blade maker in Baoding. "BPF" stands for Baoding Propeller Factory, which the CPC considers a state secret. Baoding, China, circa 2000.

At it's core, this is a simple case.

**The Aviation Industry Corporation of China ("AVIC") promised it would provide funding for wind power projects,**

but never funded a single project,

**And promised it would not compete with Soaring Wind,**

but started as new "subsidiary" and developed wind power projects in direct competition with Soaring Wind

Image 9: A slide from the claimant's lawyer's opening statement at the arbitration proceeding. Dallas, August 2014.

5 July 2015
2015年7月5日

Mr. Liu Zhongwen
刘忠文先生
Chairman of the Board
董事长
AVIC Huiteng Windpower Equipment Co., Ltd
中航惠腾风电设备股份有限公司

Dear Chairman Liu,
尊敬的刘董事长:

Thank you for kindly inviting me to meet with you in Beijing. For twenty years, face to face meetings with AVIC and Tang officers have yielded some of the best results that our companies have accomplished together and, especially now with our ongoing litigation, provide a model for creating mutually beneficial agreements.

谢谢您诚挚地邀请我到北京与您见面. 过去二十年来, 在与中航集团及美腾官员面对面的会议中, 我们双方共同取得了极佳的成效; 此外, 特别是在目前进行的诉讼案, 面对面的会议亦达成双方互惠的协议.

You may have not yet learned that AVIC representatives filed two false criminal reports against me personally in the USA. Because China does not provide travel visas to those it accuses of crimes, I will not be able to meet you in China. We would, of course, be delighted to host you in Dallas. If the non-stop flight from Beijing to Dallas is not convenient for you, I would be glad to meet you in our country's capital, Washington D.C.

您尚未知晓, 中航集团的代表人在美国已经针对我方, 发出二份错误的犯罪报告. 由于中国政府无法提供旅游签证给被控告者, 所以我无法前往中国与您会面. 我们当然很高兴在达拉斯接待您. 如果您不方便搭乘从北京到达拉斯的直航班机, 我们也很乐意在美国首都, 华盛顿, 与您见面.

Tang Energy Group, Ltd. □ 4925 Greenville Avenue □ Suite 1020 □ Dallas, Texas 75206 USA

Image 10: A July 5, 2015 letter to HT Blade's Board Chairman, noting the oddity of their invitation for Jenevein to visit China at the same time AVIC was pressing detectives in California to prosecute him as a criminal.

Image 11: In a picture taken on March 18, 2022, 109 empty strollers are seen arrayed outside the Lviv City Council, highlighting the number of children killed in the ongoing Russian invasion of Ukraine. (Photo : Yuriy Dyachyshyn/AFP via Getty Images)

Source: Bill Chappell, "109 empty strollers sit in a Lviv square, representing children killed in the war," NPR, March 18, 2022. https://www.npr.org/2022/03/18/1087536180/empty-strollers-lviv-children-killed

Image 12: The Dabancheng wind farm in Xinjiang, called East Turkestan by Uyghurs, circa 1999.

# Chapter 9

# In Vino Veritas

**SF**: I say this as a compliment: Tang was as gifted at pivoting as Dirk Nowitzki or Luka Dončić from your hometown Dallas NBA team.

**PF**: Ha! And like them, we were mavericks.

**SF**: Touché. So pivot number one was from natural gas-fired power plants to wind farms. And pivot number two—occasioned by the collision of the US and Chinese aircrafts on April 1, 2001—was a pivot to . . .

**PJ**: . . . manufacturing wind turbine blades.

**SF**: This was a plan hatched on the day of the collision when you went to a scheduled meeting with AVIC to discuss collaborating on wind farms.

**PJ**: Yes. As mentioned, Tang and AVIC had worked together very well on the Dunhuang natural gas power plant near the western end of the Great Wall. And even though project financing retreated in the wake of the 1999 Belgrade bombing, and NUON and EdF avoided committing any funds to us in the first quarter of 2001, we had remained hopeful. Naïve, perhaps, but hopeful.

One thing we haven't previously discussed that gave us some optimism was that China seemed to be on the path to becoming a member of the World

Trade Organization (WTO)—an outcome I supported. As you probably know, most countries aspire to join the WTO because it greatly facilitates international trade, making it easier for all parties to make money and create jobs.

Admission requires meeting certain minimum standards, and the PRC was not in the inaugural class.

After years of negotiations, however, Zhu Rongji, the PRC's premier and second (some argue third) most powerful CPC member, was strong-arming reforms in the PRC to open markets and reduce tariffs. Premier Zhu was also addressing concerns about corruption and lack of transparency. He may have been one of the smartest politicians on the world stage. He understood that the PRC had to look to external laws and powers to get the CPC to change its approach to the economy.

When the PRC won admission, its people had more work, and more ways to make money, and Americans had to work fewer hours to buy the same blue jeans and washing machines they needed. For Tang, this created a higher demand for electricity, which grew the need for our expertise in energy. It's worth noting that Premier Zhu's actions did more to lift Chinese standards of living than any other CPC member since Deng Xiaoping. Current General Secretary Xi Jinping should take note.

**SF**: As you awoke on April 1, 2001, China's admission to the WTO was still uncertain—it did finally happen that December—and then the planes collided. So, goodbye optimism?

**PJ**: Never tell optimism goodbye! History supports the optimist! Besides that, you need optimism to be a good spouse, parent, friend—and author!

**SF**: Tracking the evolution of the Tang/AVIC relationship through HT Blade is essential to understanding the devolution that led to the celebrated Soaring Wind Energy (SWE) dispute. Begin by taking us into the room where pivot number two happened after learning of the collision of the aircraft.

Who was there? How many beers were consumed before someone said, "Hey, maybe it won't be viable for AVIC and Tang to build wind farms together, what say we partner on manufacturing turbine blades instead? After all, they don't require project financing."

**PJ**: That's a lot of ground to cover. The overall view starts with Deng Xiaoping, long before my first trip to the PRC, goes through sunny pastures, and ends with Xi Jinping's ascension to paramount ruler within the CPC.

Xiaogang Village marks the starting point in 1978. Others pick Deng's southern tour of the Shenzhen area between Hong Kong and Guangzhou in 1992. But Deng watched the Xiaogang Village's transformative success. There, the CPC began to allow communes to keep or trade amounts of crops they grew over a specified threshold. Before that, under Mao Zedong's programs, PRC peasants turned *everything* over to the state, and the state allocated back to them amounts of grain determined by the party. Tens of millions of Chinese died of starvation under Mao's policies.

Xiaogang's simple change, which Deng permitted, pollinated a surge in agricultural production over the following years. Moreover, it cross-pollinated innovation, job growth, wealth creation, and even joyfulness among people living in the PRC.

Between Deng's igniting PRC prosperity and Xi's inhibiting it, we worked with Chinese people who saw outcomes that raised both PRC and US standards of living. US-PRC cooperation allowed PRC citizens to work for higher wages and US workers to spend less time working to buy things they wanted.

Tang's overall trip ends with Xi, who is throwing the Chinese, and any other population the CPC can corner, back under the maul of Mao's policies. Understanding this last point bears on your question about who was there. While our counterparties from AVIC were not competing to become the PRC's paramount leader, they belonged to *guanxi* factions that, fewer than ten years later, began warring with each other to determine the PRC's next paramount leader.

Since winning that fight in 2013, Xi Jinping has "disappeared" around two million CPC members, including some of the participants at our meeting. "Disappeared" refers to people who the PRC takes into custody while providing as little information as it chooses, as infrequently as it chooses. Writing descriptively about them and other participants could jeopardize their careers, their families' welfare, and even their lives.

If you like, I can tell you about the tone and tenor of our meeting. It may open a few rare views of tension inside the PRC.

**SF**: Please do.

**PJ**: We had scheduled meetings with AVIC on April 2, 2001. The airborne bumper plane game over Hainan Island happened the day before, resulting in the death of the Chinese pilot, Wang Wei (sounds, coincidentally, like "Wong Way"). It stunned us all.

For context about the game: The PLA Navy is developing, among other ambitious weapon systems, submarine warfare capabilities. This concerns the US Navy, which flies reconnaissance aircraft that can track submarines. To disrupt the US reconnaissance missions, the PLA flies fighter planes close to and around US aircraft. In Wang Wei's case, he flew his J-8II interceptor into a US EP-3 reconnaissance aircraft.

Back to our meeting. When we met, we all wore our professionalism in trim grooming, buttoned jackets, and tight faces. Dutifully following Communist Party decorum, our AVIC hosts opened with the agenda we had planned for weeks and tweaked before the war planes bumped in the sky over the weekend.

Non-Chinese foreigners are relatively free from having to follow cultural protocol. That made it easier for me to toss etiquette aside, interrupt the agenda, and say I was really worried that the incident with the war planes from our two great countries could doom our shared hopes for project finance. The silence of others around the table suggested their relief that I had spotlighted the elephant in the room. It also showed they feared commenting on the incident. The PRC media had kept its comments to the most objective of facts, devoid of spin or blame. General Secretary Jiang Zemin had not returned President George Bush's calls.

Taking advantage of the silence and relieving our counterparties of pressure to respond, I talked about the bigger picture of what we were doing. I noted that our two countries brought considerable benefits to each other and the world. Our success on a business level depended on deep understanding of each other. It also demonstrated possibilities and opened paths to realize those possibilities for our countries. Together, we were creating jobs in both countries and advancing stable relationships for Chinese and Americans. For world prosperity and peace, the most important bilateral bond to build is the one between the United States and the PRC.

With my own doubts for our continued success, I recognized their sense of dilemma. But I could talk about it. They didn't know if they could or where to start talking about how the incident might affect our business prospects. The party sets bounds on what its subjects can do, on what they can say, and now, under Xi Jinping, on what they can even dream. In warfare, diplomatic interactions, and business negotiations, this characteristic of overbearing control allows outsiders to maneuver more quickly than party members can. Looking forward, military combatants, diplomats, and businesspeople can leverage this dynamic.

After less than an hour of the much longer planned session, our host proposed breaking for lunch. Wait staff soon brought libations. I remember reminding our hosts that as an American working through jet lag, I lacked the strength of Chinese men to drink *moutai*. I did concede to drinking *píjiǔ*, or beer. Candor floated as alcohol flowed.

AVIC's employees told us that the blandness of the PRC media reports indicated the party was having a hard time figuring out what position to take regarding the incident. The observation made sense. The interesting part is that CPC supporters were openly voicing, among themselves and in front of foreigners, concern for the CPC's difficulties in making decisions and the limitations of its choices. Observing that Walmart alone bought billions of dollars of goods from PRC companies every year, one participant expressed hope that the party wouldn't "screw up."

I don't remember how much Tsingtao beer and *moutai* we drank. It certainly lubricated the conversation. Fundamentally, however, we had spent years getting to know each other. We had developed high degrees of confidence in one another. Our own, shared *guanxi* provided a safety net of relative comfort. Few political or commercial leaders get to do that. Instead, they fly into Beijing or Shanghai and meet with other really important people, ink a few pages, then fly out.

Now back to your "pivot" question. *In vino veritas.* We talked about the government-to-government or military-to-military situation; we also talked about our business situation. The embassy bombing and the planes colliding stand out as business-killing events. But they also stand out from a whole field of challenges in the PRC for deploying project finance. Seeing our glasses half full, we discussed opportunities:

1. The PRC was changing and growing fast. Those changes included improving laws to protect investors, inventors, and innovators. Fernando Vila, a Partner and CFO of a private equity investor once told me, "I'd rather invest in a country growing at 8 percent a year than one growing at 3 percent."
2. Wind energy businesses were attracting investors. We could tap that money flow directly through an IPO, or indirectly by selling turbine blades to wind energy developers who drew in lots of investment capital.
3. Consumers all over the world bought things made in China. If we could make something the wind industry needed, we could develop our own success.

Luckily, a year earlier, while I was leading Tang efforts to secure project finance, Yih-Min had begun to explore making blades for wind turbines. He had persuaded Wu Gang at XWEC to test one set of blades that AVIC made in a propeller factory in Baoding, about 100 miles south of Beijing. The test was working.

Disappointed by one failure and fueled with alcohol at lunch, the wind blade experiment turned our thoughts to growing a business with fewer threats from external factors. The idea made sense based on the environment and our combined abilities. PRC laws may not have protected or supported project financing, but PRC conditions did still support making things and selling them around the world.

Our reasoning: AVIC makes wings, propellers, and blades for planes, helicopters, and fans. Tang knows how to grow businesses. Together, we could develop our success. By the end of that year, 2001, we had made our first few sets of giant propellers for WTGs. As you know, much success was to follow.

**SF**: A lot of our future conversation will focus on the Tang/AVIC joint ventures—positive and negative—that basically grew out of this meeting—including SWE in 2008. Before we start on that journey, can you tell me if the fallout you anticipated from the collision of the planes did indeed materialize? Were your fears that this would kill the ability to build wind farms in China founded?

**PJ**: As others have observed, working with China requires a taste for bitterness. Yes, the belligerent acts vitiated commercial finance for wind farms in the PRC. But through diplomacy, US and PRC political leaders were able to avoid a serious confrontation and save face with their own constituents. This allowed established investment and supply patterns to continue. The timing of events, however, did kill our project because it hit us before we had secured financing and established a commercial investment pattern for wind farms.

**SF**: No offense, but why did AVIC need you, or any foreign partner for that matter, to participate in the business of manufacturing wind turbine blades in its own country?

**PJ**: Fair question. No offense taken. There were several advantages to AVIC for working with us. Most reflect learning how to work with oddities the

CPC creates for people living under its auspices. First of all, it was a new idea for AVIC to make blades, or propellers, for wind turbines. Even today, people working inside a CPC-controlled company can't directly come up with a new idea without peers shredding them over it. Bold subordinates can, however, suggest maneuvers to ride foreigners' innovations in case those later benefit the CPC, especially its armed wing, the PLA. The successful, bold subordinates give their bosses a way to deny involvement with a failure and to take credit for success.

In terms of *mianzi*—US leaders should learn to exploit this feature of PRC culture—masking involvement in failures allows the leader to save face, while taking credit for success allows the superior to gain *mianzi*. The subordinate can benefit either way because he or she empowered the superior.

At the time, the party had directed SOEs to learn "management science" and glean technological know-how from foreigners, especially Americans. In our case, if the venture failed, AVIC subordinates could point to party direction and blame the Americans. Of course, if we knocked the ball out of the park, they could round the bases like Babe Ruth. And that's what we did.

Lingering on innovation for a moment: Years later, with staggering breadth, the party enshrined approaches like this in its Innovation-Driven Development Strategy, not so much to nurture innovation within the PRC, but to acquire innovation through whatever it takes and wherever PRC patriots find it. Party organs fund about 600 different talent recruitment plans that seek, among other goals, to appropriate IP to CPC-controlled entities.

Another advantage: The fact that very large SOEs, like CNPC, wrote publicly and positively in Chinese about Tang was very helpful. It contributed to solidifying our relationship network, or *guanxi*. This network complemented AVIC's, and brought it opportunities, both domestically and internationally, it may never have developed without us. Because of Tang's relationship with XWEC, Goldwind became HT Blade's first customer.

It surprises Americans, but Goldwind and AVIC—two Chinese entities—couldn't easily talk with each other. They came from different, siloed ministries and had to struggle to figure out which ranked higher than the other in Confucian hierarchical terms. We, the lowly foreigner, could serve as the conduit that enabled both companies to improve their absolute positions.

I need to make this point again: Yih-Min and I didn't just want to make tons of money, we wanted to lead clean energy production. We also wanted to raise standards of living in the PRC.

This needs more explanation because some criticize our commitment to doing well by doing good in the PRC. Critics say we helped the Chinese. Well, we did. We also helped ourselves and other Americans, directly. By doing well in the PRC, we created jobs in Texas. The most obvious include the basic work of making a business run—engineering, welding, administration, and accounting in our own shop, and external accounting, law, engineering, and finance in other organizations.

Indirect effects blossom in transportation, construction, and infrastructure sectors and beyond. Consultants describe the multiplicative values that grow from overseas business effects. We've all heard that all politics is local. While that's certainly true for getting votes in a democracy, commercial effects in Lubbock and Dallas can impact commercial effects in Lahore and Doha.

Political leaders could look to business practices for models of success and failure. Tang had sustaining successes and one terminating failure. In our interactions with Communist Party-controlled companies, we had to know and show we were willing to fight to protect our core interests, though we feared having to actually fight. Our adversary could access the PRC's treasury—no kidding. Because of that, we had set up conditions at HT Blade so every dollar gain for us created a three dollar gain for AVIC, and every dollar loss for us created a three dollar loss for them.

As Tony Stewart, a brilliant and devoted lawyer with Jones Day, put it: *We could look into the abyss.* I didn't appreciate the thoughtfulness of Tony's comment then. Now, I see how right he was. We could stare into the abyss knowing AVIC profited more by avoiding it and lost more if we fell into it.

For several years, this approach worked. Then Xi Jinping came along to show us and the world that irrational behavior—which in this case meant taking actions that harm one's own interests—can actually cause the counterparty to injure itself.

We didn't expect Xi Jinping, or any other PRC leader, to throw the PRC or its entities into the abyss. But, by supporting "wolf warrior" behavior among the CPC's diplomats, taking fish out of other countries' oceans, and agitating for war in the South China Sea, General Secretary Xi has done just that—pushed the PRC into the abyss. In doing so, he may drag the world over the cliff and into the abyss with him.

Today, political leaders could use models from business that generate truly distasteful commercial effects for the CPC as the PRC's belligerent behavior grows. For example, simply tie the PRC's cost of capital to the number of military sorties it flies against Taiwan's airspace. Commercial actors know how to do this.

**SF**: What were the next steps after those initial discussions in April? I know the HT Blade venture was up and running very quickly—by the end of 2001. I assume there were contracts to be drawn, partners to be identified, responsibilities to be determined, investors to be found, capital to be contributed, and a business plan to be drawn.

**PJ**: Yes, indeed. By the end of 2001, we had already turned a small profit. But we were still scrambling to complete documents, secure approvals, and protect investments. Several months earlier, following PRC processes, we had set up a working committee with AVIC that laid the foundation for forming ZhongHang (Baoding) Huiteng Windpower Equipment Company, Ltd.—or "HT Blade." In the PRC, entities' names can reveal connections, which can assert importance in a Confucian order, as well as intentions.

In HT Blade's case, *zhong* (in Chinese: 中) stands for China and shows a direct tie to the PRC. The PRC calls the territory it governs *Zhong Guo*, or "middle people"—*zhong* for middle, and *guo* for people, or country. ("Middle" refers to that hierarchical population in between heaven and earth.) *Hang* (in Chinese: 航) stands for aviation. So, *ZhongHang* refers to "China's Aviation" or AVIC, the PRC's sole supplier of military aircraft equipment. *Hui* (in Chinese: 惠) means benefit or kindness, and ties in an AVIC subordinate unit's name, Huiyang Propeller Factory. The *teng* in *Huiteng* refers to Tang Energy Group. *Huiteng* suggests the joint venture intends to bring "soaring benefit."

Our naming suggestions inserted a little American rebelliousness. We're used to Sam Walton sneaking his last name into Walmart, or Home Depot straightforwardly reflecting its function and wares in its name. The Chinese convention is set up to show Confucian hierarchies, which Americans historically dismantle. Just think of the Chinese reaction if Tang meant "sinking" rather than "soaring."

While attending to tactical details, we eked out some strategic gains. By strategic, I mean we put certain resources in place that would help HT Blade achieve its business objectives. Yih-Min led our effort. We suggested Zhang Lin become the chairman of the board, and, after much handwringing, AVIC agreed. He was a career engineer who had become party secretary at an AVIC gas turbine power company. ("Gas turbine power" refers to using the power in a combustion turbine, also called a jet engine, on the ground or on an airplane wing.)

As time went by, Zhang Lin's aversion for risk helped Tang because that characteristic allowed bolder colleagues to bear the consequences of taking new directions. Another Mr. Zhang, Zhang Ziguo, became HT Blade's general manager. This Zhang was a boon, as he would take responsibility by the horns and get stuff done. But that came with a price.

Years later, at a board meeting, a CPC board member raked General Manager Zhang over the coals for building or acquiring molds for a new, longer wind blade. Zhang's decision put HT Blade in a position to win a contract from a European wind turbine maker. The potential revenue justified the not-specifically-approved action. Our general manager had done what the business needed, even while knowing he might have to endure what the CPC would consider humiliation in front of the HT board. And that he did.

Yih-Min was our man on the ground in China. In October, Mr. Zhang and Mr. Huang Yun, President of China Aviation Industry Gas Turbine Power (Group) Company, an AVIC subsidiary, hosted me when I visited. After the trip, I wrote to thank them for their hospitality and "a lot of good work with the start-up of [HT Blade]." I added: "I am also favorably impressed with the near-term market for Baoding's blade production. Thank you for your kindness in hosting me and, more importantly, for the work you have done to improve the Baoding wind blade company's market position."

**SF**: What work was that?

**PJ**: HT Blade, mostly because of Tang, was getting its blades on wind turbines. But a handful of cash flow-positive efforts does not make a business.

**SF**: Are you at liberty to tell us the dollar amount of Tang's investment in HT Blade and its initial percentage of the company?

**PJ**: Our initial placeholder investment was all of $5,000. Over the years, we reinvested dividends and added several million dollars of growth capital.

**SF**: You began your operations in Baoding.

**PJ**: That's right. The very first sets of blades were built in an existing AVIC factory. Remember, the A in AVIC stands for "Aviation," and it's a state-owned aerospace and defense company. AVIC was already experimenting with different uses of different materials. What I call "fancy fiberglass" was one of them, and one of the uses for it was rowing shells. While that interested me because I row for exercise, making blades for wind turbines with composite technologies fit in AVIC's remit. And whether it's a blade for a wind turbine or a helicopter, or a propeller for an engine, or a wing for an airplane, those are all airfoils, which very much interested AVIC—how you design them, how you make them, how you maintain them.

So part of the reason why AVIC was making blades for wind turbines was because if you know how to make a really long wing or long blade for a wind turbine (Image 7a), you can take that know-how and apply it to drone technology, or to flying high-altitude, long-endurance airplanes.

**SF**: I'm curious. As an American, did it give you pause to be partnering with the PRC's defense arm in developing technologies that had the potential to enhance their military capabilities?

**PJ:** Yes, it did. Not to make excuses, but we were working in a complex environment. Overall, our balance favored us and the United States. First, on the simplest level, the CPC could have gotten what we showed them from publicly available resources. In contrast, we were bringing back insights that still matter to at least some in the US government. Others can gauge that value to the government better than I can. I don't know what questions or gaps in knowledge it had at the time.

Second, we were creating "capitalist roaders," to use a Mao-era term of condemnation. Capitalist roaders often guard their awareness of benefits from allowing individuals to express talents more freely than the CPC currently allows. Concealing cognizance of a more self-fulfilling system builds pressure within the communist system works until the pressure ruptures its containers.

Though honoring all people's expressions appeals to me, I fear the potential of an explosive change in China. Xi Jinping acts as if the party can contain the people's frustration. It can, until it suddenly cannot. Today, his apparent plan to choose a successor depends on competition—likely fatal competition. If the over-pressurized environment in the PRC doesn't relieve some of that pressure before Xi dies, expect a violent release when he does.

Third, the overall balance between the value we brought versus what we got, tipped in their favor. This is especially relevant in a country-to-country comparison. It's popular to say the United States got China wrong. That's not quite right. It's too early to tell. A rigorous analysis, like an internal rate-of-return calculation, could assess the benefits—or long-term effects—and answer the question, "Did we get China right?"

**SF**: If I had taken a tour of that first manufacturing facility, what would I have seen?

**PJ**: Well, not much—a bunch of grim, gritty, and sweaty men in gray work clothes using old technologies for bending metal into fan blades and helicopter propellers. For wind blades, we used what the industry calls "hand layup" (Image 7b) to spread the fancy fiberglass into the form and shape of blades. We made the internal supporting structures, or ribs, out of old-fashioned fiberglass. Still, "not much" can tell you a lot about another country's military capabilities.

Technically, I should never have been allowed in that factory. The CPC considers its location, the number of people working there, the work they do, the tools they have, and the products they make to be state secrets. During the tour, the factory leader told me about these state secrets. After the tour, he arranged for a series of photographs with several workers, all with the "Baoding Propeller Factory" sign in the background. (Image 8) These photos become "go to jail" cards without expiration dates. Not only did they tie me to the trip, which the party can deem an incursion whenever it wants, they also identified scores of willing witnesses to testify against me.

One room we visited in the tour was different from the others. It was cleaner and brighter. All the old gear had been removed. It held just one long clamshell mold for making blades for a 600-kilowatt wind turbine. Most wind turbines in the United States are much bigger. Those first blades were less than half a football field long. Now they reach well over 75 meters.

**SF**: In 2003, HT Blade distributed profits for the first time. For reasons we'll discuss later, in 2003–2004, Tang sold 42 percent of its Hong Kong-based company, which owned a 25-percent interest in HT Blade. By the end of 2007, you were talking about going public and listing on a PRC stock exchange by August 2008. That same year you received an injection of capital from Kleiner Perkins, a venture capital firm interested in green tech.

**PJ**: Yes. By 2008, HT Blade had been global for a few years and was the second largest pure blade manufacturer in the world. The company was valued at $1.8 billion, making Tang's interest worth $450 million.

**SF**: The *New York Times* recently wrote the following about Chairman Xi's global efforts:

> China's top leader, Xi Jinping, founded the Belt and Road Initiative a decade ago to use the country's economic might to enlarge its geopolitical heft and counter the influence of the United States and other industrialized democracies.
>
> China has since disbursed close to $1 trillion to mostly developing countries, largely in loans, to build power plants, roads, airports, telecommunications networks and other infrastructure. Mr. Xi has used China's cash and infrastructure expertise to tie together countries across Asia, Africa, Latin America and parts of Eastern and Southern Europe.
>
> Belt and Road has established for China a role in global development rivaling that of the United States and the World Bank. But for all the influence it has brought Beijing, the initiative has contributed to unaffordable levels of debt for dozens of poor countries. China also directed contracts to its own companies and in some cases built expensive, subpar projects that have not spurred economic growth. (Keith Bradsher, "China Invested $1 Trillion to Gain Global Influence. Can That Go On?" October 16, 2023)

Is the United States doing enough around the world to expand its influence? Should it? What are the takeaways from China's efforts?

**PJ**: Let's start by calling what it really is. When you cut through the "initiative" wrapping, you find a deliberate, strategic, diplomatic-commercial offensive.

In Chinese, *yi dai, yi lu* (带一路) means "One Belt, One Road," or OBOR for short. "Belt and Road Initiative" represents the CPC propaganda department's effort to turn our thoughts to OBOR's potential for good works. "Initiative" deliberately hides the strategic offensive objectives of OBOR. For Chinese language nerds, dropping the dash between the two characters can render an abbreviated but still proper translation of "Belt and Road." "Initiative" remains propaganda.

Every year, countries, commercial interests, or influential leaders within those countries accept loans and loan terms under OBOR. As time passes, assumptions about borrowers' abilities to repay and OBOR lenders' benevolent intentions perish. Sri Lanka couldn't service its debt, so it ceded the Hambantota marine port to PRC operators. Indonesia still holds obligations to the PRC for power plants they equipped, built, and financed, even though those plants generate electricity less than half the time expected. Venezuela still repays debt to the PRC in barrels of oil, regardless of the market price.

First, OBOR seeks to develop militarily useful ports and bases around the world. At over $1 trillion—yes, that's trillion with a "t"—the strategic offensive has secured critical locations for overt, covert, and clandestine operations. Three out of hundreds of examples touch on its military usefulness:

- Djibouti: a military base at the mouth of the Red Sea
- Margarita Island, Panama: a port installation built on top of Teddy Roosevelt-era US fortifications on the Atlantic side of the canal
- Piraeus, Greece: port facilities that could facilitate equipment deliveries to Ukraine

Second, OBOR seeks to bend or buy political will to accept or support Beijing's positions publicly. An undisclosed portion of the $1 trillion of OBOR funds compromise political leaders around the world. As I mentioned, ZTE appears to have had a CBO—chief bribery officer—for some time. Much of OBOR spending has gone to corrupting politicians internationally.

Is the United States doing enough? Yes, on quantity. No, on quality. Americans support causes around the world generously. In recent discussions about spending US taxpayer money to counter OBOR investments, government officials tend to want to match PRC spending. That's poor quality for several reasons.

OBOR has overstretched PRC coffers—remember, the CPC needs cash. To yield more bang for each taxpayer buck, the United States could erode the value of OBOR investments. Building different kinds of swarming capabilities at facilities near OBOR projects can attenuate OBOR project values.

For even smarter effects, US leaders could help OBOR debtor nations extend loan terms, lower interest rates, and reduce principal amounts. Just quantifying loan proceeds that went to paying bribes opens potent possibilities—so potent that some nations' officials will oppose them.

Other internationally expected lending provisions, which OECD and World Bank documents cover, augment desired effects. A strategy of codifying, call it, "generally accepted lending standards," plays to America's strengths and attenuates CPC capabilities to export oppression around the world. In fact, if I were designing a US counteroffensive to OBOR, I would propose "attenuation" as the guiding principle.

Showing financial sophistication, the Communist Party has tapped American investors and taxpayers for much more than the OBOR loans and investments. Over the past two decades, trillions of US investors' dollars have supported PRC companies. Sadly, or at least ironically, investments from the United States have freed up PRC cash reserves to fund OBOR dreams. Attenuating the PRC's access to US investments just a little bit could induce behavioral changes.

As Air Force Brigadier General Robert S. Spalding (retired) notes in *Stealth War: How China Took Over While America's Elite Slept* (2019), America's elite have slept through the CPC's brilliant and deliberate insinuation of personnel into and effective authority over hierarchies of multilateral institutions like the World Bank to favor Chinese positions over the United States and other countries. With a bit of coordinated narrative and commercial diplomacy, the United States could turn this around for pennies-on-the-dollar gains for US taxpayers. Such a turnaround would, of course, attenuate the CPC's capability to export fear, injustice, and oppression.

Every year CPC leaders court leaders of smaller countries. OBOR advertises its intent to spend a trillion dollars (that's right, $1,000,000,000,000) outside of the PRC to facilitate projects in smaller countries.

As we'll discuss later, the bankruptcy in California of AVIC USA, an SOE, shows (again) the fusion of the PRC's diplomatic and commercial efforts. Court records tie the bankruptcy to the same time period during which AVIC USA's parent company, AVIC International Holding Company (AVIC IHC), was funneling cash to political leaders in the Solomon Islands.

The CPC throws small, deceptively low-grade challenges at the United States every hour of every day of the year, and over time, these minor hazards can add up to major threats. Through their PRC-dependent operations, American companies see these challenges in real time. This view from-the-field can provide indications and warnings (I&W) of changes in PRC behavior, often before American diplomats can. The bigger payoff is understanding that while US political leaders make domestic decisions quickly and ardently, their relatively slow and anemic globally directed actions allow international threats to grow more virulent even as those hazards fester. American companies are used to working on tight time schedules and habitually thinking through their responses to a range of possible future occurrences in markets, or from competitors. They've tested their thoughts about what it would it take to attenuate the CPC's unwanted behaviors more often than their peers in government. The challenge is how to turn the CPC's actions back against their own interests. American companies must think about what they can do to make little wins on the field every day.

Dissecting I&W illuminates what it would take to erode the effectiveness of the CPC's unwanted behaviors. Comprehensive agreements, treaties, or accords attract us all. We cannot win every engagement with our CPC counterparties, but we should train ourselves to play a long season and aim to win more often than we lose.

## Chapter 10

# Mr. Vice President . . .

**SF**: I want to hear all the details of HT Blade's remarkable rise, but before that, let's quickly talk about four other energy-related endeavors that were born over this time period and how they informed you. One took place in Jamaica with a Chinese company. One took place in China with an American partner. One took place in the United States with a Chinese company. And the fourth took place with AVIC in China.

**PJ**: AVIC was actually our partner for the Jamaica project, too. This was a 122-megawatt power plant that would be powered by fuel, not wind. The plant constructor was another Texas company, which was working for the project owner, Jamaica Public Service Company (JPSC). US-based Mirant—which, coincidentally, had purchased our power plant in Wichita Falls in 1999—owned 80 percent of JPSC. Unfortunately, the Texas company was having a hard time keeping up with the construction and attendant documentation. Enter Tang and AVIC.

**SF**: You already had a relationship with Mirant. Did you need AVIC?

**PJ**: One of the things AVIC can do really well is put a bunch of engineers together to make sure plans get produced—the as-built blueprints, the schematic plans, the one-liners, and so on. So that was an area in which we could work together. Remember, we had successfully partnered on Dunhuang. At this time, we envisioned building power plants—either natural gas or wind-generated—around the world.

**SF**: What happened on this project?

**PJ**: Mirant went broke. At the time, it filed the biggest bankruptcy case . . . *ever*. To collect the several hundred thousand dollars Mirant owed us for our work in Jamaica, we would have had to spend at least that much on legal fees and such, and then wait an unknown length of time for an uncertain recovery.

**SF**: The wind farm partnership in China I alluded to was with GE, which—according to *Forbes*—was the world's fifth largest corporation at the time.

**PJ**: Yes. Tang entered into a joint venture, called Rolling Hills, with GE Wind. The aim was to build a wind farm in northern China using project finance. We came together to try to make a point to the political leaders in Beijing: *If you do this, you can access a lot of cash to build wind farms in your country.*

**SF**: And the result?

**PJ**: No letters to the Whirlygigs, as there was nothing to write home about. The demand for GE wind turbines grew so much in the United States that GE couldn't afford to sell turbines into the PRC market. We spent two years developing Rolling Hills only to sell it to Hong Kong Power and Light. We didn't want to, but GE wound up having priorities other than completing our wind farm together. We got our money back and even made a little bit. But it wasn't the outcome we wanted.

**SF**: The third endeavor to note during this period involved your friend from XWEC, Wu Gang, who in 1997 had founded and become the powerful chairman of Beijing-based Goldwind, the wind energy behemoth.

**PJ**: Yes. Goldwind wanted to establish its international credibility by equipping a wind farm in the United States with wind turbines. Exporting Goldwind turbines to the United States would show that the company had met the rigorous quality control standards for equipment and could operate in the most prestigious market in the world.

Wu Gang thought I might be helpful. He came to Dallas. As I mentioned, we hosted him at our house. I also took him for dinner to—of all places—the Dallas Petroleum Club. Maybe because there wasn't a Wind Club! There, I outlined the plan Goldwind would later adopt to enter the US market. The discussion was easy for me because I could just about follow a table of contents from my project finance closing binder. We developed the Goldwind business plan for them, and they executed it successfully.

**SF**: We hear a lot about how the Chinese rip off American technology, and you've mentioned you took steps to prevent them from being able to fully understand your processing equipment. Do you think Goldwind pilfered the design and operation of its turbines?

**PJ**: No. But later, companies like Sinovel, another PRC-based wind turbine manufacturer, according to news reports, stole about a half a billion dollars' worth of IP from a US company, American Superconductor.

**SF**: Wow. What's the remedy for that kind of activity?

**PJ**: Sometimes there is no remedy because the theft destroys the victimized company and leaves it with too little cash to sue the aggressor and with no hope of recovering property even if successful in litigation. CPC-controlled companies hide behind a Great "legal" Wall. After supplying hydrogen sulfide-laden drywall to American consumers, a representative for China National Building Materials bragged to reporters that all their assets were in China. Other companies have brought suits in the PRC. Some PRC courts have found in favor of IP theft victims but awarded only pittances.

Three whammies for you: One: The US Department of Justice estimates that PRC theft of US IP alone ranges from $200 to $600 billion *every year*. Two: PRC-based companies can instruct MSS—a CPC-controlled organization that some compare to a massively funded CIA—to acquire specific technologies. MSS often does so by whatever means necessary. Think about that for a moment: If you're a US company wanting to get an edge over an international competitor, you don't get to task the CIA for your competitor's secret sauce. Three: US companies hesitate to reveal IP thefts.

Every year, the PRC invests in US start-ups, and every year, some of those investments fail. But some make money. In either case, PRC investments in US start-ups feed lessons to the CPC's PLA and make it more difficult for the US Department of Defense to incorporate those companies' IP into its own systems.

It's easy to say, *Well, the US government should do what the CPC is doing*. We need to go beyond responding to a statist approach with our own statism. Doing what the CPC does can weaken us. Instead, we can enforce old structures and create new ones that raise the costs of CPC investments in fledgling US companies as well as the uncertainty of their long-term, accessible value. At the same time, we can protect US nongovernmental investors' support for innovative companies by reducing their investment costs and raising the certainty of their access to long-term value.

**SF**: The fourth project, also with AVIC, involved neither natural gas nor wind, but rather introduced technology aiming to curb pollution from Chinese coal-fired facilities.

**PJ:** Yes. Our first prototype plant was in Shanxi, which is one of the dirtiest provinces in the world. Meijin Energy's steel plant outside the capital city of Taiyuan, about 300 miles southwest of Beijing, emitted severely polluting coke gas. It makes your eyes sting, your throat scratchy, and limits visibility. It's horrible pollution to put in our earth's atmosphere anywhere, anytime.

Mike Graul, one of the most creative engineers I've ever worked with, conceived a plan to take waste gases from the mill and use them to fuel a jet engine, which would power an electricity generator for the mill. It was a win-win proposition. We reduce their costs and pollution enormously, and we make money. We hoped to be in production by February 2009.

Before you ask, let me say something about coal-generated power. Wind and solar energy sources can bring benefits to many people. Those sectors had plenty of room to grow. They cannot, however, keep the lights on at emergency rooms or maternity wards at hospitals, which need to be open at all times. They cannot provide the refrigeration we need to store food, medicine, and other products. Supply intermittency raises their costs.

Democracies will continue to use natural gas to generate electricity. The PRC will continue to build new coal-fired power plants. For millennia, people have been making trade-offs based on cost and reliability. For a few decades, Americans have been telling themselves renewables have no adverse consequences whatsoever, and that with significant investments in new technologies and electrical transmission assets, renewables can address all our energy needs. Pushing this dream pushes people, starting with the poorest, beyond reach of basic conveniences that require electricity.

Kleiner Perkins sponsored a meeting at the Aspen Institute in the summer of 2007. Despite the prominence of expressive communicators like Thomas Friedman and Al Gore, Kleiner invited people like me who were just trying to improve the production and delivery of cleaner energy. The first afternoon, Friedman led cheers for Gore running for president. And Gore led cheers for *no more coal-fired power plants anywhere.*

At the breakfast panel the next morning, two men from China and I sat six feet from, and facing, Gore. The Chinese men froze. The thought of saying something wrong to the former Vice President of the United States locked their tongues. Surrounded by their silence, my tongue wagged, "Mr. Vice President, I have been working a long time to provide cleaner energy. In China, our choices do not include not building new coal-fired power plants. We can, however, encourage using technologies that burn coal more cleanly."

Not wanting to force a response, our discussion moved on to other aspects of the PRC's energy market. But that afternoon, at the public forum in the big tent in Aspen, John Doerr from Kleiner interviewed Gore. During the interview, Gore led an altered cheer: *No more coal-fired power plants anywhere without carbon capture and sequestration technology!*

I hope my point stuck. Energy choices include several factors people have been trying to balance, for better or worse; cleanliness, reliability, and cost are among them. Incremental improvements, deliberately and persistently pursued, create sustainably established clean energy communities.

**SF**: Point taken. What happened with the Meijin project?

**PJ**: Sadly, the two PRC companies, Meijin and AVIC, began to disagree, and failed to make their required investments. We pressed our contractual option to sell our interest back to the joint venture. But the spat between the PRC companies slowed resolution for years. Finally, in 2021, we sold our interest for about three-quarters of our original investment.

**SF**: Four very different efforts. Beyond, *you win some, you lose some*, is there a common theme, a particular takeaway from them? Do these kinds of ups and downs, dreams and disappointments, simply come with the territory of being an entrepreneur?

**PJ**: Broadly, yes. Entrepreneurs expose time and money to uncertain outcomes. Working in the PRC expands that range of uncertainty.

**SF**: Let's get back to HT Blade. You started in 2001, and by 2005 you occupied more than 90 percent of the 600- and 750-kilowatt turbine blade market in China. Revenue was over $25 million. In 2006, revenue was about $80 million. That's quite a trajectory for just five years.

**PJ**: Yep. HT Blade caught the wave we had expected in 2001. Wind farm installations were rising dramatically in China, and around the world.

**SF**: So by that time were you selling beyond China?

**PJ**: Yes, we'd gone international. But before diving into that, let me throw you a couple more numbers. First, remember the general manager Mr. Zhang who we talked about earlier? He started at HT Blade with a CPC-established salary of about $500 per month. General managers like Mr. Zhang operate with responsibilities similar to a CEO. Yih-Min and I argued that Mr. Zhang should get paid on par with his global peers, that a PRC national champion like HT Blade should show respect and appreciation for its CEO in line with global best practices. Within a few years, HT Blade raised Zhang's salary to over $10,000 per month, with additional annual bonus potential.

A second "numbers" story: One day, from the conference room in HT Blade's first separate building, which flew both PRC and US flags at equal height, I looked out over the parking lot. It held two company cars, a small company pickup truck, and about a hundred workers' bicycles. Just a few years later, standing at the window in the conference room at HT Blade's newer corporate headquarters, I looked down and out over the parking lot. It now had about a hundred employee cars and about two hundred bicycles. We were doing well *and* good.

As for going international: We started HT Blade small. We invoked Mao to secure AVIC headquarters' support, saying even the Long March began with a first step. Once we solidified a foothold in China, we looked abroad. I led European and US efforts, talking to equipment makers like Acciona, Siemens Gamesa Renewable Energy, GE, and Nordex; government-controlled or -regulated generators like EdF and Energie und Rohstoff GmbH; and developers from New York, Spain, and Turkey. AVIC led discussions with potential Asian wind blade buyers from India, Japan, Thailand, and elsewhere.

**SF**: What constitutes a set of blades and how much does one cost?

**PJ**: Your typical WTG uses three blades that constitute a set. Each set of HT Blade's blades costs a few hundred thousand dollars. As blades get longer, they cost more. For relevant magnitude, blades make up a little more than one-fifth of the overall WTG cost.

**SF**: When you made the decision to go global, what preparations did you have to make in anticipation of more demand for your product? Did you need more capital? Greater manufacturing capacity in terms of space and labor, etc.?

**PJ:** You're spot on. The bloody truth about success is that it takes investment to sustain success—investment from outside and investment in more people and more equipment and space.

We were making turbine blades in Baoding. To shorten shipment times, recruit more workers, increase capacity, and manage costs, we wound up establishing two other manufacturing plants—in Jiuquan in western Gansu Province and Tianjin on the sea side of coastal Hebei Province. We grew HT from nothing to the second biggest blade maker in the world, putting it in position to be a Chinese champion, a global champion of Chinese capabilities.

**SF**: Was there something special about your blades that facilitated such growth?

**PJ**: We thought so, and certainly stressed that in our marketing material, which read, in part:

> Using aviation expertise as a competitive advantage, HT developed a proprietary blade tip technology to increase aerodynamic performance and decrease operational noise; HT's patented structure damping technology is used to produce blades especially suited for China's unique wind characteristics.

**SF**: Who held the patents?

**PJ**: HT Blade. Our engineers worked on improving designs every year. Wind blades go to, well, windy areas, which causes stress to the blades. When winds get too high, the WTG has to stop the blades from turning. While our engineers made our designs special, our competitors designed their own solutions to the same problems. Hours in operation prove one design or another better.

**SF:** This may be naïve, but how do you actually go about selling turbine blades? I can't imagine you lugging samples to potential customers like, say, a pharmaceutical salesperson. You're selling blades that run 50 to 75 meters long.

**PJ:** Canny contrast. You're right. Not even magical origami could fold a blade into a briefcase. But blueprints, specifications, process audits for quality, shipping weights, and prices can. GE provides an example. It manages its supply chain with brutal efficiency. To even have the chance to sell to GE for its WTGs, you have to triumph over the company's gauntlet of engineering reviews.

Before you start, you have to provide a compellingly competitive budgetary price. The whole time you're running the engineering gauntlet, GE is calculating costs for each component and each manufacturing process phase. At the end, if you pass, the company may have helped improve your process, design, or both, but you have also exposed all your costs, which puts GE in the advantageous position of saying they like your product, but not your price.

In the PRC, we held an advantage that annoyed GE. Paraphrasing their words, PRC authorities treated HT Blade as 100 percent PRC, but GE as 100 percent foreign. It irritated GE that foreigners—that would be us—owned 25 percent of HT Blade, while GE operated with only 5 percent foreigners.

**SF**: What was your specific role?

**PJ**: I built relationships. And I had to travel a lot internationally to do so: China, France, Germany, Holland, Japan, and Turkey. I also traveled domestically: Lubbock, Houston, New York, San Francisco, Cleveland, and Greenville. I'm sure I left out places.

Showing up matters in and of itself. Showing up with positive track records advances conversations. Then, you have to show you know how to assure quality throughout a manufacturing process, from ordering input materials to latching a blade on a wind turbine hub in the middle of nowhere, where it's windy. That took an engineering team as well as people who could facilitate communication. Getting engineering teams to open specification notebooks almost always reflects progress. Getting those teams to discuss weights, pressures, bolt hole sizes, and placements shows the promise of closing a financial agreement.

**SF**: A big question: With the company growing rapidly and profits distributed for the first time in 2004, why did Tang sell a significant share of its interest in the venture around that time, reducing it from over 40 percent to just 25 percent?

**PJ**: From scratch, we had created a company worth almost $2 billion. To compete globally, we needed to access world financial markets. That pointed to taking HT Blade public or offering HT Blade stock on public stock markets. Taking HT Blade public could also capture some of the value we had created for our investors and families.

Our team at Tang had no experience taking any company public anywhere, much less in the PRC. That lack of experience drove and focused the impetus to sell part of Tang's ownership position in HT Blade.

A few years later, when an IPO became even more of a possibility, we engaged a boutique investment bank to manage the process of selling a stake in our interest in the blade business. Investors like Kleiner Perkins groom or find public company CEOs, and regularly take companies public. They place large bets on companies they think can grow and go public. They call themselves private equity investors partly because they can buy interests in companies at private valuations and realize significant gains when investee companies sell at public market valuations.

If you accept their money, you get their expertise and their very active advice. You also align your interests very strongly. From our perspective, we wanted help navigating pathways to an IPO; we did take money off the table, which reduced our potential gain and assured us some profit on our initial investment, but we increased our odds of launching a successful IPO.

**SF**: HT Blade was going like gangbusters. It was already the second biggest manufacturer in the world. An IPO was being considered. Patrick Jenevein was doing well by doing good. So of course it was time for another pivot! Time to start talking to the PRC's aviation and military arm about building wind farms in the United States and elsewhere around the world, and teaming up with China's biggest defense contractor to manufacture blades for wind turbines in the United States—which, frankly, sounds counterintuitive.

**PJ**: I think I can explain to you why that made reasonable sense, Steve. What didn't make sense was for our PRC partner to think that after forming SWE with Tang, and committing to invest over half a billion dollars in the venture, they could pull the rug out from under us and, like so many others had, we'd "go gentle into that good night."

**SF**: You spoke about helping China's Goldwind start doing business in the United States. That was over fifteen years ago. According to the news website *TechHQ*:

> Conducting business in the US as a Chinese-native company has grown increasingly difficult since 2019. Escalating US-China trade tensions have led some companies to set up overseas to avoid attention from the US government. Donald Trump's (first) term as President of the USA added fuel to the fire, but under Joe Biden's administration, friction has continued as the US and China battle for

global tech pre-eminence. (Molly Loe, "Businesses are leaving China for US expansion," June 16, 2023)

What are the implications for the governments and citizens of these two countries?

**PJ**: Oh my. Troubles ahead, especially for people living under CPC rule. Xi Jinping continues to draw more and more authority unto himself for making decisions and determining courses of action. That bodes ill, especially for people living in the PRC. They suffer deprivations of freedom first and most of all, including attendant declines in living standards.

It bodes ill, too, for Americans working with or relying on PRC entities. The sheer scale of US-PRC commercial transactions leads us to expect tensions to grow, and for more of those to become disagreements that reach courts. Americans keep courts plenty busy with our own disagreements around transactions we memorialize.

Still, PRC standard operating procedures condone what Americans call theft. The PRC even codifies what Americans call theft into laws that apply to Chinese people everywhere. Our starting points differ so much we can't see that what Americans call illegal or unethical activity constitutes moral, patriotic behavior in the PRC. If we can't pin starting points, we may never align efforts to reach the objectives we do share. Failure to align efforts, in turn, lengthens time to reach agreements, threatens product shortages, reduces prosperity for all, and could presage conflict beyond competitive commercial endeavors.

## Chapter 11

# SWE Will Be the Exclusive Vehicle

**SF**: Another scene: You've described harrowing airplane flights within China in the late 1990s, during which adult passengers were often sick and children routinely relieved themselves in the aisles. What a difference a decade makes! It's late April 2009, and your fellow passengers are again Chinese. But this time you're not flying from Urumqi to Aksu. You're flying from Chicago to Duluth with executives of AVIC. It's a long way from Beijing to Chicago, much less Duluth. Will you explain what you and top brass from the PRC-owned aerospace and defense conglomerate are up to?

**PJ**: The child in the airplane aisle provides a regular yarn that should temper Kimberly Clark's hopes for selling diapers in the PRC, but it happened just once. On another flight, adults began preparing their boiled chicken lunch by lighting an open-flame stove!

As for your question: We were flying from Chicago to Duluth to visit the headquarters of Cirrus Aircraft to discuss making wind turbine blades. Having taken delivery of my own Cirrus N868TW in Duluth some years earlier, I knew Cirrus could certainly make blades for wind turbines. That was because they used composites to make airplane wings, just like HT Blade used composites to make wind turbine blades. (By the way, "868" is a lucky number sequence in Chinese, Tang Wind Energy inspired "TW" in the tail number, and all nonmilitary US-registered aircraft tail numbers begin with "N.")

**SF**: Ah. At the end of the last chapter we hinted that you expanded, or at least hoped to expand, operations with AVIC to the United States—even though that seemed counterintuitive to me. After starting in 2001, HT Blade had soared—so much so that an IPO with an investment bank-determined value of $1.8 billion was on the horizon. And Tang had a 25 percent interest in that.

**PJ**: Exactly. I suppose we could have rested on our laurels, but we saw the opportunity to make more laurels. I know you are going to ask: How? When Yih-Min and I think about strategy, we try to gauge the obstacles to achieving objectives, and then match resources to reach those goals. Here we modified the Chinese military leader Sun Tzu's simple but effective models in ways other diplomatic and commercial leaders negotiating with CPC-driven entities can follow. Our efforts led one Chinese associate to observe that we were "more Chinese than the Chinese."

**SF**: I'm sure there are some diplomats and business people interested in your mantra. Please share.

**PJ**: Okay:

1. Clearly understand and state your own objectives. Think of this as knowing and clearly articulating what you want to achieve.
2. Clearly understand your counterparty's objectives. Think of this as a KYC (know your counterparty) exercise.
3. Start early with the truth and stick to it. Truth nurtures trust. (Trust protects creativity. The current CPC administration distrusts everyone.)
4. Know what you have and must protect to achieve your objectives. (Paraphrasing Horace Greeley, concede what you can but secure what you must.)

5. Firmly defend your objectives with a real commitment to walk away unless an agreement supports them. Negotiate to advance your objectives actively and consistently. Finally, let the CPC surprise you with responses you find favorable.

Listing these steps cannot capture the tone or drive that invigorates interactions. Unlike many diplomatic negotiations with CPC representatives, we were negotiating not just to avoid loss; we were negotiating to win. A great company builder in Texas, Jere Thompson, would remind me, "Keep the main thing the main thing."

In our strategic setting, the main thing was making HT Blade's IPO successful. Matching resources to that goal, Yih-Min assessed that HT was under-resourced to take a really good shot at knocking that IPO out of the ballpark. With that focus, we asked ourselves what we could do—in addition to bringing in those with IPO experience—to make our desired outcome more likely. Our answer: *Sell more blades for wind turbines worldwide.* Then we asked: *How can we do that?*

We figured our best shot would be to create a credible customer for buying and installing lots of WTGs. To do that—develop wind farms that would buy lots of WTGs—Tang formed a new entity, SWE. We hired a full development team, leased and equipped an office in Austin, and turned the development team loose. When negotiating to buy WTGs for the wind farms the team would be developing, SWE would require the WTG manufacturer (say, GE) to price the overall equipment package using wind blades from HT Blade. This would drive revenue for HT Blade and, perhaps more significantly, validate the quality of HT Blade's products.

**SF**: So what opened your eyes to the US market?

**PJ**: I think you know me well enough by now to know that no market was ever off our radar. Prior to 2007, Tang had developed one wind farm inside the city limits of Lubbock. That 10-megawatt wind farm used ten WTGs made by an AVIC subordinate, Huide, which owned part of HT Blade, and thirty blades made by HT Blade. That was significant because it showed we could actually get Huide gear and HT blades into the United States. We could get Huide and HT Blade paid, and get Tang paid for building and operating the farm. In other words, we could make money if we did things right in the States.

Another development around this time encouraged us: GE's partial pivot to selling more WTGs significantly raised HT Blade's prospects for putting blades on their equipment.

**SF**: You were already manufacturing blades in China and selling some of them abroad. So why consider manufacturing in the United States?

**PJ**: Ships carry compact, dense products very efficiently. Shipping something light and very long, like wind turbine blades, costs a lot. Those costs help drive manufacturing site selections. Plus, wind turbine blades do not travel well. In addition to being well over half a football field long, they are relatively light and fragile. A fair amount of cargo gets busted up as it crosses the ocean by ship. Being made of fiberglass, the blades are susceptible to chipping. It made much more sense to manufacture them as close to the wind farms as possible.

**SF**: Translation: Manufacture in the United States?

**PJ**: Yes, if possible—particularly if we were going to be doing a significant amount of business in the United States. Thus, the visit to Cirrus.

**SF**: This may sound naïve, but why did you need a Chinese partner like AVIC for expansion into the United States?

**PJ**: For several reasons. Let's begin with the old-fashioned notion of honor. We'd built this company, HT Blade, together. We worked well together. We were growing the company in a lot of places. So let's dance with the partner who brought us.

On a more practical level, continuing the alliance would allow us to continue using Chinese engineers, who in addition to being very talented, lived and worked near markets that HT Blade expected to enter. Also, finding and recruiting aerodynamic engineers is tough in the United States. We could do an awful lot of really good engineering in China that we could export around the world—and make good money.

We weren't abandoning our efforts in China. Indeed, we continued to see great possibilities there. Still, success in the PRC rides on the whims of the CPC. Because we were working with Communist Party-controlled companies, we had to keep demonstrating our value to the party. The best way to protect our position was to consistently demonstrate that we could grow the company. We constantly needed to prove that we were valuable to them, because as soon as the party figures you're not valuable to them, they ditch you. There was then, and still is, political pressure inside China to remove the foreigner's head.

Running SWE to develop wind farms was a different matter. HT Blade sold equipment to WTG manufacturers, who then sold to developers like SWE.

**SF**: Enter AVIC?

**PJ**: Yes, but not immediately. In October of 2007, as a matter of courtesy, we told AVIC of our plans for forming a wind farm developer. We didn't think they'd be that interested. First of all, they couldn't use US tax credits. Also, we didn't think they could keep up with commercial cycles in countries ruled by laws rather than bureaucracies, and they couldn't appreciate that other countries allowed their citizens to own land, much less the mineral stores under the land.

We said, in effect, "We'll do this, and AVIC will still make money because HT Blade will be selling more blades, and you are a stakeholder in that." But they wanted in. Indeed, they persisted.

**SF**: Why?

**PJ**: Hindsight helps understanding. Initially, we thought they just wanted to be part of a particular entity that they thought would grow. But later, we found out that a five-year plan provided strategic direction from the leadership of the CPC, telling AVIC: *Grow your wind business.*

**SF**: And how did AVIC turn your initial "no, thank you" into a "yes, please"?

**PJ**: By saying they'd put in $600 million.

**SF**: I can understand how that might be persuasive. Your response was what?

**PJ**: We said, "OK, we'll find a way to let you in for 20 percent."

**SF**: I'm imagining the television show *Shark Tank* and your fellow Dallasite Mark Cuban saying, "Six hundred million dollars for 20 percent? You're valuing your company at $3 billion, and I don't even see a sales sheet here."

**PJ**: That's right. We were ambitious, no doubt about it. Essentially we were saying: *With $600 million to pursue these projects, we can build a multi-billion-dollar company. For a "sales sheet," we've already identified plenty of worthy places to put wind farms. We're going to go get financing. If you want to provide $600 million, that would be great, and we'll give you a priority return and 20 percent thereafter.*

Respectfully, Mr. Cuban, you're thinking like a democratic capitalist! We were dealing with a Communistic imperialist mind set.

**SF**: Meaning?

**PJ**: Following World War II, the United States and similarly-minded nations tried to move away from great powers initiating wars to claim, control, and consume resources—like coal, oil, minerals, rare earths, grain, etc. In imperialism's place, they sought to develop a system of laws for allocating resources without war. Broadly, we call this law-based system "capitalism." Until we imagine some other way to allocate resources around the world, imperialism and capitalism fight it out for dominance. Since World War II, Communist Russia, and then Communist China, led—and continue to lead—worldwide efforts to restore imperialism.

This "either-or" description simplifies the messier implementation of systems that include aspects of both imperialism and capitalism. In real-world practice, a mix of policies places countries along a spectrum with the two concepts at opposite ends.

In a joint venture structure, AVIC's imperialistic setting drives it to want, more than anything else, control over the joint venture. And AVIC can intimidate. We knew they wanted at least 50 percent ownership, because that amount implies control. Once AVIC showed its commitment to fund the joint venture, *we* quickly took the initiative to propose ownership interests. Doing so created a position that we could defend and leverage. When dealing with Communists, imperialists, or other bullies, you never know when you need leverage to protect yourself.

**SF**: How so?

**PJ**: Compared to Tang Energy, AVIC was always the gorilla in our relationship. Some financial reports peg AVIC as the third largest defense contractor in the world. Others grade AVIC lower. The opacity that Communism imposes makes accurate ranking difficult. Negotiating successfully with the CPC, or CPC-controlled entities, requires knowing your end goal without letting your apparent positions reveal it. Sun Tzu cautions, "Strategy without tactics is the slowest route to victory, tactics without strategy is the noise before defeat." Besides that, the party almost always assumes your beginning position hides what you might find acceptable. Is it a game? Yes. Does it take more time than it should? Yes. Did our ambitions make it a game worth playing? Yes. But with protections.

To protect our position, we knew we needed the agreement to specify that the SWE parties would resolve any dispute in the United States. First, we thought that the fear of US dispute resolution would help avoid disputes. Second, if a threat of legal fight in the United States failed to dissuade bad acting by AVIC, then we would have a chance of prevailing against the AVIC gorilla. With high confidence, we could count on PRC courts to rule against us. Besides, the cost of litigating in the PRC concerned us. We would have accepted almost any US venue for jurisdiction. We asked for Dallas, Texas, and got it. File that away, because it will become critically important.

**SF**: I'd like to step back and ask you a bigger question. When this was all happening, were you thinking: *This is the business I'm going to be in for the rest of my professional career because it's a good money maker, and it's only going to get bigger and I can do well by doing good*? Or are you one of these guys who while working on one thing is thinking about the next thing. Maybe thinking: *If we're doing well with wind, maybe we'll be able to get into solar, or maybe we can take glacial water and do something*. I guess what I'm asking is, where was your head during this time period?

**PJ**: Big question. At the time, I was focused on making HT successful. My thinking was: *We've got this opportunity, now let's complete it*. But I also know there will always be something else that I can do as long as health allows. There are always ideas that come around that are fun for me to consider working on. From experience and education, I know that history has its up and downs, and it's best to make hay while the sun shines.

**SF**: With AVIC promising to invest $600 million, I can see how you would be keenly focused on SWE. Talks with CATIC, originally an AVIC subordinate, began in October 2007, and by the end of January 2008 you had signed the MOU. By its own terms, it was supposed to take effect on June 1 of that year.

The MOU stated that "SWE will be the exclusive vehicle for both Tang and CATIC interest in the wind industry" and the geographical area would "initially include North America, Central America and South America. Expansion to Europe, Africa, and Asia is designated for future expansion." Furthermore, CATIC was to be "the primary source for development funds, while Tang was to be responsible for general management as well as wind farm development."

Some of the signatories are familiar. There's Tang; your company the Nolan Group; Yih-Min Jan's family entity; AVIC USA; some other investors; and one Paul Thompson, who looks to have gotten an interest without investing cash. Can you tell me a little about him?

**PJ**: Paul and I had known each other since his days at GE as a knowledgeable and helpful sales engineer. Later, he became head of Lubbock Power & Light and helped Tang develop the 10-megawatt wind farm in Lubbock's city limits.

Paul became SWE's general manager. Mirroring the PRC's practice of using American names for PRC entities and individual titles, we used "general manager" for Paul's title to raise his stature when working with AVIC personnel. When the PRC uses an English word like "bank" to describe an organization, it makes an impression that may belie its actual function. In the PRC, banks do have banking functions, but, unlike US banks, they also carry out myriad PRC government functions and instructions. We trusted Paul and let PRC personnel know that by giving him the title of general manager. Paul earned ownership if SWE performed well. Jim O'Bannon—another luminous lawyer from Jones Day who guided us through the legal choices around commercial and corporate decisions—shrewdly commented that we must think very highly of Paul to offer this component of compensation. Jim was right. We did.

We should note one more thing here. After Liu Rongchun, vice president of AVIC IHC, signed the MOU, AVIC was the last to fund its investment commitment.

**SF**: Are you comfortable telling me how much Tang, Nolan, the other investors initially invested in SWE? And when was that money due?

**PJ**: Among the 28,000-plus pages filed publicly in US district court after we were forced to litigate with AVIC to enforce our rights, you could find that Paul invested no money and that the rest of us together invested about $350,000. These investments came in September and October of 2008. AVIC sent its money, the last and remaining $350,000 of the first investment tranche, in November 2008. Those amounts do not include the millions that Tang spent to develop SWE's business.

**SF**: On June 1, 2008, what is referred to as the "SWE Agreement" went into effect, formalizing the MOU executed a few months earlier. In accordance with that MOU, SWE was created effective that date. Almost a year later, on April 28, 2009, Tang and AVIC Trade and Economic Development (TED) met in Chicago—a city reasonably accessible to all parties—and signed what came to be known as the "Chicago Agreement." Over time, AVIC representatives used "AVIC TED," "CATIC TED" and "CATIC-TED" to describe the same part of AVIC. Among other things, the agreement states:

> Both sides agree to develop wind power projects together through cooperation and finish the development of wind power projects for total capacity of 200 Megawatt within 5 years after this preliminary agreement becoming effective. "CATIC-TED" will totally finance 300,000,000.00 US Dollars in wind power projects development, in which 200,000,000.00 US Dollars will be used to purchase related wind power equipment from China, 100,000,000.00 US Dollars will be used to purchase services including, transportation, warranty services, after-sales services, operation services and related spare parts and consumables parts.

The Chicago Agreement called for Tang to perform a "preliminary assessment" for projects in the United States, but CATIC TED would be responsible for the "entire project development."

**PJ**: Yes. By the way, CATIC stands for "China National Aero Technology Import and Export Corporation." After CATIC ran afoul of some US export provisions, it changed its name to the "Aviation Industry Corporation of China," or AVIC.

**SF**: The portion of the agreement quoted above suggests AVIC's "alter ego" CATIC TED was putting in $300 million. Where does the $600 million figure come from?

**PJ**: You cut through the confusion of AVIC's subsidiaries' names well. Three hundred million was to be AVIC's equity investment, through any one of its subordinate units, and they were going to lend us an additional $300 million that we would invest as our equity, making us fifty-fifty partners. For the work we did on the ground, we would be paid operating expenses—salaries, rent, travel, etc. But we wouldn't get any return on our investment until AVIC got back the sum of money it had put in.

**SF**: No profit for you before the venture realized at least $600 million. How many wind farms was that going to take, and did you have a sense of how long it might take?

**PJ**: We expected to reach that level in three years. The Flat Water Wind Farm in Nebraska, which we'll talk about later, cost about $100 million to get to commercial operations. Do the math and you'll see that just five wind farms could have easily deployed and generated a return on the $600 million investment.

**SF**: Obviously, you were okay with this.

**PJ**: Yes. So long as AVIC held up its end of the bargain. As I said, they were going to pay our salaries and other operating expenses. Also, we intended this arrangement to commit them. We were putting a lot of skin in the game. We were committing our professional futures to this one business line. We wanted to make money. One of the things we had to do to make money was keep our partner from eviscerating us. And one of the ways to do that was to tie them to our success. Maybe that was a little blunt, but we considered the relationships and the plan deliberately.

**SF**: Please tell me a little about your meeting in Chicago.

**PJ**: We had been working our backsides off looking for US customers, looking for wind farms, acquiring a wind farm development team, setting up the Austin office, talking with wind farm financiers, and more. The Chicago Agreement referred to projects that AVIC had reviewed and wanted to pursue. We stayed far ahead by outworking AVIC and had a slew of projects for them to approve. PRC Minister of Commerce Chen Deming's presence in Chicago, and his attention to our collaboration, encouraged us all.

Minister Chen and I talked for about twenty minutes after the signing ceremony. He had written an editorial—"Strengthen U.S.-China Trade Ties. Now is no time for protectionism."—published in the *Wall Street Journal* the day before. We talked about how our efforts fit in with his broader objectives, and the overall importance of the US-PRC relationship. He even autographed my copy of the *Journal*.

Although there was cause for excitement, we didn't celebrate that night. AVIC personnel wanted to hang around their political leaders. I wanted to get ready for our early morning flight to Duluth with Cirrus Aircraft cofounder Dale Klapmeier.

**SF**: Within twenty-four hours of signing the Chicago Agreement, you were winging your way to Duluth with some of your new AVIC partners to tour the Cirrus facilities. You already knew the company, as you said.

**PJ**: Through events for Cirrus pilots, I had met Dale, who, with his brother Alan, founded Cirrus. After building a prototype of an aircraft in their parents' barn, Alan and Dale had built quite a business, eventually selling a majority share in 2001 to Crescent Capital, the US arm of the First Islamic Investment Bank of Bahrain, now called Arcapita.

Even though they're single-engine piston, Cirrus airplanes stand out for at least two reasons: First, Cirrus includes a parachute for the whole airplane. You cannot buy a Cirrus that does not have a parachute for the plane. I'm not talking about parachutes for separate individuals in the plane, but an airframe parachute for the whole plane. Second, the Federal Aviation Administration considers Cirrus aircraft "technically advanced airplanes."

Because Cirrus utilized fiberglass composites and carbon fiber spars to make their wings—which are just another airfoil—they had the manufacturing know-how and facilities to expand HT Blade into the US market. Already, it looked like AVIC and Tang's newly formed joint venture, SWE, was driving demand for wind turbine blades in the United States. Now we wanted to talk with Cirrus about the possibility of partnering with, or perhaps even acquiring, them. Dale and another Cirrus Aircraft pilot flew two planes to Chicago to fly us up to Duluth.

I had first told Dale about our needs. I'd then told Cirrus's President and CEO Brent Wouters, as well as AVIC, that Cirrus had not only the place, but the people with the know-how to make high-quality wind turbine blades. Cirrus could teach HT Blade how to assure and improve quality control all the way from receiving raw materials to delivering high-quality composite airfoils that would perform in the field and air as customers and investors demanded.

It would have been a nightmare to try to get our CPC comrades to come to the United States and establish that supply chain effectively. Cirrus already had it. They had the same supply chain that we needed, because making an airfoil, or wing, for a plane is the same as making an airfoil, or blade, for wind turbines.

That AVIC could buy Cirrus made a lot of sense for them. At the time Zhang Xuming (aka Sherman) said, "General aviation is gonna take off in China." Whether he was right or wrong is a whole 'nother conversation; there's no general aviation in the PRC to speak of right now.

Anyway, to make sure the Communist Party approved our going out and making this idea work, we wanted to show them they had something else to gain, and that was to buy Cirrus Aircraft and develop the general aviation industry in the PRC. Cirrus earned state-of-the-art prestige and was the best-selling airplane in the United States for a while.

It was such a good idea that, on one trip to Beijing, I received a formal request to meet with an AVIC Heavy Machinery bigwig in his office. With the value we were creating, I expected to discuss positive developments. With just me, his translator, and him in his office, he wailed away at me. He said in effect, *It was my idea for AVIC to buy Cirrus. I told AVIC they should do this.* And he listed the same three reasons for doing so that I just did.

**SF**: Ha. About a month after you took AVIC representatives up to Duluth, they returned the favor. But instead of taking you to northern Minnesota, they invited you to be their guest at the Paris Air Show. There you were to continue discussions with Cirrus executives and talk about the possibility of AVIC acquiring Cirrus. I'd ask, "Why the Paris Air Show?" But I know how I'd answer that: "Why not?" But seriously, what do you remember about the Air Show and the discussions with Cirrus?

**PJ**: Every airplane buff wants to go to the Paris Air Show. Its history of aeronautical firsts, its glamour in the City of Light, and its chance to show off on a world stage attracts everyone from private pilots to giant companies that make airplanes and the cargoes they carry—commercial and military. I wanted to go see airplanes and flight demonstrations!

I'm sure AVIC's employees wanted to see Paris. I was thrilled to meet them in a country where I could easily read signs and communicate with locals. One of Tang Energy Group's analysts who spoke Chinese met me there.

I was so comfortable in Paris that I told Zhang Ziguo, HT Blade's General Manager (who we talked about earlier), that I would meet him for dinner anywhere in the city. I would be happy to dine at any Parisian bistro or restaurant. I could avoid *moutai baijiu* and drink French wine. I was feeling good.

Zhang left a message later that we would meet for dinner at . . . Restaurant Pekin. My throat clutched. Of course, Paris has Chinese restaurants. Of course, my AVIC colleagues wanted some like-home cooking. I breathed in and hopped on the Métro. Walking up to Restaurant Pekin, I saw a whole wall of wine. I thought, *this is going to work out just fine*!

Sitting down with my AVIC colleagues and seeing a small table on wheels with a dozen different French wines supported my expectation of being able to enjoy a nice glass of wine. Then, General Manager Zhang reached under the table, and, as he was saying "We brought *moutai*," pulled up two bottles of the potent liquid and placed them on the table. My spirits flagged.

As executive vice president, Mr. Xu Zhanbin led AVIC's group. Xu Zhanbin later became AVIC's vice general manager and eventually the deputy commissioner and small group leader of the Commission for Science, Technology and Industry for National Defense. His presence at the dinner, and subsequent title elevation, suggested that the CPC found extraordinary value in controlling Cirrus.

Toward the end of dinner, Tang's analyst handed Xu Zhanbin a folder and explained—*in Chinese*—that it contained commercial information on Cirrus. Our dinner partners froze as they watched this young, European descent, female speaking Chinese to one of the highest-ranking men in all of AVIC.

**SF**: Shortly after the Air Show, in July 2009, AVIC HQ created *China Aviation Industry General Aircraft*, a wholly owned subsidiary, to acquire Cirrus Aircraft. I was surprised to learn that after the Paris meeting you didn't hear about the Cirrus acquisition until after it closed in June 2011.

**PJ**: Steve, it surprised me, too. No one at AVIC breathed a hint about their efforts to acquire Cirrus. We don't act that way. If you bring us an idea or help us develop an opportunity, we always "dance with the one that brung you." The disappointment in AVIC's behavior surprised us a little bit. As a backhanded compliment, their slinking around confirmed how well we could anticipate CPC-directed behavior. Their shifty behavior also revealed their hidden desire for Cirrus's expertise. The biggest surprise was that the Minnesotans, too, were sneaking around with AVIC. They were sabotaging our position (and its transparency) to their benefit.

Years before, in 2006, author Anchee Min came to a literary festival in Dallas. Taking her to the airport, my wife told Anchee that I had been working with the Communists in China. Immediately, Anchee responded, "Have they fucked you yet?"

You may wonder why we didn't establish a middleman fee before going to Paris. We would have loved to earn a deal fee or introduction commission for conceiving the idea and making the Cirrus transaction work. But we kept our eyes on our IPO prize. Continuing to add value to AVIC showed we were always trying to be a good partner. Not fussing about a fee that may have approximated $2 million seemed reasonable to forego to ensure an IPO that, at $1.8 billion, would—with our 25 percent interest—create $450 million for Tang's investors.

Within days of completing the acquisition, AVIC surprised us. It turned Cirrus into a threat to national security by contracting to provide primary AVIC-Cirrus trainers to the US Air Force. Years after that, around 2019, I pointed out to US Air Force Lieutenant General VeraLinn "Dash" Jamieson that the tie-up virtually ensured PLA pilots had access to training modules designed to give US pilots an advantage. Compared to CPC intentionality, Americans' actions appear to just bumble along.

**SF**: In this chapter we discussed the Chinese acquisition of a US company. I know Congress has long been wary of certain acquisitions, particularly in the high-tech sector. But recently attention has shifted to Chinese acquisition of farmland. As NBC News put it:

> State and federal lawmakers are pushing to regulate foreign ownership of U.S. real estate because of fears that Chinese entities are creating a national security risk by amassing swaths of U.S. farmland, some of it near sensitive sites. (Laura Strickler and Nicole Moeder, "Is China really buying up U.S. farmland? Here's what we found," August 25, 2023)

I know there was such a push in your home state of Texas. What are your thoughts?

**PJ**: Again, broadly: The US government may not know about land that CPC-controlled companies own or control in the United States. Our government simply has not done the work to be able to tell Americans what US land the PRC controls. PRC-based WH Group owns Smithfield Foods, which owns about 150,000 acres in the United States. Another PRC-based and PLA-affiliated company, GH America Investments Group, owns about 200 square miles of land in south Texas.

In February 2023, the *Dallas Morning News* ran an editorial I wrote to help Texas faithfully address this challenge to US core values.

The amount of land CPC-controlled entities own, however, matters less than where they own it. Land positions provide not just surveillance capabilities, but opportunities to disrupt critical US infrastructure. Think of the ability to damage cables, pipelines, and electric distribution lines near or on remote farmland. Think of the ability to dump pathogens or poisons in water supplies.

When I raise these concerns to our government, I often hear, "The CPC would never do that." They may be right. But read what the CPC says in its internal documents. My own experience supports expecting the CPC to do—or at least try to do—what it says it will.

Our way of evaluating prudent action blinds us from appreciating the CPC's fixation on absolute control and their abject disregard for individual rights. We are used to our system of laws protecting us. We often cannot imagine the vicious brutality that the CPC inflicts, even on its own citizens. Two successive US administrations describe the CPC's actions against Uyghurs as genocide. Yet our country's political, media, commercial, and religious leaders seldom bring it up, much less systematically highlight the abuse or create pressure for the CPC to relent.

Instead, with our habitual and healthy self-criticality, we blame ourselves for the CPC's callousness. We say, "We got China wrong." No, the CPC got it wrong. In the long run, the CPC's inhumanity will undo the party. It's telling, if not ironic, that the CPC makes a show of demanding self-criticism from those who offend the party. Americans routinely and freely criticize themselves; we make America stronger through the process. It's as if the CPC appreciates this, but just keeps getting it wrong.

Still, we must be wary. Before it falls apart, the CPC may cause severe harm to Americans in the United States. The CPC is using US land locations as staging areas for possible future operations. In Texas, CPC agents could use GH America's sought-after interconnections with the electrical grid to disrupt power transmission. In California, unreported stores of biological agents co-located with thousands of rodents set the stage for devasting bacterial or viral attacks.

US political actions show ham-fisted responses. We must protect our own strengths, imposing costs for abuse of our institutions on bad actors, not on our own law enforcement.

# Chapter 12

# If You Want to Provide $600 Million . . .

**SF**: We've discussed many instances in which you were up in the air—literally or figuratively, or both. I wonder if you'd describe another one for us. It's late November 2010—more than a year after signing the two agreements that formally launched SWE, and more than a year after visits to Cirrus Aircraft in Duluth and the Paris Air Show. At this moment, you're in your own airplane on your way from Dallas to Corpus Christi on Texas's Gulf Coast. It's a spur-of-the-moment trip. What's this all about? Also, when the heck did you have time to learn how to fly and get your pilot's license?

**PJ**: I'll answer the second question first. Besides being a whole lot of fun, flying a small airplane makes reaching wind farms quicker, easier, and often cheaper.

Earning pilots' privileges and responsibilities also raised my *mianzi* with AVIC. Many times, as I met with representatives who worked for AVIC—the PLA's sole supplier of military aircraft equipment—I was the only pilot in the room. That gave me perspectives that none of them could match. They couldn't even imagine a route to learning to fly their own airplane. I picked up an ace in the game of "face."

An example: When an AVIC delegation visited us in Dallas, we budgeted a half day for the delegation lead Xiao Jinping (a made-up name to protect him from a possible CPC "invitation to tea") and his translator to fly to

Lubbock. Mr. Xiao wanted to see the AVIC-equipped wind farm there. The purpose drove the event, but the opportunity to score points for America with a prominent AVIC leader delighted me.

The day before the flight, I told Mr. Xiao what to expect, and that he could bring a knife (in Chinese, a *dao*). At the airport, with my credentials, I escorted him and his translator to my plane—a Cirrus SR22. After helping my passengers get in and buckled up, I radioed the tower with the current weather code and requested clearance to taxi.

The stalwart Communist sat beside me with eyes wide open. He had never been behind the windscreen of an operating airplane. Cleared for takeoff, we flew under instrument flight rules right over the middle of the Dallas Fort Worth International Airport, one of the world's busiest. He could see planes heading in toward our wing and descending beneath us to our right, and planes flying away from and ascending above us to our left.

Passing north of downtown Fort Worth, I pointed out the World War II mile-plus long bomber factory, where Lockheed Martin now makes F-35s. Satellite reconnaissance provides more detail than we could see, but flying within sight of the major military endeavor took his breath away.

Flying south of Wichita Falls and Sheppard Air Force Base, a NATO pilot coordination facility, I showed Mr. Xiao how he could follow the T-38 fighter trainers on one of the flightdeck screens. Using their transponders intermittently made them appear to disappear and reappear. Based on radio traffic on the approach to Lubbock, I told him to expect to see a flight of two T-38s that were flying ahead of us. The flight stunned both the leader and translator. They couldn't comprehend how the US government trusted citizens with airplanes in shared airspace.

Flying back to Dallas, I remembered to ask Mr. Xiao if he had brought that *dao*. He laughed. I pulled two knives out of my pocket and told him I'd brought an extra in case he had not. Okay, a bit smart-alecky, but I was also showing off the freedoms that Americans take for granted. When resisting CPC pressures, sometimes a little (attempted) humor helps highlight key differences.

The knife showed that we could trust each other within the plane. The CPC teaches its citizens not to trust each other, much less to fly around the PRC. It even puts airspace under the control of the PLA. In the United States, civilian authorities administer our airspace.

Speaking of trust, in that year-and-a-half between the signing of the agreement and the flight to Corpus Christi, we searched and found many wind farm projects for SWE.

**SF**: And how exactly did you do that? How does one go about finding wind farms in the USA?

**PJ**: Entrepreneurs find ways to make opportunities work. How? You find a person or company that has what you want and ask, "Can we work together? Can you teach me?" We found a way to build power plants in the PRC; we could find a way to build wind farms elsewhere.

We tried lots of approaches. We called anyone we could think of who might have an interest in, or was currently developing, a wind farm. We hired a wind farm development team from an oil and gas company. We could honestly say that we had a $600 million commitment from the PRC to develop wind farms globally. Developers called us back.

We were already talking to GE about putting HT Blade blades on their WTGs. Over the years, we had purchased hundreds of millions of dollars of equipment from them on the gas-fired power generation side. It was easy to ask, "Who's developing what? Do you know any developers who need help?"

Paul Thompson's Rolodex still included current GE employees whose jobs depended on selling turbines, both the combustion-engine and wind-driven types. They could help us help them by introducing us to developers—potential customers for GE—who might need help or money preparing their wind farm dreams for construction.

**SF**: So, by the time you took off for Corpus Christi in November 2010, had you found any projects?

**PJ**: Absolutely. Just two that we started—Flat Water in Nebraska at 60 megawatts and a Corpus Christi project at 9 megawatts—exceeded $100 million. And we had many more. Here are the particulars about the first two.

Flat Water Wind Farm, LLC was being developed in southeast Nebraska by JUWI GmbH, from Germany. Omaha Public Power District had contracted to purchase the facility's electrical output. Commercial operation was projected to begin in mid-December 2010. JUWI's Flat Water Wind Farm fit our objectives almost perfectly. JUWI was reducing its US exposure, operations could start relatively soon, the project needed financing, and we could choose WTGs that would use blades from HT Blade!

Texas-based Gallop Power, an entity that Tang Energy funded to meet its commitment to AVIC under the SWE Agreement, provided the "physical description" for tax credit financing:

> The Facility consists of forty General Electric 1.5 MW wind turbine generators on 80 meter towers, approximately 80,000 linear feet of buried distribution and collection system, approximately 45,000 linear feet of improved and new infrastructure roads, approximately 3,050 acres under 35 year wind lease agreements . . .

We brought this opportunity to AVIC in February of 2010. They never responded. The silence sowed concern. We brought it up again four months later in an email that was also met with silence. Stretched between our good faith action and AVIC's silence, we began to look for a bailout in case we needed it. Fortunately, a Spanish company, Gestamp Wind, wanted to add US wind farms to its portfolio. When AVIC's silence became a loud refusal to commit investment funds, Gallop Power completed development and sold the profitable property to Gestamp.

Delving into the opportunity and then digging out of it spawned many stories. You may find two especially interesting: First, building wind farms requires many studies. One of those considers the effect of a tower failure. With equipment that weighs about the same as an M1 Abrams tank attached on top of towers 80 meters tall, people understandably care about towers falling. At Flat Water, if one of the towers on terra firma in Nebraska had fallen to the south, parts of it would have landed in Kansas.

Second story: T. Boone Pickens, the legendary business magnate, had conceived a plan for an electric transmission project from the Texas panhandle to the Dallas-Fort Worth area. It was so ambitious that we wondered if he also planned to use the extraordinary right-of-way for a pipeline to bring panhandle water to parched suburbanites. Regardless, to back up his scheme, Boone had made a commitment to buy something like 1,000 GE WTGs. When his project failed to achieve certain approvals, he had obligations to buy WTGs that he couldn't use. Learning of our work, he approached us.

You may have gathered that we do a fair amount of homework—not that we get it right all the time, and not that we don't make mistakes. But when Boone told us he had renegotiated his deal with GE, we knew he had only reduced the number of WTGs he was obligated to buy, and GE had given him no money back. In effect, by halving the number of WTGs he was obligated to buy, Boone had just doubled his commitment fee for the rest of the wind turbines. When he told me I couldn't get a better deal on turbines, I thanked him graciously. Separately, I congratulated the Gallop Power team for negotiating a better deal with GE than Boone had been able to.

**SF**: What made Flat Water a good investment?

**PJ**: In short, Flat Water had the wind and all the agreements, permits, plans, projections, and backstops to support project finance and tax credit investments. That means that all involved saw a path to making a reasonable return on their investment and were willing to expose their investment or balance sheets to the range of uncertain outcomes for wind farms. It also meant, bluntly, that we had done a really good job.

**SF**: In a June 21, 2010, email, Tang reminded AVIC USA's Sherman about the Flat Water opportunity, and also sent information he had requested about a second opportunity.

**PJ**: Yes. This was a $20 million, 9-megawatt, construction-ready wind project located in the Port of Corpus Christi. It was also attractive, as it already had a long-term power purchase agreement with a major electricity supplier, Champion Energy Services, to provide all its power to a US government facility. The Harbor Wind Project, as it was officially called, also had all the necessary permits and approvals.

**SF**: So where did SWE fit into the equation?

**PJ**: Gallop Power found the project and contacted the initial developer, Revolution Energy, a company based in Colorado and Texas. Revolution had done a great job of laying the groundwork—obtaining the permits, the interconnect agreement, and an electricity sales agreement. But Revolution was running low on funds. Its weaknesses played exactly to our strengths. SWE could provide cash to complete development, and could then direct equipment selection, including driving sales revenue for HT Blade.

**SF**: You mentioned financing. Was the $600 million AVIC had promised to commit—or some portion of that—sitting in a bank somewhere when the opportunities for Flat Water and Harbor Wind materialized?

**PJ**: You're a grand, if tormenting, inquisitor. AVIC told us the money was in an account in China and was ready to go whenever we showed them wind farms. But we never saw it, and certainly didn't have access to it.

Adding to our torment, deeply rumbling political turmoil was beginning to affect behavior across the PRC. General Secretary Hu Jintao's second term was coming to its scheduled end. Factions supporting Xi Jinping and Bo Xilai, who both wanted to succeed him, were colliding. Their struggle for position, while not always apparent on the surface, had deadly consequences for their networks' members. Their mostly murky confrontations paralyzed decision-making.

At HT Blade, routine decisions, like approving promotions for an engineer or someone on the sales team, stagnated. I'll never know if my fellow board members supported either or neither faction. Later, AVIC firmly adopted CPC-promoted patriotic practices of impairing foreigners' positions.

These manifestations—eruptions, really—of CPC power point to a concern and an opportunity. The concern: Xi Jinping's ascension to paramount leader, and his interruption of leadership succession patterns, guarantee longer and lethal competition for his successor. While these battles will focus on combatants within the CPC, they could spill over the PRC's borders.

The opportunity: Knowing that factionalism with the CPC is already formed, and transforming, US leaders can (and should) find positions within the factions that support US interests. Just one example of combining aspects of concern and opportunity may help. Xi Jinping faces terrible troubles domestically. These troubles raise the risks of war. As unpalatable as it may be to help Xi Jinping in any way, US leaders could acknowledge PLA power and invite Xi to direct that power toward securing Russia's borders, made restive by the erosion of Russian military might. Explicit support for something that Xi is already undertaking gives him "face" at a time when a nod of US-conferred legitimacy could help him manage internal forces.

**SF**: Did the fact that this was a $600 million commitment also give them pause? That's a lot of money.

**PJ**: Yes, it was and is a lot of money. Still, it was less than two years of revenue for HT Blade. The wind market was experiencing tremendous growth around the world. To play and win, we needed to plan and act ambitiously. We'd already demonstrated success working on big projects. Success for SWE would mean even greater success for HT Blade as it planned that $1.8 billion IPO. HT Blade needed the international presence and revenue SWE would generate to expand and perhaps surpass LM Glasfiber (now LM Wind Power) as the number one blade manufacturer in the world. That was going to be hard, but SWE gave HT Blade a better chance.

The Cirrus connection was a really good idea that would raise HT Blade's production and profile. It was a plan built out of a fear of falling behind by not growing quickly enough. The strategy actually helped ensure our success. But then the Communist Party nixed the IPO.

**SF**: You say that almost casually, but this was huge, right? The IPO was going to be your golden ticket. Why did they nix it?

**PJ**: Nothing casual about it. "The foreigner was going to make too much money." That's a quote. At dinner, after a board meeting, away from the notetakers, and after alcohol had loosened lips, a fellow board member proclaimed the cause of HT Blade's IPO failing. Even though AVIC would reap three times more than Tang, the Communist mindset couldn't abide the foreigner (us!) making a strong multiple of its investment.

We needed US government involvement to change the party's decision, and we knew we wouldn't receive it. No rescue. No 911 call. We had to protect or preserve what we could and live to fight another day.

We climbed every rung of the "go public" ladder. But when we got to the last approval—from the China Securities Regulatory Commission (CSRC)—they declined us. As I said, one reason was because the CPC didn't want foreigners to make too much money. But looking back, I see there was a second reason: We—really *I*—didn't play the inside game right.

**SF**: Meaning?

**PJ**: As we've discussed, in 2007 we sold part of our company that owned a direct interest in HT Blade to private equity investors led by Prax Capital and including Kleiner Perkins, Draper Fisher Jurvetson, and DT Capital. Well, there was another party who wanted in—a guy named Winston Wen, who controlled New Horizon Capital Partners. Sporting an MBA from Northwestern University's Kellogg School of Management, and, more importantly, as the son of Wen Jiabao, the PRC's powerful premier, Winston exercised influence over New Horizon.

Others have written about the Wen family wealth. When Winston called me one night with a proposal to buy part of our interest at a share price considerably below what Prax et al. had just paid, I declined. I don't remember the exact evaluation, but let's say we had sold stock for $100 per share; he was offering something like $60 per share. Well, it turns out I should have said yes, because that $40 per share difference was my insurance to get past the CSRC. But silly me, I was thinking like a democratic capitalist.

**SF**: I see the connection between the experience with HT Blade's thwarted IPO and the eventual thwarting of your efforts to engage AVIC in the wind farm projects. Simply stated, when doing business with the Chinese, the winds blow hot and cold—and are often unpredictable.

**PJ**: I need to nitpick with you for clarity. When doing business with "the Chinese," you're dealing with some of the hardest working, deeply compassionate, persistently innovative, and absolutely straightforward people you will ever meet. The CPC, however, creates and maintains—through massive repression—an environment that threatens and oppresses all people. The Chinese people suffer these injustices most deeply and most frequently.

The Communist Party does blow hot and cold, as you point out, but the people (in the *People's* Republic of China) endure what they must. Even so, the party is often predictable. It takes work to make reliable predictions—a slog that requires eating, drinking, bunking, and toiling through obstacles with Chinese people in the bowels of their working environment.

**SF**: Your reference to the Cirrus airplane you were able to purchase thanks to your business ventures in China brings us back to the flight to Corpus Christi. This is approximately five months after that June email apprising AVIC of the wind farm project there, as well as reminding them about the Flat Water project in Nebraska. Had you received any response?

**PJ**: No. We had, however, learned that in September, an AVIC subordinate unit called AVIC International Renewable Energy (IRE) had been created.

With the stated purpose of becoming involved in wind farms in the United States and other countries, this new operation seemed to be in direct competition with SWE. And on the face of it, it looked like it was in breach of our agreement with AVIC, which called for all of SWE's signatories to be exclusive partners in the development of these projects. While it sure looked like AVIC was forming a competitor, we hoped that they were abiding by our agreement.

AVIC IRE's principals—including Chairman Liu Rongchun and Vice President Xu Hang—were coming to Texas in November 2010, along with their boss, the new chairman of AVIC International Wu Guangquan. Mr. Liu, or Leo, you'll recall, had signed the Chicago Agreement on behalf of AVIC. As we understood it, the purpose of this trip was to introduce Chairman Wu to AVIC's businesses in the United States. Knowing this, I planned a dinner at Royal China to discuss our ongoing collaboration and press for project approvals and funding. That dinner was scheduled for November 30.

Now—at last!—the flight in the Cirrus. A few days before our scheduled dinner, I learned that these AVIC honchos were going to be in Corpus Christi. If you are so disposed you can see part of their trip to Robstown, Texas—near where we were hoping to get involved in Harbor Wind—on YouTube.[2] So I flew there to learn more about Tang's joint venture partner's activities.

When I showed up at the hotel where the AVIC delegation was staying, they were surprised. Chairman Wu actually appeared to respect my bold move. He knew full well that I was poking my partner to learn its intention, and its capability to act on that intention. Quickly, with steel-cold confidence, he asserted his dominance in our relationship, saying that since I flew my own plane, I must know something about the risks that AVIC might face if it bought an airplane piston engine manufacturer.

Parse that for a moment. At the time, only Continental Motors and Lycoming made piston engines for airplanes. I knew AVIC's trip itinerary included a stop in Mobile, Alabama, where, you guessed it, Teledyne Continental Motors operated some of its facilities. So Chairman Wu was

[2] ixpoze, "AVIC INTERNATIONAL VISITS ROBSTOWN TEXAS USA," February 21, 2012, YouTube video, 17:10. https://www.youtube.com/watch?v=8d319YKt_Cc

letting me know that AVIC was about to spend a lot of money buying Continental Motors, and there was nothing I could do about it and no way Tang could enjoy any benefit from it.

Indeed, a few years later, a filing with the Stock Exchange of Hong Kong revealed that AVIC bought Continental Motors because it was supplying engines for some US military drones. Purchase price: $186 million. As much as US outfits like the Congressional Research Service, the CIA, and others try to calibrate the intent, effect, and threat of activities like this, Congress and the Executive Branch seem to dismiss these as balance sheet maneuvers—buying a company or capability and putting that asset on CPC-controlled balance sheets. It's worth repeating: The CPC has turned US balance sheets into battle space.

So, yes, I flew to Corpus Christi to check on Tang's partner and found discomfort where I had hoped to find comfort in AVIC's intent to abide by our agreements. Two days later, in Dallas, my friend April at Royal China prepared a sumptuous Chinese dinner featuring recipes from Wu Guangquan's hometown. The dinner truly impressed and flattered him. Chairman Wu even asked his personal assistant to give me one of the watches AVIC makes for CPC taikonauts, or astronauts.

At dinner, of course, I brought up our business plan, expressed our hopes and expectations, and asked why no money had been sent as per our agreement. To my frustration, I received no clarity. At the time, it wasn't clear what AVIC was doing, but it was clear that Chairman Wu, despite his cordiality, didn't give a flip about me and wanted to promote himself in the Communist Party. He was one of the Communists who subscribed to the belief that if you cut off a foreigner's head, that's a good thing—a good and patriotic thing to do.

After supper, outside Royal China, Mr. Liu, aka Leo, did something I've never experienced before with a PRC business associate. He hugged me. We had addressed the thorniest parts of the SWE Agreement. We had learned to respect each other—sincerely, deeply. As Chairman Wu was ascending, Leo was leaving the role that had advanced our cooperation constructively. Today, I wonder if Leo was simply expressing appreciation for our work together or if he was showing sadness that AVIC's stance was growing hubristically aggressive.

**SF**: If I'm not mistaken, that hubris started to become apparent relatively quickly.

**PJ**: Absolutely. Just a few months later we received some very disturbing news. AVIC'S new company in the United States, Ascendant Renewable Energy, had named its president. He was none other than Paul Thompson, the former general manager of SWE.

**SF**: You mentioned Chinese purchases of two companies in the United States, Cirrus and Continental Motors, which afforded the PRC opportunities to enhance its military capabilities. I'm sure there are more. Does the United States do a good enough job of vetting these transactions?

**PJ**: Bluntly, no. Let's look at just one angle of effort, the Committee on Foreign Investment in the United States (CFIUS). Laudably, CFIUS aims to respond quickly to commercial requests. However, commercial complexity contains more factors than CFIUS specialists can address in their working time frames. Those factors range across considerations of geography, technology, ownership, pursuit of capabilities, intent of purchasers, and hierarchies of control, among other things. By the time analysts receive a particular research task under review by CFIUS, they may have just three days to deliver a final, comprehensive report. Compare that to the months, even years, that two parties to a transaction have to prepare an application for approval.

Think, too, about the amount of money the transaction participants can spend to exploit vulnerabilities in the CFIUS system. Some lawyers devote significant portions of their careers to learning CFIUS processes so they can win approvals.

Not only does CFIUS face a mismatch in the time and money available to understand approval requests, it also lacks a "devil's advocate." Two parties show up as common advocates for one deal and ask the government agency to please approve it. No party appears in front of the government with opposition to the request. The CFIUS approval process appears to assume judicial characteristics, but neither budgets nor protagonists support this facade.

Furthermore, CFIUS lacks the tools or authority to impose sufficiently flexible conditions on the wide span of transactions applicants ask it to approve. Generally, it can only grant or deny an application to approve a transaction. Authorizing CFIUS to add broader conditionality to approvals could improve its effectiveness. Conditionality could include requiring financial deposits to ensure the acquirer acts as professed.

The CPC also exploits the systematic vulnerability of providing a single test point of legitimacy. After AVIC bought Continental Motors, China's biggest defense contractor used its resulting posture to buy a European manufacturer that provided aviation engines for US military drones. Limits on CFIUS's authority and resources keep it from detecting results like this that ensue from its approvals.

Not only does CFIUS approval confer apparent legitimacy on an acquirer, that badge also effectively locks out, or raises the costs for, others to right wrongly reasoned approvals. It seemed simple to allow a PRC-based company to buy 200 square miles of Texas desert, but that ranch land sat right underneath the airspace of Laughlin Air Force Base. Then, after the purchase, the company sought to power up the ranch spectacularly. Two hundred square miles of electrified property appeared right under the air space of what is perhaps the most important flight training base in the United States, threatening the women and men who fly these planes into war.

As European reviewers of foreign acquisitions assume the acceptability of CFIUS-recognized buyers, so do many legislators across the United

States. In my testimony to the Texas legislature, a congresswoman asked me, "Doesn't Washington protect us from this kind of threat?" I answered, "No ma'am. They don't."

She, like most Americans, views CFIUS approval as an endorsement. The inclinations to rely on CFIUS's effectiveness and to avoid the time and cost to challenge potentially threatening foreign acquisitions generally dissuade US citizens from taking actions to oppose malign foreign investments. By trusting the ability of our fellow citizens to make, and act on, good decisions, the United States could and should augment the single federal CFIUS gate that fails to protect us. We should empower US citizens, perhaps with whistle-blower provisions, to take deliberate action against PRC agents prowling around looking for a vulnerability to exploit.

## Chapter 13

# How Do I Get It Back?

**SF**: I want to jump ahead a few years to yet another pivotal meal. But I promise we'll backtrack to cover the events that led up to it. This meal takes place not at the Royal China in Dallas, but rather in Fullerton, California, in the coffee shop of a hotel AVIC had recently purchased from Marriott. It's March 2014. You're having breakfast with a character we've already introduced—the president of AVIC USA, Zhang Xuming, or, as you called him, "Sherman." This is the same fellow who had previously been present at the Royal China dinner, and would soon be the onlooker at the October 2014 lunch, when AVIC's lawyer Paul Ma seemed to threaten you and your family.

Your smartphone rests innocently on the table as you and Sherman talk. Or should I say, not so innocently, because, unbeknownst to Sherman, you are recording this conversation—*legally*. You have checked with your lawyers who have assured you that in California, Person A (you) may record a conversation with Person B (Sherman) without permission as long as Person B has no reasonable expectation of privacy. Because you are conversing in an open breakfast area in the hotel, Sherman cannot successfully argue he had such an expectation. Indeed, some years later he will try to argue this . . . and the court will side with you.

A couple of questions: Why does AVIC own hotels? And why the subterfuge? You've already mentioned you provided the CIA with information when you were in China, and that you periodically had contact here at home with the FBI. Were you working undercover for either of these agencies?

**PJ**: No, no, no. No Jack Ryan or Jason Bourne stunts here! I'll explain why I was recording the conversation, but first, let me note some much more nefarious cloak-and-dagger machinations made in China and exported to the United States. And yes, the recording upset AVIC; they even tried to have me jailed in California.

You asked why AVIC owns hotels? The simplest explanation is that AVIC, like other corporations, makes investments in businesses or markets or properties that will offer a reasonable rate of return. But there may be another reason. Hotels offer a wonderful way to mine data and keep tabs on people the PRC might be interested in tracking—and even trapping. It's a relatively simple way to know where someone is, has been and, and—even more concerning—will be. I have no doubt my friends in China would have loved to know if, say, I was in Paris at the same time as a manufacturer of wind turbines. Indeed, MSS used knowledge of a hotel visit to trap a Uyghur leader from Turkey not too many years ago.

Now to your question about why the subterfuge. On March 22, 2014, we were five years into the SWE Agreement; more than three years had passed since the dinner in Dallas. We had brought several viable projects to AVIC. In person and in correspondence, we had asked numerous times what AVIC's intentions were regarding SWE. We had not seen a penny of the $600 million the Communist Party had committed to invest; we hadn't seen evidence of funds held in escrow. Indeed, we had not collaborated on a single project.

And if all this wasn't enough, we'd seen evidence suggesting AVIC was actually competing with SWE to develop wind farms—in violation of our agreement. As you might imagine, we had put a great deal of time and money into identifying potential projects and developing them. We could quantify the hours and money spent, but how can you measure the rise and fall of hopes and dreams, the commitment of the most productive years of our lives and careers?

Why the subterfuge, the surreptitious recording? Because we knew our adversary and the range of actions they could take to break us. We owed it to ourselves, our employees, and our investors to determine if SWE could be salvaged and finally move forward as agreed and contracted. And if it couldn't be salvaged, we owed it to same bunch to pursue legal remedies and remuneration for monies spent and opportunities lost.

After talking with our lawyers, we developed a strategy. Before the statute of limitations could shut down our opportunity to pursue legal remedies, I would engage one last time with AVIC representatives with the hope of reaching an understanding that could keep SWE alive. As the chances of that outcome appeared slim, I would record—legally, under California law—the conversations to preserve evidence if we had to initiate litigation.

Sherman was one of three AVIC reps who I ended up taping. The others were Xu Hang, aka Mr. Shoe, our AVIC TED contact who was vice president of AVIC IRE; and Paul Thompson. As we've discussed, Paul was SWE's general manager. But he had also moved onto the AVIC payroll, serving as president of Ascendant, a US subsidiary of AVIC IRE.

**SF**: Got it. Let's go back now to detail the particulars that led you to this breaking point and the breakfast with Sherman. What happened after your dinner in Dallas where you received the ambiguous hug from Leo and the cold shoulder from Wu Guangquan?

**PJ**: While the meal itself pleased us greatly, the discussion of SWE's future did not. So we followed up. Two weeks later, in mid-December 2010, we emailed Xu Hang. We referenced the business purpose of SWE "to promote the Chinese wind turbine sales and develop wind farms in United States." We then noted that we had been keeping AVIC informed of all potential projects, none of which had resulted in collaboration.

We thumped AVIC again with what you might call a passive-aggressive passage reflecting what I had learned on my impromptu trip to Corpus Christi. Leaving there, I had gone to the airport at the same time as AVIC and saw them talking to a local US congressman. I took off about the same time they did, and, noting their King Air's call sign and talking with their pilots about weather and traffic patterns, I knew who to listen for on the air traffic control radio. I learned that AVIC's plane exited its flight pattern and flew low over other wind farms that appeared to interest them. We had already learned that in October 2010, AVIC had created, in the words of Xu Hang, "a specialized company working for AVIC and AVIC Intl. Holding and focusing on renewable energy business all around the world." In the US, he said that meant "wind project development including investment, operation and maintenance." This new entity was AVIC IRE. (By the way, looking to 2022 and adverse-to-US interests, the Communist Party used AVIC International to funnel money to political families in the Solomon Islands.)

**SF**: Wait. Wasn't wind project development what AVIC was supposed to be doing with Tang in SWE?

**PJ**: Exactly—and *exclusively*. Ever so politely, using AVIC International to include behavior by its many subordinate units, we called them out:

> We learned that AVIC International is considering some wind projects in the U.S. As partner, we are ready to provide resources AVIC International will need to evaluate the projects and add value to serve Soaring Wind's business in U.S. Our understanding is that Tang and AVIC International shall develop wind projects together in the U.S. through Soaring Wind. As you know we are working on the 9MW Corpus Christi project. We recently planned to loan $6.5 million to the project. AVIC International is welcome to jointly participate in the project with Tang. If you are interested, [we] can send more project information at your request.

**SF**: I can understand the agita. What was AVIC's response to Tang's email?

**PJ**: To the specific email, no response. To our long line of effort, an ugly snub.

**SF**: A few months after that Dallas dinner, in February of 2011, AVIC did follow your suggestion to buy Cirrus Aircraft.

**PJ**: Yes. With the purchase, Cirrus became a subsidiary of the PRC aviation and military complex. Not what I had in mind. If AVIC intended good, it could have brought up its changed expectations and even proposed a $5 million finder's fee. When it hid its actions, it strongly suggested an abusive course to our relationship.

**SF**: Did you ask for a finder's fee? Five million dollars is five million dollars.

**PJ**: No. And beyond that, we actually divested ourselves of the Flat Water and Corpus Christi projects. Why? Because the SWE Agreement was still binding on all of us. We felt like we owed a duty of loyalty to our partners. We had become involved in those opportunities only because we thought they were going to become SWE projects, i.e., in collaboration with our partner AVIC. Even if the CPC drove AVIC to cheat, we were not going to cheat. I figured—okay, *hoped*—we were still going to be partners in SWE for a long and highly profitable time, and I wanted to restore the relationship. (A psychiatry journal may want that story.)

**SF**: Looking at the timeline, the acquisition of Cirrus wasn't the only February surprise. That same month AVIC IRE created a company in the United States called Ascendant. Xu Hang was a director, and none other than Paul Thompson was named CEO. At some point it became apparent Ascendant was indeed doing what Xu Hang had mentioned in his October 2010 email, namely, developing wind farms in the United States—but not with SWE. Please explain what you learned.

**PJ:** I believed Paul when he told me AVIC set up Ascendant to make it easier for AVIC to get money to SWE. (Remember, names tell you something: "Tang," "Soaring," and "Ascendant" all mean "rising, lifting up.") Though learning of Ascendant's formation only after the fact, it was still AVIC.

**SF**: Turning back to a time and event sequence, I don't see any SWE projects detailed between the creation of AVIC's US-based Ascendant in February of 2011 and your breakfast with Sherman.

**PJ**: That's because there weren't any. Over the next three years, we brought several other potential SWE projects to AVIC's attention, but the silence became deafening.

**SF**: So AVIC just washed its hands of manufacturing blades and developing wind farms in the United States?

**PJ**: Hardly. Simply put, AVIC tried to wash its hands of doing business under the terms of the SWE Agreement. But our so-called partner was quite busy dirtying its hands with a number of projects, most of which rightfully belonged under the SWE umbrella. At one point, Paul told me that if I knew everything about an AVIC effort to develop a wind farm in the Pacific Northwest, I'd "have to take a shower." Thankfully, the Obama administration stopped the project—which would have overlooked a significant US military installation—from being built. Even more interesting, because it presaged other aggressive CPC activities in US courts, AVIC's collaborator there, Ralls Corporation, sued CFIUS to determine what facts and processes our government used to reach its decision to deny the project. You might be thinking, "What could clever PRC lawyers do in litigation to boost PRC national intelligence efforts?" If you're not, you should be.

**SF**: What was your response to AVIC's activities, or lack thereof?

**PJ**: Understandably, you may question our rationality, but we doubled down and worked harder. As you might imagine, all of us at Tang were continually disappointed, often frustrated, and persistently surprised. We were proposing projects that had the potential to make all of us and AVIC some money. But as I think you know by now, optimism tends to overbalance my pessimism.

Adding to the case for optimism was the fact that while AVIC was acting badly, it was obfuscating its behavior. Whenever we asked questions, AVIC would reply that it was continuing to abide by the agreement, supporting SWE, and working with the PRC bureaucracy to move funds. Unknown to us at the time, it was inducing others to shirk their obligations to us. AVIC apparently enticed Dallas lawyer Steve DeWolf—who had worked with us since 2003 to find, evaluate, and secure wind farms—to flip sides and perform these services for them. Later, during dispute resolution, the lead arbitrator scolded Steve for his apparent ethical breaches, even though our dispute addressed only AVIC's breaches.

**SF:** It seems the truth of AVIC's breach became pretty evident in 2013. In June of that year, Tang wrote a letter to Xu Hang referencing Ascendant and proposing what appears to be a radical course of action:

> Considering that AVIC International is not willing to get Tang's involvement to develop wind projects in United States, which is against the agreement of Soaring Wind, Tang proposes selling its interest in Soaring Wind to AVIC International. Then Soaring Wind and Ascendant will no longer compete with each other and should work together towards the long-term strategy of AVIC International in US market.

What was the rationale for selling your interest in what seemed—at least at the beginning—to be the dream project following many years spent toiling in the literal wilderness?

**PJ:** The SWE Agreement committed us all, each to the other, for at least twenty years—potentially the most productive years of my life. Through our agreement, I made a pledge to AVIC. I also had duties to my family and to Tang's investors to do well and good for them. Looking back, I recognize signs I didn't see, or couldn't believe, about our partner.

The likelihood of having to fight AVIC scared the dickens out of me. It is huge. It designs and builds weapons to kill Americans. It enjoys access to the PRC treasury—a national treasury with something like $3 trillion in foreign currency reserves. It can, and did, hire top US law firms. As Guo Wengui, a wily Chinese refugee, told me years later (in English): "AVIC MSS same." (As noted earlier, MSS refers to the PRC's Ministry of State Security.)

We sincerely preferred selling to suing, as selling would have avoided a fight with the behemoth and allowed us to redirect our careers. AVIC rejected the proposal. Although I wanted to see the SWE glass as half full, well before this exchange I knew it was moving toward empty. So, what to do? Once you make the decision that you have to do something to protect your position, a new phase starts.

To recover damages, you have to gather evidence that shows bad behavior, and damage resulting from that behavior. To win a judicial determination—that is, to win in court—you have to bring solid evidence. We knew AVIC and DeWolf and Wu Guangquan would dodge all they could, and that AVIC would assume it could crush little bitty Tang Energy—even in US courts in Dallas, Texas. Knowing a fight was coming around the bend, we began gathering ammunition.

Gathering ammunition meant getting AVIC to admit it was doing what we knew it was doing: turning down potential SWE wind farm projects in the United States while funding other such projects through entities established to compete with SWE. But we needed more. Thus, the tape-recorded conversations.

**SF**: A few months after you sent that letter, you engaged in what seems to be an eye-opening and surprising exchange of emails with Xu Hang. On November 1, you sent an email referencing the opportunity to partner in a "good wind project (in Texas) that meets the requirements that AVIC International stated before."

After again noting AVIC's refusal to participate in Flat Water and Corpus Christi, you concluded:

> Tang has made persistent & deliberate efforts to fulfill its commitment to the $300 million wind project funding agreement

> signed by AVIC International and Tang in 2009, which was witnessed by Chinese and US top government officials in Chicago. When will AVIC International respect its $300 million commitment to fund the wind projects in [the] United States?

Two days later, Mr. Xu Hang responded:

> AVIC International has already provided a total of 50 million USD in financing to wind power projects in the US and will keeping trying in the future. As a commercial company, any business activity must be in line with the company requirements.

Talk about a smoking gun!

**PJ**: Isn't it though? As a lawyer, you know the term "admission against interest." That was exactly the kind of evidence we had to evoke—indeed, *provoke*—AVIC to give us. PRC companies may choose to ignore US court orders to provide evidence. PRC litigants in the United States may claim the evidence doesn't exist and that, if it did, it would exist only in the PRC and violate PRC laws if provided. We pricked AVIC's—more specifically, Xu Hang's—sense of superiority over us to trigger that eruption of critical evidence.

Xu Hang provided that admission in the email you rightly called a "smoking gun." It was also a starting gun. It confirmed what we thought we knew and started the three-year clock under US statutes that limit the amount of time plaintiffs have to sue after they know someone has harmed them.

**SF**: A month before recording Sherman, you recorded a conversation with Paul Thompson in your office, on February 21. My reading of it is that you were trying to establish several things "on the record." First, who had undercut the highly profitable HT Blade, and why? Second, what was Ascendant's relationship to AVIC and Paul's history with Ascendant, and how were all of AVIC's subsidiaries structured and operated? And third, would Paul acknowledge that AVIC—through Ascendant and/or other entities—had failed to live up to its obligations under the SWE Agreement by turning down projects you brought them and funding others?

**PJ**: That's fair. You kindly left out that a recording keeps up with a conversation better than note-taking. You also used a hot-button word: *subsidiaries*. I describe AVIC's—indeed, any PRC SOE's—subsidiaries as "subordinate units" because SOEs organize themselves like military branches. In a centralized command and control model, subordinate units may exercise tactical autonomy, but they enjoy no strategic separation, or independence, from their superior. While allowing the freedom to implement commands, a higher authority determines the subordinate's mission and decides what resources the subordinate unit can use in its assignment.

Academically interesting organizational questions about how six US military branches stack up against one hundred CPC militarized branches abound. But think of what this means for budgeting. We've trapped ourselves into looking for PLA budgets that look like US Department of Defense budgets. US think tanks and government bodies compare US military budgets to only a fraction of PLA-tagged outfits that look or sound like US military branches. This self-imposed blindness hands the CPC a strategic win—"strategic" because we allow the CPC to hide enormous investments in capabilities aimed at defeating us.

Back to your point: I'm sorry we couldn't avoid fighting AVIC in US courts, because winning required us to present evidence of party behavior we deeply understood, but few Americans knew about.

As we contemplated the necessity of going to court, we knew we'd have to establish a direct link between AVIC and the behavior of its subordinate units, which were breaching the SWE Agreement. One way to pry evidence from AVIC about the bad actors was to leverage internal rivalries. An example of that was to ask if a man named Wang Bin had sabotaged the SWE relationship. Wang Bin was the president of Avicopter, AVIC Helicopter's branding name in English.

Avicopter had sought more involvement with or control over HT Blade. Feigning suspicion for the source of tension among SWE's owners by asking Paul about Wang Bin's possible role diffused blaming Tang's own SWE partners. It also created a situation where we would learn by either a yes or no answer if Wang Bin had created the SWE tension.

**SF**: Why would Wang Bin sabotage such a profitable business?

**PJ**: Rivalries within AVIC, indeed within the CPC, involve powerful factions, or *guanxi* networks. When they bump each other, career fatalities occur. When they collide, fatalities occur. AVIC Heavy Machinery had outmaneuvered Wang Bin's company, Avicopter, to lead HT Blade's daily operations. Having failed to take over a cash-cow asset in AVIC's stable of companies, Wang Bin may have wanted to degrade its value for a rival within AVIC. He could also cloak his undermining of HT Blade's value as patriotic. As noted, one HT Blade board member told me the CPC didn't want "the foreigner to make too much money." The foreigner was us, our company: Tang Energy.

Probing Avicopter's leader's role in causing us trouble presented the tension as a problem Tang and AVIC Heavy Machinery needed to solve together. That made answering my question easier. No matter what the answer, it also allowed us to gather evidence and test AVIC's veracity.

**SF**: Wang Bin also figures in your conversation with Paul about the creation of Ascendant and his hiring, and even its suspicious naming.

**PJ**: All of the above, yes. Wang Bin served more as a foil than a player. AVIC IHC orchestrated Paul's hire. To add insult to injury, when AVIC named their new venture "Ascendant Renewable Energy" (in Chinese), it stole our name: "Soaring Wind Energy." The words, as mentioned earlier—"Tang," "Soaring," and "Ascendant"—all connote lifting up or rising. Today, the churlishness amuses me. It would have surprised me if Wang Bin had been involved, but asking about him allowed even a negative response to help lead to a positive identification. The important point was that AVIC was stealing our people, projects, and opportunities—and even our name!

**SF**: From the discussion about naming, you moved to the activities of Paul and Ascendant shortly after that entity's creation. There seems to have been some fishy activity from the get-go.

**PJ**: Well, yes. "Fishy" reflects a Judeo-Christian-Islamic value framework that ties individual behavior to honor and applies laws to all people, including political leaders. The CPC uses a Confucian lens to blur the significance of any individual's behavior, including responsibility for behavior that breaches agreements—except to the extent that it promotes accretion of power to the party.

Watched by the CPC, AVIC's leaders reviewed probably twenty wind projects we had sourced. Flat Water in Nebraska and two Texas projects—Cirrus 1 and Spinning Star Energy—were just three. Paul sourced others. Paul being an SWE owner and former employee, AVIC apparently recruited him to bring projects directly to AVIC's Ascendent Renewable Energy.

Since we had generously made Paul an equity partner without requiring him to invest actual money, you might wonder why he took the job with AVIC. With a $600 million promise, AVIC enticed us all to pledge our abilities to SWE. Then, it indefinitely delayed funding its promise. That meant SWE couldn't pay its employees, including Paul. I'm sympathetic to him. He had a family to support. AVIC put him and us in a position of unpleasant choices.

**SF**: At one point, you asked Paul, "So who at AVIC is calling the shots?" Paul tells you things have changed over the last six months, that AVIC appears to have no interest in the wind farm projects he brings them. You indicate you are still "pitching stuff" without success. He adds, "It's almost like rats leaving the sinking ship on the renewable side."

**SF**: Was Paul cooperating with you at this point, or was he playing both sides, holding back information?

**PJ**: Two things were happening here: One, Paul was trying to figure out how he might help. Two, I was trying to figure out what AVIC was doing and what role on what side Paul might play.

**SF**: Was there a legitimate reason for AVIC to reject the projects you brought them? Was it a bad deal for them financially? Was the renewable energy business losing—excuse me—the wind in its sails?

**PJ**: No, we were bringing really good projects. Our own returns on time and money invested depended on making money from good projects. Broadly, the wind energy business was screaming along on a broad reach. Individually, projects caught those winds with varying speeds. We sailed for project profitability. However, two factors made it difficult for AVIC to find winning projects on their own. First, they lacked the discernment and ability to engage with stakeholders that decades of experience brings. Second, representing the CPC, AVIC included PRC national security objectives that they didn't reveal to us. Remember, Paul told me if I "knew everything about" a project in the Pacific Northwest, I'd "have to take a shower."

**SF**: Paul even confesses paranoia regarding the money he's being paid because the answer to the projects he pitches is always, "No." You respond that you still feel the obligation to bring any wind farm project to AVIC. Then there's an important turn to a discussion of the way AVIC conducts business. After you note that AVIC moves people like Xu Hang, Sherman, and others from entity to entity, Paul volunteers, "They're cooking the books." He surmises they are moving millions of dollars from one entity to another as well. "They're just playing fast and loose with the money . . . Follow the money."

**PJ**: Oh boy. That can open Pandora's box. The party moves people and money around as it sees fit, regardless of frameworks we consider legal, or what investment bankers and corporate lawyers put in public offering documents. A short version of a long story about cash and the books helps get to the point: After the HT Blade-Avicopter fallout, the general manager of AVIC's subordinate unit, which managed HT's daily operations, took cash from HT Blade. Comparing year-end 2010 books to subsequent accounting periods, we found what we assumed was an $8 million accounting error. It took almost six months of our persistent queries for AVIC to fess up that its subordinate had taken our cash to make its payroll.

**SF**: These shenanigans became a major storyline in the subsequent arbitration proceeding. AVIC alleged that your real reason for bringing the action wasn't breach of the SWE contract, but rather anger over malfeasance at HT Blade, which cost you hundreds of millions. Let's defer this discussion until we get to the hearing.

Back to the recording with Paul. You recounted a discussion you'd had with Sherman: "I told him, 'You know, Sherman, it really was wrong of AVIC International to start Ascendant. They should have been running all this business through Soaring Wind.'" Paul replied that he'd told Xu Hang the same thing, and the response was, "Ah, that's sort of seen as a failure and we want to distance ourselves from that."

You then reprised a conversation with Sherman about AVIC's conduct. You didn't remember his exact words, but it was something like, "Yeah, that was wrong. Patrick, you write the letter that says it was wrong. I, Sherman, can't write the letter, but if they show it to me, I'll say, 'Yeah, it was wrong, and you need to do something about it.'" Meaning business should be run through SWE. To which Paul said to you: "You know, politically, I think someone went, 'That's a turd. That's Sherman's baby.'"

**PJ**: The Communist Party's fickle mix of fragility and power makes it dangerous to criticize. My letter of criticism would certainly fracture CPC sensitivities. While the CPC can wreck me financially, it can destroy Sherman's family. Being more realistically aware of both US and PRC strengths and weaknesses, Sherman knew AVIC would ask him about critical communications from Tang. He also knew how to play the situation. He could, in effect, say, as AVIC's leading representative in the United States,

"I [Sherman] understand the foreigner's position because I understand their laws and culture. Think about the letter and your response from their point of view." Sherman saw gain for AVIC in the SWE Agreement, and also risk in abrogating that agreement.

Paul listened to the Communist Party line. He sensed the CPC's desire to get more out of SWE, even by taking its projects, hiring its general manager, and diverting its financing. Paul also watched other AVIC officers blame Sherman for his caution. Their assumptions and behavior reflected their personal growth and career progression. In the PRC and in AVIC, growth and advancement depended on building *guanxi* with powerful people and organizations. In the officers' view, mighty AVIC could and should crush tiny Tang, even if that meant breaching the SWE Agreement.

With leadership turnover in Beijing, AVIC officers sought to forge their own successes by any means available, and on their own terms. Calling previous accomplishments insufficiently aggressive evoked patriotic cheer, and because patriotism to the CPC trumps acting legally (especially according to foreign laws), that opened the range of behavior available to AVIC representatives. In this political environment, AVIC officers denigrated earlier accomplishments. It was only natural to disparage their architects, too. The situation made Sherman an unjustified, but convenient, target.

**SF**: And then the six-hundred-million-dollar question. From the transcript:

> Patrick: How did it fail? I mean we brought—
>
> Paul: It didn't fail. I mean we did what we were supposed to do. It didn't fail the way I see it. Somebody wanted to build another empire, so you've got to go.

Harsh.

**PJ**: Harsh, maybe. True, yes, because Paul validated the success of our business plan. US projects and PRC equipment suppliers needed expertise to develop wind farms. But Paul also confirmed he was part of CPC efforts, likely unknowingly, to serially abuse those who brought needed experience to make the plan work.

**SF**: You then turned to the structure of AVIC, with its various subordinate units. What was the purpose of that?

**PJ**: Two reasons, broadly. First, Ascendant Renewable was competing against SWE, but it didn't exist when AVIC and Tang signed the SWE Agreement. We expected AVIC to argue that Ascendant, as a brand new company, could legally compete with SWE. AVIC would add to this argument that it could legally invest in new companies around the world. We had to show that AVIC had created Ascendant as a subordinate unit. When I characterized AVIC as "a single entity," Paul agreed and went on to say, "that makes all of AVIC culpable."

I should add, or repeat, that AVIC had cut off funding for Paul's salary at SWE but offered him a salary as the president of Ascendant, its wholly owned subsidiary.

Second, we suspected Ascendant had no money. Even if it did have assets, we expected AVIC to strip Ascendant of money and assets if we won a legal award. Time would prove our concern was well founded.

**SF**: Let's conclude our review of the conversation with Paul by looking at this critical exchange. As he gets ready to leave, you discuss a strategy for recouping losses resulting from AVIC's failure to adhere to the agreement. At this point you're talking about pursuing a remedy "politically," i.e., through the State Department, as opposed to litigation.

You tell Paul you'd like to be able to quote him on the fact that AVIC "pushes money from one entity to the other." You also want to be able to characterize AVIC as one entity. I love Paul's response: "I think you got to keep it simple, Patrick. You can't get off on this spellbinding mystery and intrigue. It's just, they fucking stole money. How do I get it back?"

**PJ**: Paul summarizes AVIC's theft simply and accurately. When I met with State Department representatives, they repeatedly expressed concern, interest, and sympathy. Uniformly, they asked us to keep them informed. Regardless, I failed to find Department of State officials who could appreciate benefits to Americans for resolving political issues with commercial aspects, or who could imagine a plan that might help us.

**SF**: So what was your takeaway from this conversation? Did you get what you were hoping for?

**PJ**: What I got helped. We were gathering tesserae to create a mosaic for litigation. I would like to have found a solution that avoided arbitration and going to court. Paul provided evidence as an AVIC employee they couldn't hide.

**SF**: Why hadn't Paul given you a heads-up before this? His loyalty at this point seems to be to you.

**PJ**: I don't know what Paul knew or when he knew it. He lived in Lubbock and traveled to Beijing. AVIC certainly strung him out on what it was doing. He may not have known. He may have had an inclination. Fear in his chest was probably growing uncomfortably. Paul may not have known how to make the kind of decision he was going to have to make: whose side to take.

**SF**: Let's turn now to that breakfast with Sherman, which took place in California one month later. In the transcript, he references a document you've presented to him, with several issues you wanted to discuss.

**PJ**: Again, first and foremost, I sincerely wanted to see if we could get SWE on track. Maybe understanding the closing window to avoid litigation imposed by the statute of limitations would help Sherman persuade his superiors of the urgency to act properly.

Also on my list was discussion of a resin company AVIC personnel had set up, a gambit emblematic of an often corrupt system where quality control takes a backseat to the opportunity to line one's own pockets.

Here's that story: A group of AVIC officers created a company to sell resin to HT Blade. At the time, HT Blade earned about $350 million per year in revenue. It spent about $50 million or $60 million on resin. Resin holds wind blades together in, yes, the wind. The AVIC officers' new company—unsurprisingly—persuaded HT Blade's materials purchasing department to switch from the proven resin supplier to their company. This new company, in effect, provided sticky water, which they called resin, to HT Blade. In the wind, the blades made with sticky water tore apart like old flags in a squall.

Naturally, we sought to understand why the wind was shredding our blades. That's how we found out about the change in resin supplier. HT Blade's customers wanted their money back, which we understood.

In sequence, we urged HT Blade to seek redress for the resin failures from the sticky water company. AVIC told us that wouldn't happen. And it didn't. They wouldn't tell us why. They wouldn't tell us about the sticky water company's history or its owners or show us its financials. We had to find out all we could with our own due diligence—due diligence that Xi Jinping's CPC has now made illegal to conduct.

This openly hostile sequence showed us AVIC was committed to fighting and stealing rather than cooperating and following binding agreements. We hit back—hard. I penned a letter (Appendix) to AVIC's highest level Chairman in Beijing, Lin Zuoming, who we believed knew about the cash theft and sticky water company issues at HT Blade. We understood he benefitted either directly, through participation in the schemes, or indirectly, by allowing his *guanxi* to enrich its members. Our letter took the position that Chairman Lin should know of corruption in his organization. It went on to describe those infractions in English and Chinese.

It got uglier. Should I go on?

**SF**: Yes. This intrigues me. It sounds like a lesson or pattern US leaders might learn, follow, or adopt.

**PJ**: We respectfully reminded AVIC of our history of working well together for "mutual benefit," a Chinese company popular phrase. We went on to note HT Blade's success creating a Chinese national champion. We also noted that a successful AVIC-Tang relationship was illustrating a beneficial pattern for US-PRC relationships. With the letter, we were raising Chairman Lin's personal stake in resolving, or failing to resolve, our issues with HT Blade. We couched it in terms of breaching party discipline and violating PRC law.

Knowing when the CPC's Central Commission for Discipline Inspection would be searching Lin's office in Beijing, we delivered the letter to him by mail, delivery service, fax, email, and in-person. A letter from a foreigner took away his plausible deniability of the issues that led to litigation in the United States. It urged Lin to resolve differences. Refusal to do so revealed additional evidence of the CPC's conspiratorial intent to plunder a foreigner's position.

**SF**: Did it work?

**PJ**: To channel Zhou Enlai, "It's too soon to say." But several months after the delivery of the letter, Lin Zuoming was "disappeared." And we did collect dollars in Dallas years later.

**SF**: Since the odds of Sherman being helpful in the quest to resurrect SWE were slim, I assume the default position was to get his words down in a setting like this where he'd most likely be more forthcoming than in a deposition or trial testimony.

**PJ**: Exactly. The hope was he'd confirm that all the different entities AVIC had created or spun off, whether in China or the United States, were in truth agents of AVIC—therefore making AVIC liable for acts committed by Ascendant, AVIC IRE, and others that violated the SWE Agreement.

**SF**: You cut to the chase pretty quickly, asking Sherman for direction: "If you're the only one at AVIC that thinks that Ascendant did wrong, what do we do?" He suggested you bring any evidence of wrongdoing to the attention of AVIC. After you noted the agreement included a provision for dispute resolution, Sherman offered an alternative: "We should like a kind of negotiate—very friendly negotiation. And, you know, the final, if it cannot be negotiable you may have to go to the court." How were you reading him at this point?

**PJ**: I trust Sherman's sincerity, even today. I also understand his situation requires absolute loyalty to the Communist Party. He provides informed, thoughtful, intelligent advice to the CPC. The party, under Xi Jinping, defaults to brutal rather than sensible action. Its propagandized projection of strength traps it into confrontations rather than the compromises that negotiations require. The party wants to show, again, under Xi Jinping, that it can win any fight. Unfortunately, it perceives disagreements as opportunities to fight. Perhaps ironically, the more Xi Jinping quiets voices like Sherman's in China, the more necessary it becomes for authorities outside of the PRC to establish mechanisms, like guardrails, to guide otherwise careening and, in terms of world peace and prosperity, sensible behavior from the CPC.

**SF**: You then pressed ahead, asking: "If AVIC decides, *yes, Ascendant did wrong and Soaring Wind is owed money,* who would pay the money? Would AVIC pay money?" And Sherman's response was?

**PJ**: His response was basically, "Yes." He then went on to suggest that after that resolution we could either go about our separate ways or find "a chance to work together." I expected this answer. For the anticipated litigation, I needed an AVIC officer to say so.

**SF**: You followed up with the sixty-four-million-dollar agency question: "From a US standpoint, that would be principal/agent, where the principal would be AVIC and the agent would be AVIC International or Ascendant Renewable." Sherman says, "Uh, huh." But, seeming to want more, you asked: "Would it be the principal, AVIC, saying we're taking responsibility for the agent, Ascendant Renewable?" And Sherman says: "Generally speaking should be Renewable Energy company solve this whole problem. Either have dispute and pay money or something like that, it's Renewable Energy group."

You then tie it up with a bow, summarizing, "So in that case the agent company, AVIC Renewable, would on behalf of AVIC . . . " And he interrupts, "Yes."

Mission accomplished?

**PJ:** Mission advanced. We still had a long way to go. We believed we could demonstrate, to judicial standards, that AVIC's subordinate units had breached our agreements. But if we couldn't collect winnings, winning didn't matter.

**SF**: At first, the next thing you talked about didn't necessarily seem relevant to your dispute, but by the end there was indeed a connection. Sherman told the story of a young Chinese bureaucrat who had died by suicide. Apparently he had received a significant promotion, moving from being Chairman Lin's secretary in China to running an operation abroad, and the pressure got to him.

**PJ**: Yes. The vignette showcases a handful of insights. Many who aspire to Communist Party positions want to stay close to Beijing, the center of Communist Party power. Some, like Sherman, who is shrewder than most, make it work elsewhere. More fail.

Quickly, we wonder why "suicide guy" would leave Beijing? We don't know why AVIC's Chairman Lin sent this young man to Europe. Lin may have wanted to enrich him, isolate him, punish him, or serve some personal objective of his own, like getting money out of the PRC. One thing is clear: leaving reduced this young man's access to AVIC personnel and resources.

Going abroad also raised his vulnerability to AVIC infighting for promotion. Because of Sherman's sagacity, he understood that others could blame the absent fellow for failures, with or without fact checking. In Chinese systems, failures often require punishment. It also raised his vulnerability to exploitation by foreign intelligence services. Of course, stress alone may have caused his demise. We don't know enough to reach a conclusion.

**SF**: One of my favorite exchanges takes place when you characterize the influence bureaucrats—who may be thousands of miles away from where the action is taking place—have on the Shermans of the world.

"Day to day, you need to make decisions, but day to day they think they can. That's a common problem."

Sherman replies, laughing: "So don't listen to them too much."

You respond, "Yeah. Don't listen to them too much or you'll get fired." And he says, "No problem. I'm ready. Because two months—enough is enough. I don't want to listen. The chairman knows that. I have a lot of complaint. Fire me. Go ahead."

His main complaint is that he didn't learn that AVIC had set up Ascendant in Texas, even though he was the head of AVIC USA. When you tell him he should have been told, he replies: "I should. That's why I feel very, you know, frustrated about that. How can they do that? We have Soaring. We have Soaring company. You set up for same purpose, let me know. You understand that?"

Again, with your sympathetic prompting, he acknowledges that Beijing "went around" him and that he's "very angry" at people like Xu Hang. "I say, 'Okay, explain to me.' They explain to me. I say, 'Okay. Why? Because when I set up this joint venture, Soaring Wind, we have some, you know, not compete terms, noncompetition, internal competition terms.' I said, 'You set up this company. This means we are internal competing with our partner.' Yes?"

**PJ**: I like the exchange, too. Most importantly, it shows that Sherman and I liked working together, liked building good relationships and opportunities together. It's true that working internationally exposes businesses to political fickleness. Government support can wax, wane, and thwart individuals' efforts to promote peaceful, prosperous accomplishments.

Sadly, the exchange confirmed in detail AVIC's systematic abrogation of our agreements. Even sadder for me, I understood that Xi Jinping's wolf warrior growls were tearing apart friendships and opportunities to build trust, jobs, and prosperity for people around the world.

Sadder still, my mind keeps a list of old friends I would like to see, I would like to ask about, to whom I would like to say, "I remember the good we built together. I remember you." With the protection of the US government, I would.

**SF**: Sherman counseled you to bring your complaints to "more than one channel," saying he had done just that on your behalf. Then, speaking about you, he said, "As a partner, you try your best to help, but finally you lose. You lost, you know, investment and everything. Time, effort, everything."

You then say: "Well, I can see how showing that the evidence of what we lost would be helpful to resolving a problem, resolving a dispute. That's a good idea."

Sherman: "Maybe they just have it and they don't care. But they must care. You know, people suffer from that. They should care about that. That's what I'm—when I commit to the partner, I always think about other partner. That's how you win the game. If you want to get something from your partner and you don't care about them, no people win."

Did you think he was being honest?

**PJ:** Yes, I have no doubt that Sherman was speaking truthfully. He had lived in both countries, under their very different systems. He saw that a system based on transparency and truth freed people, and that free people express their individual creativities in ways that fulfill them and raise whole communities.

**SF**: Looking back at this transcript almost ten years after the recording, and several years after the arbitration proceeding, what is your takeaway?

**PJ**: Sherman and I were caught on the cusp of Xi Jinping-thought as it splashed out the fine wine of Deng Xiaoping-thought that had filled the PRC cup. In fact, Deng opened China to the world and to innovation inside and out. Deng's opening up to a rule-based order raised prosperity in the PRC and globally. Together, Sherman and I benefitted from his policies. We suffered personally and financially from Xi's restricting thoughts, his profligate use of Deng's abundances.

Xi Jinping likes to invoke the Thucydides Trap to describe the United States as a declining power, when in fact, Xi Jinping is returning China to ancient, declining power status. (Xi lives by another Thucydides quote, "The strong do what they can, and the weak suffer what they must.")

**SF**: I should note that the Thucydides Trap, a term coined by the American political scientist Graham T. Allison, posits that when an emerging power threatens to displace an existing power, war is a real possibility.

There's one more recording of note. Three days after your breakfast with Sherman, you spoke with Xu Hang. My favorite part of the conversation is when he says he doesn't want to argue with you, and you say, "Go ahead. My wife doesn't mind arguing with me."

But that's not what was important about this. Let's set the scene. You're in your car with Paul Thompson, and you pick up Xu Hang and a fellow called "Tiger" at the Dallas Fort Worth Airport. You have your phone by your side to record the conversation but have been cautioned by your lawyer to be sensitive to your location.

**PJ**: You're right. But first, did you know that Graham went to Davidson a few years before Steph Curry? For some reason, our attorneys advised me to stay in Dallas County. The highway through the airport runs down the line that separates Tarrant and Dallas counties. So I did.

**SF**: We've already been introduced to Xu Hang, aka Mr. Shoe, but who was this Tiger?

**PJ**: Tiger. Oh boy. Much younger than Sherman, and younger than Xu Hang, he dressed finer than they did, with an air suggesting he could just as easily replace those clothes as wash them. Tiger lived up to his nickname. He prowled more than he strode. He lay in wait to pounce on others for their behaviors, enjoying putting them on edge. He rationed eye contact like a humorless lord looking to affirm subservience. He wouldn't tell me his real name—even when I teased him about it. His strength swelled from the deference others showed, and his lineage sharpened his teeth—Communist Party lineage, for sure.

**SF**: What were you hoping to get from Xu Hang in this particular conversation?

**PJ**: Once again, despite all the time that had passed, I was hoping we still might get SWE up and running, and that AVIC and Tang could work together. We'd lost opportunities to partner on lucrative projects like Flat Water and Corpus Christi, but there were several other projects at this very moment, such as Spinning Star Energy, that had the potential to be quite lucrative.

While hoping for good behavior, I was planning for the opposite. Capturing bad behavior in Xu Hang's owns words would speak much more convincingly than I could. Thus, the recording. We wanted him on tape explaining his understanding of our agreement and AVIC's conduct. We wanted his words to demonstrate that AVIC knew it had behaved badly, violating the agreement.

I should add that sadness tainted my optimism that Xu Hang's admissions would help build our case should we have to litigate. Sure, truth was on our side, which would certainly help us win our case, but Xu Hang's hubris suggested much harder paths forward for two great countries and civilizations to share visions of collectively beneficial futures. He never in a million years thought that tiny American Tang—he referred to Tang as "Mei Teng," meaning American Tang—of Dallas would actually take on mighty AVIC—and the party and country behind it. A former US Navy intelligence officer later summarized, "They messed with the wrong Texan." That Navy officer was right, not because of the Texan, but because of the country the Texan had behind him.

**SF**: Despite his hubris, Xu Hang didn't present you with a confession on a silver platter.

**PJ**: No. He's smart, and he played dumb for a while, saying he thought we had suspended operations, and that he had no idea we thought AVIC had been competing with us by funding its own projects, as opposed to the ones we kept bringing them. But he knew damn well AVIC had withheld the financing originally intended for SWE, which had gone instead to Ascendant. He thought he was as clever as all get out.

**SF**: He also seemed to suggest he was unaware that SWE was formed in large part to develop wind farms.

**PJ**: That was complete misdirection. Paul asked him if he thought SWE had been created only to sell wind turbines, and thus not to develop wind farms. He said that was his current impression. Come on! He knew how to read a contract. He had drafted, in English, the Chicago Agreement.

Yes, we aimed to sell HT Blade wind blades to wind farms—but, especially early in SWE's life, developing wind farms put it in position to require wind turbine makers to buy blades from HT Blade. He darn well knew that. Still, through Ascendant Renewable Energy, he was taking the projects SWE was going to develop, the projects we brought to AVIC's attention to no avail.

**SF**: As the conversation drew to a close, Paul asked you what you wanted to do. You responded, "Make money, honey." Xu Hang agreed, saying you all had the same goal.

**PJ**: That statement *was* true but, for Xu Hang, incomplete. We did each want to make money. But, in good Communist Party fashion, Xu Hang wanted to take whatever he could get away with. In this case, he wanted to take something of high value—the business plan Tang had developed—from a foreigner. And we were that foreigner.

China's history swings from centralizing control to allowing control to migrate to the margins—to frontiers and individuals. Today's Communist Party pulls as much control and authority as it can into itself. It views collaboration not as an amplifier of it creative powers, but as an erosion of its position and strength. In every relationship, it takes as much as it can get. Even among and within PRC entities, like AVIC, officials break down collaborative frameworks to gain greater command over an entity and its resources. In contrast, most Americans share the notion that if *we work together, we both make more money.* That's why we call it "collaborating," like co-laboring. Collaborating—working together—benefits everybody.

**SF**: Were you happy with what you got on tape? What was the takeaway?

**PJ**: Happy is a tough word to apply to any part of this unpleasant experience. We did find Xu Hang's responses useful. He gave us pieces, like tesserae, that we could use to add detail to our litigation's mosaic. The arbitration panel of nine lawyers—yes, nine, the same as the number of justices on the US Supreme Court—did not let us know what evidence they found compelling. However, the recordings registered viscerally with them, revealing the dimensionality and scope of the Communist Party's subjugation of its smaller, weaker counterparties. Our lawyers could read our agreements and follow our narrative, but they were unused to wrestling with the Communist beast. Understandably, AVIC sought to suppress these recordings—unsuccessfully.

**SF**: Two months after these conversations, in June of 2014, Tang and the other SWE investors filed a demand for arbitration. Arbitration, as opposed to a trial or hearing in the courts, was prescribed by the SWE Agreement. And, to your surprise, AVIC agreed to arbitrate in Dallas. Can you fill us in on what took place on the legal front during this two month period?

**PJ**: For over two years, I had been telling AVIC, in many ways, "We have a dispute that US law will not let us ignore." Statute of limitations concerns drove us to formally initiate dispute resolutions within three years of notifying AVIC of our dispute. The closer we got to that deadline, the more time we spent with lawyers.

Paul knew of our concerns, and that we were talking to lawyers. So did Sherman, Xu Hang, and a bevy of AVIC officers. In our filing, we named AVIC entities that had demonstrated touch points to SWE's business. Signatures on related documents easily identified several. Control over AVIC subordinate units that had acted badly connected others.

**SF**: Realistically, how sanguine were you about one, prevailing, and two, collecting anything if you did? Did you expect AVIC, with all its resources—and I guess we should say threats, too—to take this seriously and try to prevail by outspending and outlasting you?

**PJ**: At the time, I saw four major battle areas: Did AVIC breach our agreement? If it breached, what damage did it do, or how much money did it owe us? If AVIC breached and owed us damages, who had legal responsibility to pay? And if we won all the above, where and how would we collect?

We also made four outcome assessments: proving AVIC's breach was highly likely; modeling the damages would be difficult; establishing payment responsibility was likely but required a lot of donkey work; identifying assets to collect against was the easiest of the four battle areas to win.

Later, to your point about AVIC outspending and outlasting us, they made me painfully aware of jurisdictional issues.

**SF**: They also made you aware that there were some personal risks.

**PJ**: Yes, frighteningly so.

**SF**: An October 9, 2023, editorial on the *China Daily* website carried the headline: "Thucydides' Trap not an inevitability as long as both sides handle ties with vision and wisdom." Do you agree?

**PJ**: Yes. Without repeating my Thucydides Trap analysis, which you can read in a *Dallas Morning News* piece from January 1, 2019, I'll say that often, and unfortunately, when the *China Daily* writes "both sides," it means that the other side needs to follow the CPC's vision and wisdom. Under Xi Jinping's policies, which threaten to return the welfare of the Chinese people to pre-Deng Xiaoping levels, China needs to develop its own vision and wisdom. We do, too.

## Chapter 14

# Overwhelmed by Lust

> Members of the panel, you all must perceive this case as complicated given the number of lawyers, given the number of parties, and certainly the number of motions and filings you have seen. I would submit to you that at its core it is not complicated.

**SF**: It's August 11, 2015. The lawyer whose words I have quoted above is your younger brother Bob. He's been providing counsel for several years regarding your dispute with AVIC. He now stands in front of the table he shares with you and your fellow claimants and their lawyers, delivering his opening statement in the matter of:

TANG ENERGY GROUP, LTD, in
its own capacity and on
behalf of SOARING WIND

ENERGY, LLC, THE NOLAN GROUP, ) et. al.

Claimants,

and

SOARING WIND ENERGY, LLC,

Intervenor,

vs.

CATIC USA, INC. a.k.a. AVIC
INTERNATIONAL USA, INC.,
GENERAL AIRCRAFT, CO., LTD.,
AVIC INTERNATIONAL HOLDING
CORPORATION, AVIC
INTERNATIONAL RENEWABLE
ENERGY CORP., ASCENDANT
RENEWABLE ENERGY CORP., CATIC
and Paul E. Thompson,
Respondents

This isn't your traditional civil proceeding in a courtroom with judge and jury. Rather, it's the arbitration hearing mandated by the SWE Agreement executed with AVIC some seven years earlier. You are in an upscale Dallas hotel ballroom, rented for the occasion. On a raised platform in front of Bob sit nine arbitrators—all men—in suits, not robes. Six were chosen by the claimants, and three were chosen by the opposition, aka the respondents. The fact that you were able to select twice as many arbitrators from a pool of Texas lawyers has already been a source of contention. AVIC and the other respondents will eventually take the matter to the US Supreme Court, which will rule in your favor because your agreement was quite clear.

Bob continues:

> This is a very simple case where the Aviation Industry of China, AVIC, made a couple of promises. First, it promised it would provide funding for wind power projects, but never funded a single project. It promised it would not compete with Soaring Wind and instead it started a new subsidiary and developed wind projects in direct competition with Soaring Wind. The promise is a simple one and is contained in the Soaring Wind agreement. The exclusive arrangement is unambiguous, and no one has disputed that it is ambiguous . . . So how did we get to arbitration?

Before we see how Bob answered his own question for the arbitrators, I have a few questions of my own. I think those of us who've come this far with you have a pretty good understanding of the relationships, ventures, agreements, overtures, disputes, evasions, alliances, breaches, losses, and threats that led you to *file* for arbitration. No need to rehash those. What's less clear is why this wasn't resolved without having to *go* to arbitration, which carries no promise of victory and can be very expensive. So, my questions: Did you want and expect this to be settled, or did you think you'd actually do better with a full hearing because the facts and law were clear, and it was on your home turf? Did you have a number in mind?

I have the same questions about AVIC: Do you think they wanted and expected this to be settled? The PRC has deep pockets. One of their lawyers had characterized you as a "flyspeck." They were the foreigners now, playing by your rules, which were to be applied by more arbitrators of your choosing than theirs. Why wouldn't they just pay you to make the matter go away?

Was there a good faith effort to settle, and did you come close?

**PJ**: First, each claimant and each respondent chose an arbitrator. There were more claimants than respondents. Then the arbitrators chose another to create an odd number. AVIC argued that the dispute had just two sides. AVIC and its subordinates appeared to hold that each "side" should choose one arbitrator and that those two would choose a third arbitrator to prevent a legal stalemate. But there was no wiggle room; we had to use the framework the SWE Agreement specified. US courts upheld the process that gave every claimant and respondent a position in the process that led to selecting nine arbitrators.

Second, the Supreme Court of the United States supported our interpretation in a very legalese way—it declined to consider AVIC's petition to throw out our legal argument.

On to costs: Early on, AVIC got comfortable foisting arbitration costs on us. They simply refused to pay. That changed when AVIC wanted to file counterclaims. American Arbitration Association (AAA) rules require parties wanting to file claims or counterclaims to pay their share of AAA charges. From an initial estimate of $500,000 for arbitration, costs quickly ballooned into the millions of dollars.

Because those numbers are so big, let's look at just the lunches for five days of arbitration trial. Lunch for nine arbitrators alone at a hotel that could accommodate the proceeding cost about $2,500, just for food. Add another $7,500 of lunch money for our lawyers, claimants, and experts.

The arbitrators, claimants, respondents, and their retinues couldn't share a room for lunch. No, we had to pay for separate rooms for each to meet outside of the big arbitration room that held the platform for arbitrators, tables for lawyers, seats for the parties involved, experts, court reporters, others who supported trial or arbitration proceedings, and two separate coffee stations.

All the arbitrators were lawyers, and, unlike judges, they charge hourly fees for conducting the proceedings—even for their time eating lunch while discussing the arbitration proceeding. Add another $25,000 just for their time while eating lunch.

Regarding dispute amounts, legal guidance on damages outweighed commercial perspectives, so yes, we sought $7.4 billion. Spoiler alert: While we could explain that amount, we blew it by seeking so much.

As for settling, we had been busting our backsides to settle for a few years. Not so AVIC, which, following Xi Jinping-thought, found support from the PRC for crushing us. To them, AVIC was the powerful one who could take what it wanted, and we were the powerless needing to suffer what we must. Thankfully, US institutions and capital markets gird the powerless to confront the powerful through a tortuously grinding process.

**SF**: Do you remember how Bob answered his own question: "So how did we get to arbitration?"

**PJ**: He began, "I'm proud to say, it starts with my brother." Then he quoted an April 1, 2013, editorial I wrote for the *Wall Street Journal.* The arbitrators knew Bob as a former judge in Dallas courts, but they knew nothing about me. He wanted to establish my credibility—my bona fides and good standing in the community.

**SF**: Over the next half hour, Bob offered a history lesson that began with your first venture with AVIC in Gansu, continued with the creation of HT Blade, and culminated in the SWE and Chicago Agreements, under which you were to partner on wind power projects, including wind farms, in the United States and abroad.

He then detailed your repeated efforts to engage AVIC in wind farm development and—at least in the claimants' opinion—their repeated failure to honor the agreements. He placed a lot of the blame on two high-ranking AVIC functionaries, Wu Guangquan and Xu Hang. Bob explained that from that first dinner at the Royal China on, Wu, the newly appointed chairman of AVIC International, showed no interest in abiding by the commitments made by his predecessors.

And Xu, aka Mr. Shoe, who oversaw AVIC's wind power initiative, stonewalled you for years before finally revealing that AVIC had spent some $50 million on projects of its own while ignoring your entreaties. You and I have already discussed those in detail, so let's let the respondents respond.

Despite an apparent conflict of interest, Steve DeWolf represented Paul Thompson. Malcolm S. McNeil and David G. Bayles, from the large, powerful, DC-based law/lobbying firm Arent Fox, represented AVIC International USA, aka AVIC USA, formerly CATIC—the AVIC subordinate unit led by Sherman Zhang, which was a signatory to the SWE Agreement. Paul Ma Ming, the lawyer who had threatened you several months earlier at the lunch in Los Angeles, also represented this entity. I can see how his presence may have been disconcerting.

**PJ**: Actually, when I saw Ma, I walked right over to him as he was talking with Sherman and asked what we could do to settle. Both expressed hopefulness, but neither suggested a solution. I still worried about my safety. When we arrived at the hotel for rehearsing and testing our arguments in front of a mock panel of arbitrators, I noticed a fancy Mercedes to the left of the entrance. It had a license plate that identified it as a PRC consular car. Quite the coincidence, eh? This only added to the stress of the days leading up to the hearing, which had already kept me from eating and sleeping well.

**SF**: What did you do?

**PJ**: I called my newly appointed guardian angel at the local office of the FBI. The senior special agent asked me to send a photograph of the license plate, which I did. The response came quickly: "Thanks, we're on it." I had no idea what that meant, but felt a little better, and went into the hotel.

**SF**: Was that it?

**PJ**: No. I still don't know the full story. I gather the consular official had not followed protocol for leaving his sanctioned location. This gave the bureau more freedom to investigate the official's actions. The FBI works with local police to look for electronic devices and, when properly permitted by authorization or agreement, enter hotel rooms where they may find material that interests them. I don't know what the FBI found or what the consular official had been up to, but at the end of our session I saw the often dour senior special agent standing near an exit, looking at me with a grin that spread from ear to ear.

**SF**: Besides anxiety, what other emotions were you feeling? I can't help but think there must have been some sadness seeing your old friends and partners, Paul Thompson and Sherman Zhang, sitting just a few feet away at the respondents' table.

**PJ**: Bigger than butterflies, it felt like Paul Bunyan was rolling around in my gut and trying to shove his fist through my throat. It felt like the beginning of existential finality.

**SF**: It's impossible to read the transcript without sensing the acrimony that permeated the hearing each and every day. Yes, there was some polite, good ol' boy Texas lawyer talk. And yes, the chairman of the arbitration panel, a Dallas lawyer named Steven Aldous, did his best to inject humor into the proceedings when possible. But this was a bare knuckle fight from the beginning. In his opening statement, DeWolf characterized you as "overwhelmed by lust for money," and claimed that "greed overcame [your] scruples and [your] conscience."

McNeil took aim, as well, when stating the respondents' theory of the case:

> My client made the terrible mistake of signing an agreement with Soaring Wind, thinking that Patrick Jenevein was going to be one of those individuals that would help him on selling wind blade equipment in the United States.
>
> They play fast and loose with the terms in this case, and the fast and loose terms are that they engage in misdirection and miscommunication and misstatement. Because there's only one agreement here that my client has signed, and that one agreement is the Soaring Wind agreement.
>
> Now, under the Soaring Wind agreement, they highlight a bunch of words here. The real word that's important is worldwide marketing . . . .Obviously, the purpose of Soaring Wind was not to develop wind farms. The issue is that when we look at this case, everything that they have to tell you is based on innuendo, conjecture, hyperbole, and, yes, unfortunately that this case has really developed through the machinations of Patrick Jenevein trying to come here and seek a lottery win.

DeWolf spoke to your motive:

> [Patrick Jenevein] had this HT Blade factory. He had 25 percent through his company. He had grandiose ideas, going to be worth

$450 million. And we don't really know why but there was some dispute that happened in China, some dispute which happened which caused that value to go south. And what he did is he made a lawsuit out of Soaring Wind Energy to use an arbitration clause and sue in Dallas, Texas. He did not want to go to China for the HT Blade dispute. That's really what this case is about. It is a dispute about them trying to extract money from some AVIC entity because they're mad about what happened in China at the HT Blade factory.

What was your reaction to that?

**PJ**: The absurd assertions both disgusted and amused me: Disgusted me because I'd devoted time, which you never get back; talent, which erodes with age; and treasure—all in order to make good work in the PRC. Amused me because Steve, a precocious performer, was showing off for his client and also trying to sway the arbitrators. To keep his insults from distracting me, I recalled asking him, before the start of an earlier deposition, if he had gotten the tight, bright red jeans he was wearing from his wife's side of the closet!

It was also amusing that his clients' superior, AVIC, had established HT Blade's value. He was saying that his client had "grandiose ideas." It was also true that we had a compelling reason for a separate case in China. DeWolf, in effect, said so.

**SF**: I want to honor your brother and keep it simple. So here goes: Among the major points of contention, three are worth noting here:

One was whether both the SWE Agreement and the Chicago Agreement were binding (your position) or just the SWE Agreement (AVIC's position).

Two was whether the relevant agreement(s) included the development of wind farms, as opposed to only marketing and selling blades. The parties' respective positions were clear here.

And three was whether the various AVIC entities were all under the control of the "home office" or whether they acted independently of AVIC HQ. At the time of the hearing, AVIC HQ in Beijing had scores of subsidiaries/subordinate units, including respondents AVIC USA, AVIC IRE, and Ascendant, the company Paul worked for, which you alleged was in direct competition with SWE.

If these entities were independent, then AVIC HQ could wash its hands of the matter. You certainly didn't want that, and thus one of the major reasons for recording Paul and Sherman was to establish the single entity theory. McNeil argued that AVIC was no monolith:

> What's happened is that the case has truly been cobbled together. [The Claimants] picked up probably 80 or 90 facts out of the universe of facts to try and say therefore there is a monolith in China and this monolith in China controls every single entity's acts and directions and control and officers . . .

Your brother spent a good deal of time addressing this issue in his opening statement, including showing the organizational chart included in the Corporate Legend.

It's rare that the public can go behind the closed doors of an arbitration hearing; privacy is a major reason why parties opt for arbitration, as opposed to a court proceeding. In this case, as we'll see later, you were committed to transparency, one might even say *exposure*. We can delve into that later.

For now, I can say I was able to access over 28,000 pages related to the case. As a result, I can also say it's clear each side went to great expense to prove whether AVIC should or should not be regarded as a single entity. The arbitration panel would eventually rule on this. Let's keep our readers in suspense on that decision, while sparing them from the particulars of the opposing theories.

**PJ:** Our global settlement agreement, filed in the California court that handled AVIC International USA's bankruptcy some years later, limits what I can discuss. However, I can provide the following observations: DeWolf, arguing for Paul, and McNeil, arguing for AVIC, wanted to attack jurisdiction for the arbitration and subsequent litigation. AVIC wanted the case in its sandbox, the PRC. Remember how the PRC wound up treating money one of its subordinates stole as income, and taxing us for the amount of money stolen? AVIC knew its hierarchical superiors controlled not just taxing authorities, but also the people's courts in the PRC.

Losing that battle, AVIC wanted to win the argument that only Ascendant held the liability bag, or only Ascendant would carry financial responsibility for any of AVIC's bad acts. AVIC didn't want a loss to expose its billions of dollars in assets to forfeiture through litigation in Dallas. This issue falls under a legal concept called "alter ego." AVIC wanted the arbitrators and US courts to believe Ascendant worked entirely independently from its handlers in Beijing.

McNeil may have believed, and certainly wanted the panel to believe, that AVIC was no monolith. But AVIC, itself, believes it's part of the Communist Party monolith of China. AVIC knows the CPC controls AVIC and courts and taxing authorities and much more in China. The CPC sets directions and controls entities and people throughout the PRC and beyond. Common sense sees AVIC's organization as a unitary pillar.

**SF:** After the opening statements, your brother began his examination of that "lustful entrepreneur"—you. How did you feel as you took the stand?

**PJ:** Confident. We had done our homework. I knew we were strongest on what we most had to win, the alter ego factor in our battle. My family and friends backed me. I wore a tie my dear friend and constant champion, Roger Horchow, gave me.

**SF:** Your testimony was the centerpiece of the five-day hearing. It took place over the second half of the first day and virtually the entire second day and constitutes over 500 pages of the 1,700-page transcript of the proceeding. You were examined and cross-examined by Bob, lawyers for your fellow claimants, lawyers for AVIC and Paul Thompson, and several of the arbitrators. We'll get to the highlights in a moment. But first, can you give me three adjectives that best describe the experience?

**PJ**: No. But a quick story can. My senior year in college, one of my housemates asked me to fill in for his club football teammate, a defensive back who had to take a music test. An hour or so later, I was wearing a helmet and pads, trying to stop an awesome running back who ran through our defensive line carrying seventy-five more pounds on his body than I had on mine. I must have tackled him ten of the twenty times he ran through the line. It hurt. Later, it hurt more. The questioning felt like that.

**SF**: Bob's first question to you summed up the importance of your testimony and the pressure you were under: "I think the panel will judge your credibility based on how you testify today. Are you ready?" And you answered?

**PJ**: "I am."

**SF**: After you quickly outlined the origins of your relationship with AVIC and the formation of HT Blade, you rebutted the respondents' assertion that your grievance with HT Blade was the "driving force" for this litigation. Bob then cut to the chase, asking you to explain why you'd formed SWE and whether it was solely for the purpose of marketing, as AVIC's lawyer had suggested.

**PJ**: As you and I have previously discussed, HT Blade needed to build a profitable relationship with an international wind farm developer that specified it would use blades made by HT Blade. SWE became that developer. The SWE Agreement was explicit about that.

**SF**: After you described how AVIC wanted to participate once it learned of your plans to establish SWE, Bob asked you about the MOU, signed in January of 2008. He wanted to know why, for the first time in your career, you would sign a noncompete clause with AVIC, and how you felt after signing.

**PJ**: AVIC had committed $600 million to SWE. We could use that money to develop wind farms. Once developed, we could finance a wind farm for construction and return development expenses with a strong profit margin to SWE. With our team and that investment, we could compete around the world. I could end my career there.

**SF**: To refresh our memory here, after the MOU was signed, the SWE Agreement became effective in June 2008, and was signed in May 2009. Then came the Chicago Agreement, which outlined the $600 million AVIC would be investing. You acknowledged the agreement didn't specifically mention SWE, but rebutted AVIC's claim that SWE wasn't tied to this particular agreement, which was signed in April 2009.

**PJ**: Yes. We had to start without AVIC's promised financing. We had made promises earlier, and we were keeping those promises. We believed in our plan, in ourselves, and in our partners. Xu Hang told us we needed the Chicago Agreement to meet approval requirements for moving US dollars out of China. He even wrote the Chicago Agreement—in English.

**SF**: We can see how Bob is building the case here. First the history with AVIC, then the agreements. And now on to the projects you brought them—Flat Water and Corpus Christi—and their response.

**PJ**: Several folks from AVIC wanted SWE to succeed. Several encouraged us to keep working, to keep bringing good projects to them. AVIC loved our work. We made them look good. Perhaps we made wind farm development look easy. Xu Hang once said he learned more from me at a lunch than he had in two weeks of study about developing wind farms. Nevertheless, we could barely get an answer from AVIC, much less a commitment on those projects.

**SF**: I think your exchange with Bob regarding Flat Water was telling. You acknowledged selling it for a profit but said you would have liked to hold onto it longer. Indeed, you said the fact that you sold it "pissed off" your other partners. So why sell?

**PJ**: If I can quote from the transcript:

> Because AVIC had not participated with us and we thought we were in the business to participate exclusively with AVIC. So when they did not participate in the project, we felt like we had to sell it. We could have held it. I would have loved to have held it.

**SF**: Bob's direct examination went on for some time. I want to note some of the important points you made before we turn to your cross-examination by DeWolf and McNeil.

At the end of 2010, when you heard AVIC was creating AVIC IRE to go into the renewable energy business, you were, you told Bob:

> . . . quite pleased because here they were telling me that they're going to bring more resources and going to pay more attention to meet our objectives. One of my problems was I couldn't get a response. I mean, we keep pounding on AVIC by e-mails, by phone calls, by trips to China saying, "You know, come on. We need to catch up. We're bringing all these projects."

As you entered 2011, you felt "very positive" about your relationship with AVIC, and you felt even better when you learned AVIC had created Ascendant and it would be headed by Paul Thompson. You told the arbitrators:

> I thought it was great. Paul is somebody that I talked to almost daily, either by phone or by e-mail. Paul was somebody that would return my call, and, frankly, if Paul was going to stay up late into the night to talk to folks in China, that was a burden off of my shoulders.

Of course, at that time you didn't realize Ascendant was going to be a competitor.

**PJ**: Correct.

**SF**: Bob continues to take you on this journey year by year. That was 2011. We can sum up 2012 with this exchange:

> Bob: How did the business of Soaring Wind change as you rolled into 2012?
>
> Patrick: We told AVIC that we can't keep leading the wind farm development like we had been leading it. We'd already spent pretty close to $50 million on trying to bring projects to them. We couldn't keep doing that. They knew that—and they clearly didn't respond to us. So they said they would take the lead, that they would do more to develop the projects and that they would let us know what we could do specifically for bringing Power Purchase Agreements, for bringing tax equity, for bringing project finance structuring that we knew a lot about.
>
> Bob: When Paul Thompson and Steve DeWolf generated some positive press on the Cirrus project, how did you react?
>
> Patrick: I was thrilled. I thought that was an indication that we were moving forward. And even at the time Paul Thompson was saying, you know, "We still need your help on getting a Power Purchase Agreement for that project."

You explain that nothing came of this, however, and you got no response in 2013 when you brought another potential Texas project, Spinning Star Energy, to their attention.

We can see Bob is stressing that you kept trying to engage AVIC and were getting nowhere. And then we get that November 2013 bombshell email from Xu Hang, in which he says AVIC has invested $50 million in projects in the United States. Bob says: "All right, Patrick, when you got this e-mail, what did it mean to you?"

There's a long pause before your brother says: "It's okay. Take your time. Take a breath. They need to hear your answer." Take us there, please.

**PJ**: That email is when I really knew AVIC, with all the help it could get from the CPC and the PRC treasury, was trying to crush us. Before that, the dispute seemed commercial. At that moment, I realized it was existential. Yes, it was emotional. I had invested some of my life's most productive years with an outfit, the CPC, that cared nothing for anyone's life or career except to the extent that that life advanced the party's possibilities.

**SF**: And you finally answer, "That's when you know they're taking it all." That is heavy. I know you had previously gone over your testimony in anticipation of the hearing. This doesn't seem studied.

**PJ**: It wasn't. You asked earlier how I had answered, "Are you ready." I answered, "I am." As it turned out, I only thought I was. Bob's question culminated in my realization like an unexpected gut punch. Indeed, the CPC was taking everything it could—money, time, blood, sweat, tears.

**SF**:

> Bob: So in five years you hadn't developed a wind farm. Why hadn't you personally—you had the expertise. Why didn't you go out and develop a wind farm in those five years? What kept you from doing that?"
>
> Patrick: My commitment to my partner.
>
> Bob: How did your focus change?
>
> Patrick: To trying to figure out what the hell happened.

Bob's examination concluded with discussion of the recordings of Paul and Sherman, and then a discussion of your calculation of the damages you were seeking—more than $7 billion. The vast majority of this was what is called "expectation damages." These were calculated based on the fact that if SWE had proceeded as planned—a wind farm usually lasts for twenty-five years—the income would have been in the billions.

The amount also included $55 million in reliance damages—money Tang had invested in reliance on AVIC's promise and agreements, seeding the business you had agreed to build together. Also, there's a figure that jumped out at me: some $3 million Tang had advanced just to try the case—almost $800,000 in attorneys' fees to date, hundreds of thousands more on preparation of exhibits, etc., and a considerable sum on security.

**PJ:** Those are all commercial factors. None address the years AVIC and the CPC took away, which we'll never get back.

**SF:** When Bob finished, he used a term that to those outside the profession might seem a little discomfiting: "Pass the witness."

**PJ**: Yes. He was passing me over to questioning by AVIC's lawyers. I expected highly personalized attacks.

**SF**: If I were to use three adjectives to discuss the cross-examination by DeWolf and McNeil, they'd be: contentious, fiery, and insulting. But to be fair, they raised some legitimate points. DeWolf, for example, asked if you could have withdrawn your initial $350,000 SWE investment and just walked away. He questioned how you could ask for damages having made money on Flat Water and Corpus Christi. He asked why you did business with other AVIC entities in the midst of this dispute. He suggested that another entity—Prax Capital—was funding this lawsuit for you, characterizing it as a scam, a "Shanghai Shuffle." He said the agreements specifically limited the amount of damages you could seek, and asked if AVIC and Ascendant had the same officers.

**PJ**: Wearing his other hat—entrepreneur—DeWolf may have wanted his own access to AVIC's $600 million commitment to fund wind farms. Sure, he could color events as if they contradicted my position. As a litigator, he spins yarns for a living. He could not, however, change the truth. The truth left him with few choices.

Steven Aldous, chairman of the arbitration panel, looked askance at DeWolf's fact twisting and context bending. Prax Capital, a Spanish private equity firm, had invested in Tang's Hong Kong company that directly held the investment in HT Blade. Prax had nothing to do with Tang forming SWE. DeWolf fabricated his assertion that Prax was funding litigation expenses. Bob summarized the Prax fiction well, saying, "This is the biggest example of a nonissue that there is in this case."

**SF**: DeWolf did seem to score by presenting an email from SWE's CEO to Paul Thompson:

> DeWolf: Now, isn't it true, sir, that at some point the real business purpose of Soaring Wind Energy was just to sell wind turbines and blades, not wind farm development?
>
> Patrick: Never was—that was never true.
>
> DeWolf: . . . talking to Paul and he says, "I've spoken with Patrick about our conversation. We agreed on the following. SWE's main concern is to sell turbines." And then it says in the last bullet, it says, "If we run across a project that requires us to spend money for development or purchase a partially completed project, that would be beyond the scope of Soaring Wind Energy's—that would be beyond Soaring Wind's scope and financial resources. You should pass these on to Patrick if he has an interest." Do you see that, sir?
>
> Patrick: I see that.

**SF**: Then he just moves on. Am I wrong that he scored there?

**PJ**: He may have scored. We ran a good shop and worked a good plan. As hard as we worked, we were never perfect. In the end, we scored more wins than losses—a clear way to measure even US foreign policy relative to the CPC-PRC.

**SF**: It seems like the tension was building, or perhaps friction is a better word. A few examples:

> DeWolf: Isn't it true that since Soaring Wind came into existence you have had disputes with most of the folks you've worked with?
>
> Patrick: No, I would not agree with that.

And:

> DeWolf: Isn't it true that while Tang was a member of Soaring Wind, Tang made multiple presentations to companies trying to do wind projects and never said it was part of Soaring Wind or the—under the reservation of Soaring Wind or under the auspices of Soaring Wind?
>
> Patrick: I don't think that's true. But I'm having a hard time understanding your—the construction of your sentence. So I can tell you that I—we talked to several companies. We were looking for wind projects all around the world. We talked about our relationship with AVIC and the exclusivity thereof, which was one of the reasons why companies talked to us.

And finally:

> DeWolf: So, sir, we're getting down to the end of my questions for you. Isn't it true that the reason why you have brought this lawsuit is because you want to get back at AVIC because of the HT Blade dispute?
>
> Patrick: Absolutely not.
>
> DeWolf: Now—
>
> Patrick: I don't even understand the question, but it's certainly not true.

**PJ**: At times, I could tell DeWolf's antics were impressing the panel . . . unfavorably. One of his questions started with something about how I had "extrolled" Chinese virtues. For a moment, I thought about asking him if that was the word for trolls coming out from under a bridge. I kept the humor to myself. Today, I think Aldous may have welcomed the comic relief.

**SF**: There was no love lost between you and AVIC's lawyer, Malcolm McNeil, either. His thrust was to negate the notion that AVIC was a single entity and to suggest the Chicago Agreement was nonbinding. I could cite numerous portions of your back and forth, but let me single out two—one substantive and one to highlight the tone of his cross-examination. I'll start with the substantive:

> McNeil: You never spoke to a lawyer about drafting an agreement to be the finalized agreement whereby $300 million would be transferred to Tang, did you?
>
> Patrick: No, that's not quite true.
>
> McNeil: You didn't talk to Xu Hang about changing the signature lines on the agreement from Tang Energy to Soaring Wind, did you?
>
> Patrick: I did talk to him about that.
>
> McNeil: Why didn't you cross that out and put in Soaring Wind instead of Tang?
>
> Patrick: Because Xu Hang explained to me that the preliminary agreement for funding was a document that had to conform with the Ministry of Commerce's expectations to be able to get not just cash but get dollars, US dollars, out of China's treasury and move it into a facility that we could spend on developing wind farms in the United States.
>
> McNeil: So it's your testimony, you're expecting the panel to believe, that China suggested that they would want you to—or they would

transfer $300 million to an entity called Tang Energy Group, which isn't owned by any Chinese partner, and that comports with Chinese law more than Soaring Wind, which has a 50 percent partner and an AVIC subsidiary? Is that what you're telling us?

Patrick: You said so many things there, I don't know what the question is.

McNeil: I withdraw the question.

And now the snark:

McNeil: Did you know that in your deposition there were 88 separate places where you say, "I don't know, I don't recall, I don't know if I did, and I may have"? Did you have any opportunity to tally those up?

Patrick: I did not take time to tally my "I don't know" answers.

**PJ**: AVIC had very few facts to support its positions on substantive issues. If facts were music on vinyl, DeWolf and McNeil danced to a scratched-up record.

**SF**: Again, we could spend a long time going over Bob's redirect examination of you that followed. I recommend interested readers find the transcript of the second day of the hearing. I'll note two exchanges. In the first, Bob attempts to rebut the respondents' argument that the agreements had more to do with Tang than SWE. There was the question of whether you'd misspoken; he wanted to clean that up and, showing his impatience, keep you on point:

Bob: Okay. I'm not suggesting that Tang doesn't have interest worth protecting, but this agreement protects the interest of what company?

Patrick: Of Soaring Wind. It's absolutely Soaring Wind.

Bob: And if I wasn't your brother, I wouldn't yell at you like that.

At which point, Chairman Aldous interjects with the humor and command he demonstrated throughout the proceedings: "If you weren't his brother, I wouldn't let you."

**PJ:** I was also exhausted and should have asked for a break. I had lost context. Bob recovered well. Aldous assessed my condition and the environment well.

**SF**: The second exchange I want to highlight dealt more with personal attacks from the opposing lawyers:

> Bob: Patrick, you have—Steve DeWolf put you through a litany of what a bad guy you are . . . .Do you have an estimate of how many pages of documents you have produced in this case?
>
> Patrick: About 100,000.
>
> Bob: And over what period—how many years of your business activity does that include?
>
> Patrick: I think that's just . . . the past seven or eight years.
>
> Bob: In that period of time, and you were—your attention was drawn to some we'll call them disputes. I don't want to use a controversial term. But of those disputes how many times did you or your company get sued as a result of that dispute?
>
> Patrick: I can't think of a single time when we've been sued.
>
> Bob: Let's assume that on every dispute that Mr. DeWolf talked about and on 50 more that he didn't talk about, let's assume you were a bad guy, let's assume you got sued and let's assume you lost. Does that change whether or not AVIC promised not to compete with you?
>
> Patrick: It does not change that.

Bob: Does that change whether or not AVIC competed with you?

Patrick: No. AVIC did compete with us.

Bob: You guess that's the best they got? You know, scratch that.

**PJ:** We had worked hard and honestly. We had believed in our partners. As the saying goes, lawsuits are not tea parties. They are battles. If you're the face of a business in litigation, expect personal attacks.

**SF**: I'll get you off the witness stand shortly, I promise. But I want to point out that you were asked several questions by members of the arbitration panel, as well. I'd like to note two significant exchanges. This first one—about reliance damages—was with Gregory Shamoun, a Dallas lawyer:

Shamoun: I think I heard you correctly, you would not have spent that money had it not been for oral representations by who?

Patrick: By AVIC. We would not have spent that money if we didn't have the Soaring Wind Agreement, if we didn't have the Chicago Agreement and if we hadn't had encouragement after those agreements to go bring projects. One of our jobs was to bring deal flow to Soaring Wind.

Shamoun: So do you believe based upon the provisions in the Soaring Wind Agreement that AVIC was required to fund?

Patrick: I don't think that they were required to fund. If we brought a project that didn't meet their criteria, no, we couldn't force them to invest. We brought projects that met their criteria and they didn't invest in those. The real damages are the projects that they did do without us.

Shamoun: I just wanted to know whether or not you believed, in your understanding of the Soaring Wind Agreement, that AVIC or CATG (another AVIC-related company) was required to fund these reliance damages?

Patrick: You're going to answer that question better than I can, I'm sure, but, yes, I felt like they were required to invest in the projects that met the criteria that we had agreed on.

Exchange number two has Aldous returning to that telling email:

Aldous: This is an email from Mr. Xu?

Patrick: Yes.

Aldous: [Did] any of the $50 million that was referred here in this go through Soaring Wind?

Patrick: None of it did.

**PJ:** All the arbitrators are lawyers. Perhaps I should be by now, but I'm not. Their questions seemed to drill down on very specific facts that touched fine points of law.

**SF**: We've talked about reliance damages and the like, which arise in a dispute like this, but there's also the incalculable damage that's done to relationships. In this case, your relationships with Paul Thompson and Sherman took big hits. Paul testified that he had to go on antidepressants as a result of the litigation and gained forty pounds. He used the abbreviations for the words bullshit and chickenshit to refer to your conduct and claimed you had "betrayed" him. Ironic, considering the circumstances.

**PJ**: AVIC corralled Paul into the Communist Party's lair. They stopped paying into SWE, which provided Paul's payroll, and started paying him through Ascendant. When dispute resolution began, AVIC then forced Paul into choosing between AVIC and Tang. Talk about being stuck between a rock and hard place. Taking AVIC's side as a respondent in arbitration, Paul could continue his payroll. Joining Tang as a claimant, he may take a moral high road, but with only potential financial reward.

I don't like it, but I understand Paul wanting to blame me. Understandably, too, Paul fears AVIC. A keen observer, Bob suggested Paul's duress was tied to having told the truth about AVIC in our candid, prelitigation discussions. Back then, when he was free of stress, Paul conversed genuinely. Did AVIC get to him?

I'm jumping ahead here, but our big win on alter ego suggests the arbitration panel found Paul's conversations with me in a relaxed atmosphere more credible than his recanting under AVIC's glare.

**SF**: Under direct examination from his attorney, Sherman testified in similar fashion to Paul. He focused more on the fact that he'd been recorded without knowing it and felt betrayed, rather than on the words he had actually spoken. Then under cross-examination by Matt Bracy, the lawyer for another claimant, Sherman tried to distance himself from several of the incriminating things he said—namely, that AVIC subsidiaries were required to invest in other subsidiaries even when they didn't want to—as well as Xu Hang's assertion that as president of AVIC, Sherman was expected to provide support and assistance to the entire AVIC group. In other words, Sherman was pushing back on the single entity theory. I think Bracy won this one:

> Bracy: So when you were speaking to Patrick Jenevein and you were being recorded and you said, "For the others we like to invest some business, but the meantime we have to invest something our brother-sister company, you know, in the tier one, we don't want to," were you telling the truth?
>
> Sherman: That's why I just say fool around the conversation, the whole story is Patrick complain his partner in this and there. I just follow. I just replied, you know, to comfort him. That's definitely the situation. He come on this and that, I say, "Oh, yeah, they do this and do that." That's not—it's follow the conversation with Patrick.

**PJ**: Perhaps I should work on my sensitivity; I failed to perceive the comfort that Paul and Sherman say they were trying to provide. Both knew, as Paul

Ma had said, that AVIC had messed up. Sherman's reference to a "tier one" company at AVIC suggests alter ego relationships among the "brother-sister" companies.

**SF**: David Denney, another claimant's lawyer, also got—if I may use the words of AVIC's lawyer—the "Shanghai Shuffle" from Sherman when he showed him a particular photo.

**PJ**: Quite the showman, DeWolf risked insulting his client with the term "Shanghai Shuffle." The term denigrates both Shanghai and the people from there. DeWolf was representing companies with assets and personnel from Shanghai.

Denney's thrust falls into the "cute" category. Perhaps he wanted to add color, but he took precious time. He was following up on Sherman's earlier deposition, which Bob was leading, where Sherman denied knowing what A-V-I-C meant. Bob then asked, "How about the A-V-I-C on your lapel pin." That was an amusing moment, but reliving it helped no one. Interestingly, when I was visiting AVIC in China, subtle differences in AVIC lapel pins could indicate hierarchical positions corresponding to PLA ranks.

**SF**: One final question about Sherman. You've previously noted your respect and affection for him, and that was clear in the transcript of the recording you made. At the hearing, McNeil asked him if he still considered you a friend, and he said, "No." How did that make you feel?

**PJ**: It saddens me still. And it makes me think of all the bonds of trust that CPC actions destroy—especially within families. The party sows distrust that breaks relationships between spouses, even between parents and children.

**SF**: We come now to the fifth day of the hearing, when closing statements were made. In his, your brother returned to his original argument that this was a simple case—the parties entered into an agreement; one party didn't honor the agreement; the party that did honor the terms of the agreement suffered damages due to the action of the other party. He also noted AVIC's attempts to avoid arbitration—even though it was explicitly mandated by the agreement—and outlined numerous instances in which the opposition had failed to produce requested documents. He concluded: "It really comes down to this: Is there any justice for these Texas investors?"

Chief Arbitrator Aldous wrapped things up: "I feel like I love y'all so much, if I don't leave now, I may never leave." What did you feel like? What did you think when the hearing ended? Did you think there was going to be justice for the Texas investors? And what did you do after those five long days?

**PJ**: I felt wounded and worn out. AVIC had beaten me up with lies. We had neither time nor money to fight all their lies. But the beating had stopped. Walking out of the arbitration room, at the top of some stairs, my knees just about buckled. Several lawyers wanted to go drink. I went home and slept for four hours. When I got up, Kathy and I went to eat at a bar with an outside porch. Even though it was August in Texas, I wanted to sit in the setting sun. And we began our wait.

Our wait for the arbitrators' Final Award.

# Chapter 15

## The Evidence Is Overwhelming

> The panel of arbitrators presided over the oral hearing of the above-referenced matter held in Dallas, Texas, on August 10–14, 2015. The parties submitted post-oral-hearing briefs and proposed findings of fact and conclusions of law. This Final Award includes findings of fact and conclusions of law as required by the contract between the parties, and is based upon the testimony and documentary evidence presented by the parties at the hearing and the evidence submitted to the panel subsequent to the hearing . . . . Having received and considered only the appropriate evidence, having read and considered the written arguments of counsel, having heard and considered the oral arguments of counsel, and having reviewed, considered and followed the applicable law, the undersigned now enter the following Final Award as majority decision:

**SF**: The arbitrators' decision was rendered on December 21, 2015, more than four months after the hearing ended. Were you on pins and needles waiting for it? How were you spending your time?

**PJ:** Heck, yeah. We didn't know when we might hear from the arbitrators or what they would say in the panel's final award. I figured we would win some positive amount and prevail in our alter ego argument, which would make AVIC in Beijing financially liable for any award. In line with Paul Ma's warning that AVIC would bleed our cash, we had spent more than ten times our original $500,000 budget. We had to find cash to continue the fight. While we waited for the arbitrators' decision, I had plenty to do to secure litigation finance for the rest of the battle and to nail down where and what AVIC assets we could attach for collection. The lawyers were saying, "Any day now." One lawyer speculated on an $800 million award. I tried to focus on what I could do, securing financial assistance to continue litigation and finding reachable AVIC assets. Those two efforts consumed my time.

**SF**: Let's keep our readers in suspense for a bit longer. How did you find out about the decision?

**PJ**: I think every lawyer for all the claimants sent emails at about the same time saying the arbitrators had sent out the Final Award. I started at the front, flipped forward in the PDF version to see AVIC headquarters' liability, then skipped to the damages. Decoding the various damage calculations took building an Excel spreadsheet. That showed about $63 million to $70 million, depending on whether AVIC chose to pay or lengthen litigation, which would add interest at 5 percent annually.

**SF**: The decision runs over thirty pages. The panel obviously did its homework. There are 140 "Findings of Fact," 41 "Conclusions of Law," and 12 "Awards as Follows." The Findings of Fact begin with a discussion of the structure of AVIC, the historical relationship between Tang and AVIC dating back to Gansu, and the fact that:

> In 2007, because of its successful investment in HT Blade and the development of several wind power projects, Tang, Jenevein, and some of its investors decided to create a business to develop wind farms and promote the sale of wind power equipment as part of the development. Out of this idea came the creation of Soaring Wind Energy. AVIC HQ expressed an interest in being part of Soaring Wind Energy.

Seeing the reference to the development of wind farms must have made you smile, as AVIC had strenuously insisted that SWE was only about selling turbine blades.

**PJ:** Ah, it cracked a wee smile. After the beat down of the arbitration, the substantive victories tasted sweet. The gut of the Final Award for me was the alter ego section, which established that AVIC—the whole darn outfit—owed us money. The second most important aspect was how much they owed us. The rest still matters because it provides the detailed legal analysis that supports who owes and how much they owe.

**SF**: The section titled "Single Business Enterprise/Alter Ego" begins as follows:

> The evidence overwhelmingly shows that AVIC HQ, AVIC International, AVIC IRE, AVIC TED, and Ascendant operated as one entity with respect to the MOU, SWE Agreement, and the Chicago Agreement. AVIC HQ exercised such complete control over the other entity Respondents in this case the AVIC Respondents operate as one entity.

This was supported by twenty-one more findings.

**PJ**: Yes. Dear to my heart was this one:

> AVIC HQ maintains clear ownership control over its subsidiaries, even when it allows other entities to own non-controlling interests. Even in situations where it does not own a controlling interest on its own, AVIC HQ uses subsidiaries to maintain control. As an example, AVIC HQ unilaterally decided that it should own a 25 percent interest in HT Blade. To make room for AVIC HQ's interest, its subsidiary shareholders, Baoding Huiyang Aviation Propeller Factory and China Aviation Industry Gas Turbine Power (Group) Company, simply relinquished the necessary percentage of their

> own interests without consideration. Subsequently, even though AVIC HQ was only a 25 percent owner, it appointed the Chairman of the Board of Directors for HT Blade. AVIC HQ caused HT Blade to pay Baoding Huiyang Aviation Propeller Co., Ltd. (an AVIC subsidiary) $8 million from HT Blade's account without the consent or approval of the shareholders of HT Blade so that Huiyang could meet its payroll.

**SF**: Toward the end of this section, the Final Award uses "AVIC HQ" to talk about AVIC headquarters in Beijing, and goes on to say:

> **AVIC HQ used its subsidiaries and its control over its subsidiaries to commit a fraud and work an injustice on Claimants.** [Emphasis added.] AVIC HQ dominated its subsidiaries in the transactions at issue in this case, namely, directing the establishment of SWE and the subsequent establishment of a new subsidiary (and its Texas-based subsidiary Ascendant) intended to compete directly and effectively against SWE. AVIC HQ and its wholly owned subsidiaries created additional subsidiaries in an attempt to get around its promises made in the SWE Agreement to Claimants.

**PJ**: I know you like baseball; this was a bases-loaded, three-runs-behind, bottom-of-the-ninth-inning-of-the-seventh-game-of-a-tied-World-Series home run.

**SF**: In the "traditional" civil trial most people are familiar with, the jury receives instructions from the judge on the pertinent laws or statutes, and then applies those to facts of the case in order to reach a verdict. The verdict may include damages. In an arbitration hearing like this one, the panel of arbitrators is the "trier of fact" *and* applies the law *and* determines damages.

By a 6-3 vote, your panel concluded you were indeed entitled to damages based on breaches to the SWE Agreement, but not the Chicago Agreement, which it concluded was a "preliminary agreement to agree between CATIC TED and Tang and therefore unenforceable as a breach of contract." This eliminated recovering any of the hundreds of millions of dollars the AVIC-related entity was to invest in wind power projects, including wind farms. Also denied was the request for damages you claimed, because AVIC entities . . .

> . . . accepted Tang's work product, specialized knowledge, relationships and expertise within the industry and then used that knowledge for their own benefit and to usurp corporate opportunities to the detriment of Soaring Wind, Tang and its other members.

Still, the panel awarded you a significant sum, writing:

> The present value of the return on the $50 USD million investment is what Claimants bargained for and only an award of some amount of these lost profits will put Claimants in the same position they would have occupied had the SWE Agreement not been breached by AVIC USA and its Affiliates.

**PJ**: Briefly, this told us that for winning the series, we could apply to AVIC to recover expenses, but no one would hand us a trophy. Before trial, lawyer Ma had warned us that AVIC would resist paying anything. During proceedings, bureaucrats from Beijing even wrote the panel denigrating our evidence. Recall the smoking gun email from Xu Hang, who the lawyers call "Shoe." The arbitrators accepted only that email as evidence of damage to SWE.

Recognizing that our experience would have made AVIC's $50 million investment worth more, the arbitration panel deduced a $63 million value from that investment. To that, the panel added about $7 million in expenses, including almost $4 million in attorneys' fees and $900,000 for the arbitration hearing. Additional damages depended on AVIC's decision to pay promptly or continue, as Paul Ma had threatened, to pursue actions through district court, the court of appeals, and the US Supreme Court.

**SF**: A big question now: What was your reaction to the panel's verdict?

**PJ**: Mostly relief that we could move on, that we could get to work on collecting the money owed us. The panel also divested AVIC of its interest in SWE, which widened our range of freedom to act.

**SF**: So, case closed, eh? You collected your millions and moved on to new adventures, right?

**PJ**: Ha! Steve, we would have loved that. We still have seven more years to go in this story before the case is closed. AVIC would try to fulfill Paul Ma's warning, but it failed to appreciate the foundation US law gave us to stand on and fight. It also underestimated our willingness to use that glorious platform, which allows the meek to fight the mighty. To AVIC, we were scrappy, sure, but we were far short of mighty. Little bitty Tang was determined to use the US legal platform to swing its bat at big ol' AVIC's shins.

# Chapter 16

# The Court Finds

> The Court has carefully reviewed the motions, responses, replies, the extensive record, the applicable law, and the arbitration award. The Court finds no grounds upon which it must vacate, modify, or correct the arbitration award as to Respondent AVIC USA. The Court must confirm the arbitration award against AVIC USA because the arbitrators' ruling as to the liability of AVIC USA "draws its essence" from the Soaring Wind Energy Agreement. Accordingly, the Court GRANTS Movants' Motion to Confirm Arbitration Award Against Respondent AVIC International USA, Inc. and DENIES Respondent AVIC USA's motion to vacate the arbitration award.

**SF**: The above is an excerpt from an opinion rendered on August 9, 2018, by Judge Ed Kinkeade, who sits on the district court in Dallas. He was ruling on a motion you and your fellow claimants in the arbitration proceeding had filed almost three years earlier, on December 21, 2015. We'll talk about what it means in a bit, but first, this begs several questions. Why on the very same day, in December of 2015, that the arbitrators awarded you some $70 million, did you feel it necessary to ask a *federal court* to uphold the judgment? This was the very forum the parties to the SWE Agreement deliberately circumvented in favor of *arbitration*. Did you have reason to believe AVIC wouldn't pay up—and by AVIC, I mean AVIC USA aka CATIC-USA? Your lawyers must have prepared this motion in anticipation of the judgment coming down in order to be able to file it immediately. Yes?

**PJ**: Yes, we drafted a motion to confirm the Final Award before the arbitrators issued it. Your head may hurt following all the "AVICs" and "CATICs " The CPC uses US laws and legal expectations to tie counterparties, juries, and judges in knots. Our win in litigation cut through the confusion and established that the whole Gordian knot of AVICs and CATICs that Tang and Soaring Wind litigated against were responsible for paying us. We took seriously Paul Ma's statement that AVIC would never pay until forced to do so. We read several signals from AVIC HQ as confirming its entire organization's intent, and because the CPC controls AVIC, we understood this as the CPC-PRC whole-of-government intent to undermine the dispute resolution process it had agreed to—and dodge the resulting award. The CPC's PRC Ministry of Justice had flouted Hague Convention obligations, which requires signatories including the People's Republic of China, to deliver legal documents in the PRC from other signatories to the Hague Convention, including the United States. Other PRC officials created and submitted new evidence but scoffed at subpoenas for us to cross-examine them.

Enforcing arbitration awards requires going to court. To avoid payment, we expected AVIC to strip subsidiaries of cash and move assets out of the United States. This included any vulnerable subsidiary, not just AVIC USA. For a refresher course on AVIC's character, remember the CPC used AVIC USA's immediate hierarchical superior, AVIC International Holding Corp. (AVIC IHC), to funnel cash to politicians in the Solomon Islands. Back to SWE: We needed to move quickly.

**SF**: Over two-and-a-half years went by before Judge Kinkeade issued his opinion, during which time some 360 motions and other documents were filed with the court. The most important and most time-consuming one—

besides your original motion that precipitated the action—was AVIC's "Motion to Vacate," filed a few months later than your "Motion to Confirm." This motion said, in essence, that the arbitration panel's decision should be thrown out. I don't know how to say "chutzpah" in Mandarin, but can you explain AVIC's argument here?

**PJ**: AVIC believed it could pull victory from defeat by outspending us. Broadly, for us to win, we had to prove proper jurisdiction, appropriateness of arbitration, AVIC's breach, value of damages, and responsibility for liability. AVIC could win by defeating us in any one of these areas, plus one more: forcing us to run out of cash to continue the fight.

AVIC knew its relative mightiness to our meekness, so it sought to outspend us. The Chinese defense contractor, AVIC, hired some of America's best known law firms: DLA Piper; Bracewell; Arent Fox; Dacheng Dentons (known as "Dentons"); the small Dallas firms Walters, Balido & Crain, as well as DeWolf; Connolly Gallagher (for two suits in Delaware); and, of course, the Law Offices of Paul Ming Ma.

These firms constructed superficially sophisticated arguments around issues that genuinely challenge legal scholars, like establishing jurisdiction, and what authority determines arbitrability. AVIC even alleged misconduct by the arbitration panel. Imagine nine lawyers, several of them former judges, acting improperly in front of each other and dozens of lawyers advocating for one party or another, on a case they knew would attract lots of attention in legal communities—all the way to the US Supreme Court.

To illustrate AVIC's willingness to use tenuous legal arguments for the sake of imposing costs on us, one of the lawyers at Dacheng Dentons adopted our argument when it mattered to him personally. You'll read more about Jinshu "Johnny" Zhang later. He argued against our position on arbitrability, then turned around and adopted it in a row with his own law firm. Interestingly, that spat threw some nasty testimony into US courts. Dacheng Dentons alleged that Johnny had exfiltrated client information to Beijing; in turn, Johnny claimed the firm had forged client documents.

Along the way, AVIC initiated two suits in Delaware, where we had formed SWE. As an SWE member AVIC sued us there using the twisted logic that we had not won enough money in the arbitration in Texas—against AVIC themselves!

**SF**: I also don't know how to say, "I'm not buying it" in Mandarin, but, in effect, that's what Judge Kinkeade said by finally granting your motion to confirm the arbitration panel's award and denying AVIC's "Motion to Vacate." Indeed, he called certain of AVIC's arguments "absurd."

Not surprisingly, AVIC appealed this decision to the Fifth Circuit Court of Appeals, which also ruled in your favor. AVIC, however, remained undaunted.

**PJ**: Yes. It then filed a writ of certiorari asking the US Supreme Court to review the decision. Among other questions, AVIC asked:

> Therefore should a court confirm an arbitration Award where an arbitration panel is selected with one side of the dispute electing a super majority of the panel through an **absurd** interpretation of the parties' agreement?

I've added the bold type there just to note how AVIC turned one of the words Judge Kinkeade used on its head.

We had tried our best to follow the dispute resolution process in the SWE Agreement. No one wanted the expense of fielding a panel of nine arbitrators. But that's what the words pointed to. AVIC said we were wrong, but it never said what the right interpretation was. Judge Kinkeade essentially ruled that the parties had a right to enter into an agreement, even an unclear agreement or, in retrospect, an agreement they wished was different after dispute resolution began.

The Fifth Circuit Court of Appeals affirmed Judge Kinkeade's ruling unanimously, 3-0 in our favor. And the appellate court, based in New Orleans, affirmed it in about thirty days that spanned the Christmas-New Year's holidays and included LSU winning a national collegiate football title.

AVIC's strategic decision to outspend us in money and time forced them into taking illogical legal, or tactical, positions. Speaking of absurdities: Sherman and AVIC USA pressed detectives in two separate California counties to bring criminal charges against me for recording our conversations. Then, they sued me personally in California civil courts.

Absurdity One: Sherman and AVIC USA claimed the arbitration award against AVIC and its subsidiaries, including AVIC USA, rested entirely on the recordings I made of conversations with Sherman. If the AAA Final Award had relied solely, 100 percent, on the recordings, the arbitration record would include only a small portion of its roughly 28,000 pages.

Absurdity Two: Sherman suffered no damage from the recordings. Sure, the litigation interfered with his routine work, but no award tagged him personally. Had I conducted the recordings improperly, which I did not, and had they caused AVIC USA damage, California law allows only natural persons like Sherman, and not incorporated companies like AVIC USA, to claim damages from improper recordings. AVIC USA had to contort the suit nonsensically to claim it was damaged, as if the corporation had actually been Sherman the natural person.

Absurdity Three: Get this. At the same time AVIC was trying to have California detectives arrest me, it was inviting me to China—where authorities had already levied a tax against Tang for an amount an AVIC subordinate unit had stolen from our joint venture, HT Blade.

See Image 10 for my reply.

Guardian Angel Coda: Based on my understanding, my guardian angel from the FBI called up Detective Cormack in Pomona, California, and Detective Malone in Fullerton, California, with a similar Socratic lead of turning answers into questions that went something like this: "Detective, this is Senior Special Agent Angel in Dallas. I've got a guy named Jenevein whose litigation against AVIC is opening wide a window on an important foreign actor. I see that you may have an unusual perspective on my guy. If it's the same guy named Patrick Jenevein, can you tell me if I should trust him, or if he's duping me?" Within days, both detectives terminated their criminal investigations.

Uncomfortably, AVIC then filed a civil action against me—for three times the Final Award amount—for the damage the recordings allegedly caused. It took lots of time and money to beat their abusively ridiculous claims.

**SF**: The Supreme Court denied the writ of certiorari in October 2020, meaning it refused to hear AVIC's appeal, meaning you won. Now you could finally collect, eh?

**PJ**: If only. It turns out that virtually simultaneously with Judge Kinkeade's 2018 ruling in our favor, AVIC USA started unloading many of its assets in the States. Imagine that!

**SF**: Yes, imagine that! How and when did you find out?

**PJ:** Sorry, Steve, I can't talk about how. I can tell you we read a lot. We learned that in the summer of 2019, AVIC USA transferred more than $20 million of proceeds from the sale of investments to enter into another joint venture. This wasn't for wind power in the United States, but rather for an infrastructure project in Africa.

**SF**: The old African infrastructure gambit. I'm guessing you didn't take that lying down.

**PJ**: No. We never did lie down. AVIC had been trying to knock us down for years. An aside may interest you: That transfer helped fulfill some of AVIC's obligations to support the PRC's OBOR strategic offensive. To your point, we went back to Judge Kinkeade, told him what AVIC USA was doing, and noted, "while acknowledging that its revenues for the last two years were more than $50 million, AVIC USA was left at that point with almost no valuable assets." *Tell AVIC USA to turn over whatever is left to the US Marshal*, we asked.

**SF**: Why the marshal? And what did the judge do?

**PJ**: I'm not a lawyer, so I'll answer as I understand. A US district court can order a party to turn over assets, but it cannot take, say, the keys to a pickup truck if that's what someone complying with a court's order has to turn over. The US Marshal, not the court, handles asset transfers.

AVIC wasn't complying with the court's orders. In August of 2020, Judge Kinkeade issued another opinion. And again, it was in our favor: **"The Court finds that AVIC USA has been transferring assets to avoid this Court's judgment."** That's a doozy. Federal judges expect parties to comply with the court's orders. Judge Kinkeade then ordered AVIC to surrender its remaining assets to a US Marshal.

**SF**: And?

**PJ**: It should come as no surprise to you that AVIC USA ignored the order. So, on September 28, 2020, we filed a "Motion for Order to Show Cause to Require Catic USA to Show Cause Why It Should Not Be Sanctioned or Held in Contempt."

**SF:** I'm guessing even this didn't do the trick.

**PJ:** That's right. Less than a month later—about the time the Supreme Court refused to hear AVIC's and AVIC USA's petitions—AVIC USA filed for Chapter 11 bankruptcy. "Any act to collect, assess, or recover a claim against the debtor that arose before the commencement of the case" must be stayed under the bankruptcy codes, our nemesis argued. Ditto any sanctions or finding of contempt.

I should add here that we had previously sought payment from AVIC HQ in Beijing, which, as the parent company, was clearly responsible for its "children's"—or subordinates'—conduct, and had more than enough to pay what had grown to $85 million thanks to interest ($77 million-plus to SWE and $7 million-plus to Tang), and would eventually grow to $100 million.

Judge Kinkeade placed a stay on this effort. After AVIC USA filed for bankruptcy, we sought to have the stay lifted, but the judge again denied our motion. While the bankruptcy created potential negative outcomes for AVIC USA, it suspended legal action in Judge Kinkeade's court, which imposed more costs in time and money on us.

**SF**: So now you were in bankruptcy court in California, home state of AVIC USA. I've looked at some of the documents from those proceedings. In August of 2021, bankruptcy court Judge Julia Brand said she would allow AVIC USA to convert to a Chapter 7 bankruptcy case if it couldn't reach deals with its creditors, including you.

According to the US Bankruptcy Code:

> A chapter 7 bankruptcy case does not involve the filing of a plan of repayment as in chapter 13. Instead, the bankruptcy trustee gathers and sells the debtor's nonexempt assets and uses the proceeds of such assets to pay holders of claims (creditors) in accordance with the provisions of the Bankruptcy Code.

Am I correct that you wanted to avoid that if at all possible?

**PJ**: No. The bankruptcy trustee would have access to the bankrupt company's files and records. It could even sue the company's chain of command, or the parties who caused the debts that drove AVIC USA into bankruptcy. This scenario appealed to me.

**SF**: The bankruptcy judge stayed this conversion to Chapter 7 pending settlement efforts. She noted these had been going on since February. That's six months. What exactly was going on?

**PJ**: At the beginning of that period, Lew LeClair, our lead lawyer after the arbitration hearing, had cornered AVIC. His work won jurisdictional and arbitrability arguments, the order for AVIC USA to turn over assets, the motion to show cause for why *not* to sanction AVIC, and more—all of which forced AVIC USA into bankruptcy. To escape this trap, Johnny Zhang, who later had the lawsuit with Dacheng Dentons, approached Lew with a settlement proposal. Lew let me know about AVIC's overture. I asked how much. He responded that Johnny had framed a range in the high six figures:

> Me: You mean maybe nine-hundred grand?
>
> Lew: Yeah, that's what Johnny said.
>
> Me: Tell him to pound sand.
>
> Lew: That's what I thought you'd say, but it's the first time ever in the years we've been on this case that we've heard any movement toward settlement.

Thus AVIC launched our litigation's final leg, unveiled our mutual exhaustion, and unleashed tensions among award beneficiaries.

We did begin with a "pound sand" response. Through Lew, we let AVIC know we considered a six-figure settlement worse than unrealistic, that it would be a waste of time to even consider it, and that it insulted our leadership in front of investors, but that—depending on terms and conditions—we might consider an eight-figure sum to settle.

To help with the expense of continuing our fight, we had turned to a litigation finance company for capital, collateralized by the proceeds we hoped to recover. Our litigation finance investor salivated at the opportunity to settle and grew increasingly impatient to do so. Johnny Zhang spooked them quite effectively during bankruptcy information-gathering sessions.

Because of COVID-19, we conducted deposition-like hearings over audio-only conference calls. Johnny cunningly exploited this accommodation. On those calls, he and Sherman would sit unseen in one place, while our bankruptcy lawyers, our team, and the litigation finance crew joined from far-flung locations. Although a job requirement for AVIC USA's position of president, which Sherman held, required English language proficiency, Sherman would only answer after he and Johnny discussed the question in Chinese. Then Sherman would answer in Chinese for Johnny to translate into English. The time it took to answer even simple questions exasperated us—and the court, too.

Many criticize litigation finance investors for funding lawsuits that wouldn't reach courts without them. In our brawl, AVIC could access the PRC's treasury, literally. Thank goodness, we could access free-world capital markets.

Still, our investor pushed for a return as soon as possible. Sickened by Johnny's shenanigans, they expressed their lack of enthusiasm for financing litigation through AVIC USA's bankruptcy liquidation. They had invested with us in 2016 and simply wanted out. I believed we could recover a high percentage of our judgment with more time, and by taking AVIC USA into liquidation. Still, I respected their position and allowed their influence to push us toward an earlier settlement.

Regarding influence, others have asked if Hunter Biden and Christopher Heinz's investment with AVIC in Henniges Automotive influenced our settlement decision. We had to think about it. Hunter and Chris held apparent paper gains of 200 times their investments. They exerted no control over the AVIC-led investment consortium and couldn't sell their interests without AVIC approval. Still, their investment with AVIC in assets we might seize compounded the complexity of an already fraught decision.

Back to the process. With the possibility of settlement, Judge Brand pushed us out of the court's bankruptcy protocol and into a client-to-lawyer-to-lawyer-to-client communication pattern. I represented the client on one end. Shrewdly, Johnny Zhang, for AVIC, drafted emails to Lew that I would have to summarize for our litigation financer and other partners. Possibly trained by the PRC's MSS, Johnny worked on isolating me like a cutting horse and cowboy isolate a cow from its herd. In his communications, Johnny increasingly twisted differences in terms into my personal failures to reach agreement.

In one communication, Johnny wrote:

> Everyone on AVIC's side is extremely disappointed at your revision, which has drastically changed the basic deal terms that had been there from the onset of our settlement negotiations dating back to last February. If you recall, both of you mentioned that your clients

> (Patrick Jenevein in particular) would be receptive to the final deal terms if there had been more money on the table.

Johnny's ravings acknowledged a tactic and confirmed a strategy. Through Lew, I let Johnny know AVIC could trade terms and conditions (T&Cs) for cash. The more cash AVIC paid, the more it could have the T&Cs it wanted. So, yes, I used changes in basic deal terms tactically to our benefit. His ravings confirmed our strategic patience would win both more money and better T&Cs.

Lew and I knew our good cop (him) and bad cop (me) strategy was working. In Chinese, the equivalent terms are "white face, black face" (白脸 and 黑脸). Johnny went on to say:

> Now that AVIC had tentatively agreed to a whopping 20 percent increase of the previously agreed settlement payment, you came back to seek fundamental changes of the deal terms. The leadership held its nose and finally approved the $24 million number based upon our promise of no major changes to the deal terms. Since you have moved the goalpost again, you may as well assume any approval we previously received has been nullified. Through your effective counseling, Patrick has succeeded, again, in embarrassing us in front of the leadership.

By the time we signed, we had protected our core interests; we got what we had to get. With more patience, we may have gotten more money.

**SF**: What was the impact of Judge Brand's decision to allow a Chapter 7 proceeding if you couldn't settle? Did it create an even greater sense of urgency?

**PJ**: For me, it brought a greater sense of calm. Finally, we controlled the schedule. We weren't waiting and wondering when and what an arbitration panel or a court might rule.

Isn't it interesting that American bias assumes the Chinese epitomize long-term perspectives and patience? Here, Lew had methodically maneuvered AVIC into the ambush it had impatiently set for itself. About a decade earlier, AVIC's short-term greed undercut not only its own, but other SOEs' abilities to collaborate with entities from the free world. It took a while—a long while—but AVIC felt the heat. They needed to settle—and quickly, before little bitty meek Tang Energy from Dallas wrenched mighty AVIC's subsidiary into liquidation, and before Tang placed a trustee into AVIC USA's chief executive position. Of our two available choices, settle or shove AVIC USA over its existential cliff, it was incumbent upon AVIC to make one choice more attractive to us.

Johnny, as his bluster ironically confirmed, knew this. He sought to inject a sense of urgency among the other settlement beneficiaries. And boy did he play his weak hand well.

Warning—this may sound a bit convoluted: The number of bankruptcy lawyers in the Los Angeles area, where AVIC USA filed for bankruptcy, ensures most of them know each other. Our litigation finance team hails from California and hired Robbin Itkin to answer to both of us, as she represented Tang and SWE in the bankruptcy.

Unknown to us, Robbin had worked with John Moe at another firm years earlier. Moe was now Johnny's partner at Dacheng Dentons. Johnny used the implied professional trust among lawyers, especially law firm partners, to create a daisy chain of back-channel communications based on their understanding of the law, and their comfort working together to reach a reasonable agreement. He would confide with Moe that non-lawyer Patrick Jenevein alone was holding up the settlement. Moe would confide with Itkin. She would confide in our litigation finance group, which was mostly composed of lawyers, and then with Lew.

To some extent, Johnny was right. However, decades of experience taught me—better than any of our lawyers—how to optimize benefits from negotiating with Communist Party-controlled entities. Lew got it, but Johnny played the field of lawyers brilliantly. He preyed on their pride—

their belief that they always knew what was best for their clients—just as if he had been trained in MSS recruitment methods.

Johnny was especially effective with a younger man who replaced a veteran at the litigation finance company. The old-timer and I had worked together for several years. We understood each other's strengths and weaknesses and made better decisions together because of it. For personal reasons, he abruptly left the company. The aggressiveness of his less-experienced replacement opened a vulnerability that Johnny exploited. Just as MSS plays on people's pride to bend their loyalties and capabilities to its purposes, so Johnny turned this man's trust against me. This dynamic disrupted our cohesion and impaired our position.

Johnny's "flyspeck" email to Lew shows off his tactic of isolating and blaming me, and shaping a sense of fear among others for not settling sooner:

> I feel and appreciate your sincerity in finalizing this settlement. However, you, the litigation funder and the other claimants should no longer indulge Patrick in his real or faked paranoid [sic]. In the grand scheme of things, Patrick is but a flyspeck on the Chinese radar screen and no one in his right mind wants to see Patrick's face ever again, let alone wasting money on legal fees to go after him. It is imperative that he deliver his laundry list of "pardonable" bad acts today. In any event, the breadth of the general release, which is EQUALLY applied to both sides, already adequately covers every possible liability, even at the risk of being overly verbose.
>
> I have been formally told by my clients to read the claimants the Riot Act: either the claimants sign the settlement agreement now or we will pull the plug and repatriate the deposit money. When the settlement breaks down, Patrick's fellow LLC members will have a claim of breach of fiduciary duty against him for torpedoing an exceedingly reasonable settlement offer. The litigation funder can sue him for breach of an implied covenant of good faith and fair dealing—a funded litigant cannot unreasonably hold out for a pie

in the sky on other people's nickel. Personally I start to feel tired of a thankless job and what increasingly appears to be a fool's errand.

Thank you!

So CPC threats continue. But "flyspeck?" As I told you earlier, I looked it up and learned it means more than just a fly-sized radar return. It means a speck of fly feces.

**SF**: Let's fast-forward some seven months. On March 10, 2022, Judge Brand approves the settlement you've reached with AVIC. Only—and I say this facetiously—six years and two months have passed since the arbitration panel ruled in your favor and awarded you about $70 million. Since then, some $15 million in interest has accrued. We're talking $85 million owed to you and your fellow claimants. While our readers already know the dollar amount of the settlement, please take us into the rooms where it happened. How did you finally reach an agreement?

**PJ**: Actually, by the time of settlement, the judgment receivable had reached about $100 million. How did we reach a settlement, you ask? In short, by knowing what we had to get, what the Communist Party feared and what it had to get, and by pressing them tenaciously.

As far as the rooms where it happened, they were virtual: emails and phone calls. The last phone call came late at night.

After years of litigation, we had run up financial obligations. Those weighed heavily on us. The years had also exhausted everyone's energy levels, AVIC included. I would have pressed further. A friend who was working in Washington, DC, at the time said, "Jenevein, you have battle fatigue. I know how to recognize it when I see it; you have battle fatigue." Kathy knew it, too.

What could have been the last call invaded our bedroom just before midnight. Lew had just gotten off the phone with Johnny. AVIC had agreed to all our changes, but wanted to add a paragraph limiting what we could talk about concerning the case—paragraph 9.5 in the global settlement agreement. AVIC's message was: Take or leave it. I chose to leave it. Ever thoughtful, Lew cautioned that that response killed the deal. I understood. Lew understood. We expected opposition from litigation finance. We agreed I would call our investors and he would call Johnny in the morning.

Sure enough, intense ire slammed us both. The next night became the final last call. Lew called and said, "Guess what?"

> Me: They caved.
>
> Lew: Not exactly, but they did agree to limit the remedies if you breach the settlement agreement.
>
> Me: Somehow that's not going to help me sleep tonight.

We went on to discuss wording and implications. It didn't take me long to agree. That was early February 2022. We wouldn't see a penny of the $24 million until late April.

**SF**: The settlement agreement states that "each AVIC Party hereby specifically denies it is an alter ego of AVIC USA or another AVIC Party, vicariously liable for any act or omission of another AVIC Party, or that its conduct can be imputed to another AVIC Party." I'm confused here, because according to the settlement agreement, AVIC IHC, AVIC USA's parent company, was going to be paying the $24 million. Also, you had consistently and successfully argued in front of the arbitration panel and the federal courts that AVIC USA was indeed an alter ego of AVIC IHC. Please help me understand.

**PJ:** You have it exactly right. Consistent with its habits, AVIC HQ in Beijing wanted to change history. The CPC rewrites history to suit its purposes. It even says that to manage the future, you must control today—which you do (in part) by commanding the past. The CPC does the latter by writing and rewriting official history. CPC-inflicted injustice and oppression have sown fear and taught the Chinese people to accept the party's declarations regardless of their absurdities.

AVIC and its lawyers cannot change the court record. They can deny it, and they can spin a yarn for their minders in Beijing that they did change it. But US legal institutions and practices prevent changing the record. You may have noticed that even AVIC's highest administrative unit signed the publicly filed settlement agreement.

**SF:** *Wall Street Journal* senior editorialist Jillian Kay Melchior wrote two excellent articles about the bankruptcy proceedings. Four days after Judge Brand approved the agreement, Melchior wrote:

> The settlement includes a commitment that the parties won't "use, disclose, reference, mention, or provide to third parties any of the expert reports produced or generated in any of the Covered Cases." But expert reports are in the public record as part of the long docket for the Texas litigation, and those court records include expert reports that map out the corporate relationships and intersections among various AVIC entities.
>
> Credit Mr. Jenevein for fighting AVIC and its subsidiaries for years in court and for getting the terms of this settlement in the public record. In 2012 a Michigan consulting company, Global Technology Inc., claimed AVIC and some of its subsidiaries had breached an agreement, unjustly enriched themselves, and engaged in "misrepresentation and/or silent fraud." In 2016, AVIC and Global Technology Inc. "agreed to resolve this matter," according to court documents. But the terms weren't public, and the owner of Global Technology Inc. declined to comment. ("A Legal Settlement Shows the Risks of Doing Business in China," March 14, 2022)

**SF**: Why was it important for you to make sure these records were accessible to the public? As an aside, I'd like to thank you; it certainly made my job easier.

**PJ**: Oh my—fear and hope. As hard as I fought, the CPC still feeds my own fears. It can cause disruption and, when it chooses, severe pain.

About a month after we dismissed all the lawsuits and collected dollars in Dallas, I received an unfriendly notice from the IRS. It read like an audit notice but didn't quite reach that level of scrutiny. Our outside accountants at BDO responded that, yes, the notice was legitimate. It requested information on transactions we had made in China years earlier. It went on to ask us to identify owners and investors. The United States and the PRC are parties to an agreement that helps governments gather information on possible tax dodgers. This should irritate you. The CPC was using US taxpayer-funded resources to let us know it could still upset our routines and impose costs upon us.

On the hope side, in winning against the CPC's biggest defense contractor, we demonstrated successful approaches and illuminated characteristics of its SOEs. What we showed can help other targets of CPC fear, injustice, and oppression. Those who came before us created the environment that allowed my generation to flourish beyond all means anyone on earth had ever enjoyed. I hope I've done even a little bit to tilt this world toward extending the frameworks that benefited me. Our settlement agreement clearly indicates the CPC's desire to limit the reach of our victory. Filing it publicly provides others with a guide to lessons learned.

**SF**: So, on March 10, 2022, it's finally over. How about three more adjectives to describe how you felt?

**PJ**: Relieved. Victorious. But dissatisfied. I would like to have done more to right wrongs, to collect more for unrecoverable time lost.

**SF**: And what did you do after getting the word?

**PJ**: Word came by email, anticlimactically. It all happened at electronically enabled and COVID-19 protocol-required distances. We gathered all the needed signatures through emails and then prepared and sequenced filings with the courts—Judge Brand's bankruptcy court in California and Judge Kinkeade's court in Texas. No one had gathered to sign and exchange documents or money.

Kathy and I shared a drink in our front yard, knowing I would sleep well that night. The years of fighting had tried and tired us. Then we waited. The courts took back schedule control. We waited for those processes to play out, then waited for the cash.

Over a month later, Kathy threw a celebration party—a hot dog barbecue in our front yard for the many friends who had lent us their strength during more than eight years of dispute. Kathy's notes explained the culinary selections: "HOT DOG! At least, it's over." "BUNS—We kicked their buns." "ARTICHOKE (There are a few we'd like to choke.) ☺" The most meaningful was "CHIPS—When the chips were down, you lifted us!" And a favorite: "ROTEL QUESO—GO TELL everyone a Texan won a case-o against the Communist Party of China!"

We drank Texas-made beer and French 75s, a champagne cocktail with a devastating punch. One thoughtful friend brought a whole bag of Chinese fortune cookies.

**SF**: How did you actually collect the money?

**PJ**: Wire transfers from AVIC to Dacheng Dentons, then to Lew's firm, McKool Smith, then to lawyers, financiers, and us.

**SF**: If you feel comfortable answering: When all was said and done—forgetting lost opportunities, all the anguish, and the like—with that $24 million were you made whole for the SWE expenses, and the legal expenses as well?

**PJ**: I can tell you the outcome pleased some and not others.

**SF**: The headline over Melchior's article stated: "A Legal Settlement Shows the Risks of Doing Business in China." And in her final paragraph, she wrote that the "legal record should serve as a warning to any American considering business with AVIC, its subsidiaries or other Chinese state-owned enterprises."

Very few people have as much experience in this area as you do—both in country and in litigation. In the epilogue that follows, and in the coda following the epilogue, you will address those risks and offer your counsel to readers, just as you currently do with government agencies and corporations through your strategic intelligence firm, Pointe Bello, LLC.

Before that, however, a final question: From the time you first set foot in China in 1995 to the time your case was finally settled in 2022—through the trips to the oil fields of Xinjiang, the pilot projects, the power plant by the Great Wall, the awareness that you were bringing power and electricity to those who had never enjoyed it, the use of cleaner energy technologies, the pivots occasioned by embassy bombings and aircraft collisions, the building of a blade business valued at almost $2 billion, the meals of cicadas and camel's feet and noodles, the consumption of *moutai* and Tsingtao, the times away from Kathy and the Whirlygigs, the friendships made and lost, the exhilaration of starting SWE, and the ups and downs of the fourteen years that followed, *would you do it all again*?

**PJ**: Yes, without reservation.

After a discussion regarding government business, a friend who was about to leave his job at the Pentagon turned back to me and asked, "Jenevein, you'll have an opinion on this. What's better to have, money or stories?" Without hesitation, I answered, "Stories. Hands down."

Yih-Min and I, with lots help from others and forbearance from our families, built a great business. We tasted riches. Then the party attacked. But the attack bared tactics, exposed strategies, and revealed intent. Our stories can prime others for the CPC challenge. We've got to tell those stories. It's an effort worthy of all our brawn, brains, and belief. Freedom lovers in many places can leverage what we learned.

Few have worked with as many wonderful people from such diverse cultures and professions as history offered me. Now, we see totalitarians rising around the world. They are spearing us with the existential trial of our time. Sure, I miss owning and flying my airplane, and having the choices that piles of money make possible. Still, I'd rather have the company of friends who love, pray, and act to protect and promote freedom.

# Epilogue

## We Are Chalking Up Wins

Johnny Zhang, AVIC's lead lawyer, helped end the last chapter of this book, and offers a peek at the next chapter in my life. In March 2021, speaking for AVIC—or MSS and the CPC—he noted:

> We are aware that Patrick Jenevein has been launching publicity campaigns to . . . peddle his service to go after the Chinese . . . by someone who still harbors a quixotic ambition to build an anti-China cottage industry.

Apparently, he was referring to our company, Pointe Bello, which strives to bring clarity to Communist Party predations and build strategies that attenuate its capacities to terrify, torture, and torment. Private corporations, nongovernmental organizations, US government agencies and military entities, and others desire and need strategic intelligence for their dealings in and with today's China. We do our best to provide that.

Johnny's jab is wrong, right, wrong, and interesting in its assessments. I *did not* launch a publicity campaign. Parts of the US government *did* find our fray with the sole supplier of military aircraft equipment to the PLA enlightening and paid for additional insights. I *do not* harbor any ambition to build an anti-China business, and while decidedly anti-Communist, I'm pro-Chinese people.

In fact, the drive to transform relationships among Americans and Chinese, and the longing to alleviate fear, injustice, and oppression pushed me to write this book with Steve. Not only has he made it possible to write this much, he's also made it worthwhile and fun.

The fact that Johnny's handlers devote resources to stay aware of my efforts indicates an aggravated level of concern. If Dallas's Tang Energy Group alone could clip the party's ambitions even a little, what could Americans do if we coordinated effective actions among ourselves, and with freedom lovers around the world?

Many talk about what we should do; far too few buck up the courage to push to change Communist Party behavior. Strategically, we should focus on two vulnerabilities: the party's appearance of legitimacy and its access to cash. Tactically, transparency fights the first, and disciplined investment fights the second. Both take work.

Today, I am channeling vim and vigor through Pointe Bello, and, based on the response of those with whom we consult, we are chalking up wins. Ironically, our success could help save the Communist Party from itself. As I write this, Xi Jinping and his political party are screaming for help. Their petulant piques threaten peace in the South China Sea and prosperity globally. Few in Washington, DC, recognize the PLA's bellicosity over Taiwan as a cry for help. Fewer understand how to take that temper and turn it into geopolitical relief.

Our political leadership follows brilliant writers, analysts, and observers who describe situations and trends well. However, the change agents America needs act more than they write, which makes them hard for government authorities to find. But find them we must.

Then, I can get back to finding the Chinese friends I miss.

I began this book with a question: "What can I tell you about the People's Republic of China?" I trust that by sharing my experiences and insights, I've helped increase your understanding of the PRC—including its leaders and people. But the journey isn't quite over. When we finished the preceding pages, Steve posed twenty-one more questions about today's China. These inquiries challenged me to articulate a great deal of thinking about dancing with a dragon who we cannot and must not ignore.

# Coda: Twenty-One Questions (and Answers!)

**1. Why should ordinary Americans care about China today?**

China's people offer prosperity while their governing party threatens destruction. Chinese people living in the PRC provide extraordinary opportunities for Americans. Their talents, discipline, perseverance, and more already help advance Americans' quality of life. Their scientific capabilities and discoveries alone, including the production of therapies and medicines, keep many alive and help many more thrive. Since the 1980s, their work has allowed Americans to work fewer hours to buy stuff, from cell phones to blue jeans.

The Communist Party, on the other hand, believes it should dictate trade and transportation terms around the world, without consultation, compromise or collaboration. It believes that might makes right, that the powerful can take what they want and the weak suffer what they must. That attitude manifests most frequently and painfully inside the PRC. There, the Communist Party combines advanced technologies with ancient ideologies to torture and oppress Chinese people. Increasingly, the party seeks to export that model internationally.

For the love of individual freedoms, Americans should care deeply, first, about the 1.4 billion souls in the PRC and, ultimately, about protecting the freedoms we often take for granted in the United States.

**2. What are three basic things Americans should know/understand about China today?**

One: The CPC created the PLA first (on August 1, 1927) and the PRC second (on October 1, 1949). The PLA pledges allegiance to the CPC, not to the PRC—not to "China," and not to the Chinese people. This means that neither the PRC nor China have a military. The current leading Chinese political party controls the only military inside the PRC. History teaches the vulnerable to fear military powers controlled by a single political party, especially single political parties controlled by individual totalitarian rulers.

Two: Communist China pushes extreme uses of imperialism over capitalism. Broadly, and especially before the US revolution, which presaged imperialists' more severe decline a century later, powers around the world use and have used imperialism—conquest, occupation, and domination—to secure resources tied to lands and seas. No comprehensive resource allocation system today is completely imperialistic or capitalistic. Like a dial, those systems turn more towards one or the other, but all include aspects of both. Some identify the Magna Carta of 1215 as the beginning of a long process to diminish imperial powers. Over time and after many wars, the appeal of capitalism's use of law to command resource supplies grew. Capitalism in its simplest ideal form, instead, uses laws to regulate access to resources. Most basically, capitalism's systems of laws allow money instead of blood to allocate resources. Sovereigns throughout history have used elements of imperialism and capitalism to advance their objectives. Former PRC Premier Zhu Rongji sought to adopt capitalism's respect for law to drive PRC growth and consequent CPC power. Xi Jinping's Communist Party eschews laws it cannot ignore, and chooses imperialistic means to control resources it wants. Hardcore imperialists like Xi hold on to imperial powers to exempt themselves from capitalism's laws.

Three: Dictatorships such as Xi Jinping's operate with brutalities that democracies often fail to anticipate or even recognize. Simple respect for individual rights supports democracies, which, though imperfect in execution, foundationally seek to protect people from political parties and other bullies. Dictatorships flip this priority upside down; they protect political and other elites from the people they rule. Xi Jinping's China mirrors its imperialist external oppression with domestic repression. It chooses to rule through fear, injustice, and oppression.

### 3. Why should ordinary Chinese people care about the Unites States today?

As the CPC removes guardrails that Deng Xiaoping (China's paramount leader from 1978 to 1989) put in place to protect people from the increasingly unchallenged, unchecked imaginations of a single individual, the safety and security of Chinese people depend on external factors, outside forces using their powers to keep the PRC on a path to prosperity. In times like these, the United States becomes their best hope.

One question helps make this point: *What happens when Xi Jinping dies?* Paramount leader Xi has no apparent succession plan. That raises the likelihood of fatal struggles to determine his replacement. A Mao Zedong-like succession struggle with aspirants to the position controlling some of the world's most fearsome arsenals could spill over the PRC's borders with the speed of hypersonic weapons. An earlier coup could limit the carnage.

The Chinese need capable US leadership as much as the Americans.

Xi's totalitarian controls fix in concrete the choices of Chinese people who remain in the PRC; their futures depend on external forces having the power to break them free. Chinese emigrants seeking academic, economic, intellectual, religious, or other freedoms already look to the United States for safety from oppression in the PRC.

### 4. What are three basic things Chinese people should know/ understand about the United States today?

One: Democracies look messy. Sometimes really messy. That messiness, however, reflects the real source of power for political leaders in the United States: the American people.

Two: Many Chinese already know or understand that the US political system tells the truth more reliably than the Communist Party. Telling the truth early and often makes communities strong. If they want China to become as sustainably strong as the United States, Chinese citizens should expect truth-telling from their governing political party. All national systems take time to find truths. All suffer through the processes of getting to truth. Those who get to the truth sooner prevail.

Three: Moving too close to the pride side of the pride-to-humility spectrum of national or cultural strengths blinds the Communist Party to other's strengths and its own weaknesses. A more respectful awareness of both US strengths and weaknesses can pave the way for more Chinese prosperity.

**5. Does either country pose an existential threat to the other?**

Yes, absolutely, in three ways: two forcefully, because they can occur quickly, and one insidiously, because it takes more time.

Militarily, the weapons caches of both could annihilate entire populations within hours. This threat waxes and wanes with leadership capabilities and commitments in both countries.

Economically, both countries depend upon each other to lift their quality of life. Borrowing a description from a smart, well-informed friend, we have created the capability of "mutually assured economic destruction." If the People's Bank of China, for example, sold a significant portion of the US Treasuries it owns, it could significantly raise the cost of borrowing for US national and local governments and for US businesses. Credit card debt rates could bury US households.

The bigger threat to both, however, lies in ideology. At their foundational levels, the systems collide diametrically. One seeks to protect individuals; the other seeks to protect a few elites. If ideas from the former enthuse Chinese souls, they will destroy the ruling party. Going the other way, if CPC behaviors corrupt US leaders, US citizens will suffer.

**6. Currently, what is the best/smartest US policy with respect to China?**

With strong caveats to follow, buying as much stuff as we can.

On personal levels, buying good stuff at cheap prices stretches American families' budgets. Making dollars go farther saves Americans time at work. Over the past forty years or so, buying more cell phones, blue jeans, computers, or boots from China has allowed Americans to work fewer hours to buy what they want.

On a national security level, trade imbalances—buying more stuff than we sell—set up currency imbalances that favor Americans. In this context, trade imbalances are not all bad. When we buy stuff, we sell dollars. Think of dollars as financial souvenirs. They are not bars of gold or buckets of diamonds.

Like a seesaw, when we buy more things than we sell, we sell more financial souvenirs than we buy. Selling more US currency, in turn, builds and holds significant strategic advantages. Broadly, over a much longer period of time than the life of the stuff we buy, we control the value of the financial tokens we sell. We use the boots we buy to work. Their value changes only as our work wears them out. The value of the dollars we send to others, however, changes because of fiscal and monetary policies the United States controls.

Think about US inflation alone. As it erodes the value of dollars, anyone holding them suffers the degradation in value. If people all over the world hold dollars, and the value of the dollar falls, then not just Americans suffer. On a more positive note, net sales of US currency help the dollar hold reserve currency status. That one privilege alone effectively adds about $3,000 or $4,000 every year to every person's net worth in the United States. That's a big number. Worldwide, anyone with more than $10,000 has broken a poverty barrier into the richest 47.5 percent of the world's population. Think of the three or four thousand dollars as a 30- to 40-percent head start on the rest of the world's population, like 30 to 40 yards in a 100-yard dash.

Caveats: Don't buy products from the PRC that put kill switches for US water and electricity supplies in the hands of the CPC. Mind your medical and military supply chains. US residents depend on PRC-manufactured antibiotics, diabetes medication, and more in the medical realm. A relatively small outbreak of an engineered pathogen, for example, could wipe out the US inventory of saline bags and tubes that hydrate patients suffering dysentery. Militarily, some US weapons systems do not work without components made in the PRC. Governmental bodies cannot handle it all.

### 7. What is the worst US policy with respect to China?

Some good friends with National Security Council tours under their belts argue that the United States should "decouple" economically from the PRC. They want us to rip out roots that PRC entities have in the United States, and US entities to rip out their investments in the PRC. We respectfully and constructively disagree. Government-dictated decoupling will look like the government-directed withdrawal from Kabul, Afghanistan.

Many businesses already understand the range of threats PRC policies present in their models. Balancing the depth of their exposure with their current cash flows, businesses are moving supply chains out of China. Their balancing supports much better responsiveness to PRC changes in behavior. Unwanted PRC policies accelerate managed decoupling. Desirable policies slow down decoupling and reduce disruption.

More broadly, the US government relies too much on tariffs, sanctions, and prohibitions. These tools have their place and purpose. But they are all hammers. Sometimes we need screwdrivers, wrenches, and other tools to widen or constrict incentives that change behaviors in both governmental and commercial spheres.

**8. Currently, what is the best/smartest Chinese policy with respect to the United States?**

From the PRC perspective, recruiting smart, energetic, and rich Americans. The party maintains hundreds of talent recruitment programs. The most visible target STEM talent. Less well-known programs recruit leading political families—not just in the United States, but around the world.

At its simplest, China's state apparatus rewards recruits with cash. More sophisticated programs flatter recruits' egos. The MSS identifies the vulnerabilities of targets and exploits those mercilessly. Victims may not even know the party compromised them until long after the effort succeeds.

**9. What is the worst Chinese policy with respect to the United States?**

From the perspective of what hurts the CPC, stealing $200 to $600 billion of US IP every year is the worst. Sure, CPC-controlled companies get highly valuable IP, but this blade cuts two ways. First, US institutions suffer cuts, but, more and more, the theft enrages Americans. Second, it boldly manifests the Communist Party's disregard for laws. This degrades the party's image as a responsible stakeholder and loosens its appearance of legitimacy to rule over one-eighth of the world's population. History shows quarrelling with legitimate, united, aware, and angry democracies dooms dictators.

**10. If you had the ear of the China policymakers in Washington, DC, what are three things you'd tell them?**

Prepare. Defend. Assert.

> Prepare: Start at home. The Communist Party respects and fears other's strengths. Trust and empower American families and businesses to make decisions that strengthen the US economy. This raises American standards of living (as well as revenue to the US Treasury), reduces threats from the Communist Party, and shows the Communists a path toward raising Chinese living standards in a way that reduces chances for confrontation.
>
> Defend: Preserve the financial advantages that decades of US leadership in prosperity have accrued to the US taxpayer. Protect that position and restrict CPC access to it. Today, the party enjoys access to US investments and loans, as well as lower costs for loans because US taxpayers subsidize CPC borrowing rates at multilateral institutions like the World Bank. Simplifying the process to illustrate the point, if a PRC entity borrows money from the World Bank and does not pay it back, US taxpayers refill World Bank coffers.
>
> Assert: Take confidence in the American narrative. We aim to protect all people's rights. The Communist Party leaves two lanes for easy layup opportunities:

First, find and support factions within the Communist Party who want to move the PRC toward transparency and protecting individual rights (including the authority and responsibility to make decisions) or toward other American interests and ideals. Those factions exist. They cower under their current political masters. Savvy US leaders can play to those blocs' latent strengths without having to call them out.

Second, leverage the contradictions the CPC spouts like a nonstop fountain. The party says it will take Taiwan by force, if necessary, because China has a historical claim to Taiwan. Yet the PRC has negotiated to let Russia keep historically Chinese territories.

The CPC says China is the world's oldest civilization with unbroken continuity. Yet, at the World Bank, it claims China is a developing country. Ask: *How long will it take the oldest civilization on earth to develop*? Recognize, take, and use the CPC's own contradictions to compel both the party itself and the Chinese people to recalibrate their confidence in an otherwise unchallenged environment for setting national policies. For the sake of peace and prosperity in the world and in China—for all people and for the Chinese—use these and myriad more contradictions to nurture discussions with the CPC. Simply put, call them out on it all.

**11. If you had the ear of US policymakers in Beijing, what are three things you'd tell them?**

Listen to Deng Xiaoping. By loosening control of individuals a little bit, by pushing decision-making authority, responsibility, and consequences to families and communes, Deng enhanced the power of the party immensely.

Not just Karl Marx, but others in the West have come up with compelling country-building ideas. Chinese people outside of the PRC have relied on those ideas to generate unparalleled prosperity. Widen the CPC's consideration of other's ideas and open even more opportunities for the Chinese. Doing so, from Beijing's perspective, improves their lives and solidifies foundations for party power.

Understand that Americans cherish preservation, from oceanic reefs in the sea to atmospheric air quality all the way to space. Recent CPC diplomacy and PLA construction have attacked these ideals from beneath the ocean to above the atmosphere. Those attacks reduce the chances of constructive and mutually beneficial cooperation. Beijing can benefit from nurturing cooperation and showing appreciation for American ideals.

**12. What should US companies doing business or thinking about doing business in China know, particularly if such business will involve significant interaction with the state or the CPC?**

Any business worth circumnavigating the northern hemisphere will encounter significant open or obscured interaction with the CPC or its government. Recognizing the fact that the CPC controls every lever of power in the PRC helps US businesses gauge the amount of time, personnel, and investment to expose to the uncertainties of CPC behavior. US businesses' levers of strength—often advanced technologies or superior access to global markets—erode over time. The CPC commands its entire bureaucracy to accelerate the attenuation of those advantages. Beware the myriad vectors CPC-commanded units will take to capture US business advantages.

**13. How strong is Xi's hold over China, and would it make a difference if someone else were in charge?**

Xi Jinping fills a role, like a placeholder. Paramount leaders in the PRC seize and retain power transitorily. Still, it does make a difference who fills the role. Some work to incline the world toward peace and prosperity. Deng Xiaoping did; Xi Jinping does not. Today, Xi holds enough power to keep his job. He may cling to enough power to hold on until he dies. He is riding a tiger he fed and uncaged. Xi doesn't know how to get off without shooting the tiger in the back of the head. US policy, in response to belligerent or peace-upholding behaviors that the PRC exhibits, can and should focus on either shrinking or enlarging the area any CPC-PRC paramount leader has to ride his tiger.

**14. Should America be making a greater effort to teach its young people about China? If so, what would you suggest?**

Yes, absolutely and broadly. We should teach young and old alike about the CPC and other totalitarian regimes. We should emphasize the differences between any system of government that protects elites from the people, instead of the other way around.

Then, we should discipline ourselves, buck up our courage, and promote policies that push decision-making authority and responsibility away from our own and other central governments at national, state, and local levels and toward individuals, families, entrepreneurs, professionals, and communities.

TikTok is a good example. ByteDance controls TikTok. The Communist Party controls ByteDance and causes it to gather intelligence and influence users. The CPC considers TikTok so dangerous it will not allow Chinese people to use it. The party knows TikTok can take over minds, especially young and vulnerable ones. With a bit of discipline, US authorities could and should eliminate TikTok's abuse.

**15. What's your best guess as to what the state of US-China relations will be in five years? Ten years? Twenty-five?**

We're in for a helluva rough ride for at least the next five years. In twenty-five years, the United States and the CPC will have either avoided, or been decimated by, war—war that deploys biological weapons on a scale we have only imagined. War that overwhelms our health care system.

Adapting Andrew Gordon's observation from his 1996 book, *The Rules of the Game: Jutland and British Naval Command*, Americans have enjoyed "the long calm lee" from winning World War II and the Cold War. In that long calm lee, we have had wars of mismatched capabilities. But also during that time, Americans have complacently sunk into expectations of victory, regardless of the confrontation. We have become contented, assuming others either think like we do, or fear our military and economic power so much that we have no worries.

A few years ago, I saw a young man in Colorado proudly wearing a T-shirt emblazoned with "USA Back-to-Back World War Champ." Appreciating his pride, I shivered. It's the cohort just a little younger than him that a war would incinerate . . . before reaching the rest of us.

In reality, the CPC and other totalitarian regimes have found inadequately defended assets to attack. State-funded packs of raiders steal assets from lightly protected—relative to state powers—asset repositories: corporations, institutes and even US government offices. Assets robbed from Americans range from cryptocurrency to IP. *The CPC has turned US balance sheets into battlefields.*

The party has also exerted its influence on pressure points within US capital markets, physical infrastructure, supply chains, and government institutions and offices, not just to retard our responses and appropriate counteractions, but to selectively reward Americans who accelerate or facilitate advancing PRC capabilities.

Amazon describes Gordon's book as a "remarkable saga of genius, tragedy, and passive corruption: of how pragmatism became overwhelmed by theory and vested peacetime interests." Now, the Communist Party has corrupted vested interests to overwhelm the pragmatism US leadership showed after World War II and during the Cold War.

**16. What's your best guess as to what the state of renewable energy, particularly wind power, will be in the United States in five years? Ten years? Twenty-five?**

We may have reached "peak wind" where we should expect a decline in the growth of wind energy installations. We have learned a lot about renewable energy's limitations. We know qualitatively its strengths and weaknesses, its benefits, and many but not all of its costs. Wind energy lowers some costs. But it raises the costs of unreliability. In 2021, winter storm Uri in Texas, which derives about 28% of its electric power from wind, cost consumers billions of dollars as the Texas electrical grid ran devastatingly short of electricity. Operational accommodations for having so much wind energy on the power grid contributed to the causes of massive electricity outages. As currently deployed, wind farm installations also raise the costs of generating electricity by other means. The naturally interruptible character of wind dominoes disruptions across electrical grids. In turn, this forces traditional power plants to start, stop, and restart operations more frequently, which raises maintenance costs. Unpredictable operational cycles also push traditional power plant owners to shun investments in energy-saving technologies that work better in continuous operation. As a country, we are still seeking to balance the benefits of renewable and traditional electric power generation. While we know the character of many costs, we have not studied the costs or the unintended and unknown consequences of extracting energy from the wind. As one thoughtful lawyer, Robert Newell, succinctly observed, "Everything has trade-offs."

Disproportionately, those costs fall hardest on poor people. At a private dinner in 2007, a future Obama cabinet member remarked that climate change was a rich person's problem. Since then, policies claiming to address climate change have eclipsed policies that improve the environment in which people live, work, and play.

When loved ones show up at emergency rooms, we want the lights on. When we show up to work, we want the tools we use to earn our pay to have all the power they need. Watching baseball, we want our hot dogs hot and our cold beer cold.

Putting net-zero emissions policies ahead of scientifically feasible or financially sensical considerations can ravage environments that support people's lives and livelihoods. Worse, such mandates tie scientists, engineers, money, and imaginations to marginally evolving technologies, like wind turbines, instead of letting wildcatters and inventors work out newer energy technologies, like modular fission and nuclear fusion, that can solve our most troubling puzzles.

Your time frames trigger sirens of caution, but here goes: We will not see much change in wind energy installations in the next five years. By ten years, we'll see more deployments of other technologies. In twenty-five years, new generation technologies will push now conventional wind farms to rump status. Piles of wind blades may remind us of our overinvestment in wind energy.

### 17. What about the state of renewable energy, particularly wind power, in China and worldwide over the same time frame?

Russia's war on Ukraine has shined more light on the importance of electricity generation reliability and the strategic primacy of lower energy costs. The PRC consistently plays up wind energy investment, in large part to impress foreigner leaders. The CPC suffers deficiencies in cash and legitimacy. Playing up wind energy activities addresses both.

Economically challenged countries already shun wind energy sources for more reliable systems. Besides depending on the wind itself to blow, wind energy equipment maintenance compounds its unreliability. The equipment requires specialists and getting them, their tools, and replacement parts way up in the air on top of a swaying pole.

Lastly, governments have directed billions to renewable energy projects. In 2022 alone, the US government provided $15.6 billion in renewable energy subsidies. Voters notice that as their tax dollars rise, so do their energy costs, but their reliable access to energy falls. Sustainable energy policies make it harder for them to sustain their families.

Real people need relief now. Real people need an environment that protects their paychecks, keeps the hospital lights burning and the grocery store freezers cold, and defends them from totalitarian regimes.

**18. When you think about the world in which your grandchildren are growing up, what keeps you awake at night?**

Global leadership's lack of concern for the future. Around the world, contests for leadership positions focus on short-term gains for nearby constituents. To our peril, the contestants discount long-term effects for ephemeral near-term gains. With terrifying consistency, world leaders manipulate environmental concerns to move vast resources. Their actions do little to support sustainable efforts to continue improving environments that affirm life. Instead, they use the term "climate change" to build political power. The CPC uses "climate change" to attract investment and camouflage dictatorial intent. US officials sacrifice strategic advantages in energy availability and pricing at the expense of the country's poor.

**19. What one thing would make you sleep better?**

Term limits.

**20. If it were safe for you to travel to China with safe passage home assured, where would you go and what would you do?**

When HT Blade unilaterally recharacterized an equity investment it made to explore the US wind market as a loan to Tang, it set a trap for me. Under PRC law, as Tang's designated legal representative, I am liable for company debts, whether fabricated or real. Still, I long to visit and revisit culturally diverse, historically intriguing, and geologically complex Xinjiang. I'd like to see the karst structures in Guilin and the Shangri-La beauty of Yunnan Province. Chinese history scatters architectural gems throughout the territory. I'd love to see old friends. CPC abuses of Uyghurs and other Chinese and its threats to my travel freedom fuel my drive to write this book.

If I could return to the PRC with the might of the US Navy and Marine Corps behind me, I'd build relationships among US and PRC political and commercial parties. I'd take this book and ask my PRC counterparts to help me find mistakes I may have made. I'd ask them to help me get on with improving the world's most important relationship to get right.

**21. We've spent over a year putting this book together. You've bravely shared many experiences and insights. Are there any last thoughts you'd like to share?**

Well, while possibly politically incorrect, you asked for it!!

Experiences tyrannize our perspectives and, sometimes, lead to clarifying insights. Reading my experiences, you can calibrate my perspectives. My generation grew up yearning to protect the environment. The first Earth Day occurred when I was in seventh grade. Twenty-five years later, my observations of CPC machinations began. Over the next few decades, I watched governmental actions collide with environmental concerns. In many ways, governmental forces erode people's ability to take life-affirming action. Many political regimes—especially totalitarian ones—rank their tenure in power above caring for our world and its people. My experiences bring me to a disconcerting choice: Do I spend my vim and vigor working to fix in time an ever-changing environment, or should I nurture positive changes within the natural and political environment we live in that support and affirm life in its complexities and needs?

A photograph from March 2022 distills my dilemma.[3] (Image 11) Taken on a crisp, sunny day, it shows 109 empty baby strollers occupying a town square in Lviv, Ukraine. The scene drives attention to a truly existential, environmental peril: *Totalitarians create environments that extinguish children's lives today.* We must remember that we are protecting the environment so it might nurture life. Protecting environments that

[3] Bill Chappell, "109 empty strollers sit in a Lviv square, representing children killed in the war," NPR, March 18, 2022. https://www.npr.org/2022/03/18/1087536180/empty-strollers-lviv-children-killed. Photo credit: Yuriy Dyachyshyn/AFP via Getty Images.

sustain life requires leading with compassion for people and approaching enshrined climate change conclusions with humility.

Regarding showing compassion for people: My interactions with CPC-led companies provided firsthand proof of a totalitarian regime's disregard for individual lives and liberties. Russia's war in Ukraine is captured in daily photographs, similar to the one mentioned above, that reflect an identical disdain. When we measure concerns for the environment, we need to include concerns for how the environment supports and protects life *today*, not just in an unknown future.

Regarding ensconced conclusions about fossil fuels: At least two scientific questions support reserving some doubt, or harboring some humility, for the appropriateness of energy policies that shutter hydrocarbon production. As a wind energy company executive for over twenty years, I have spoken at symposia from Shanghai to San Francisco. Still, I have yet to find an answer to a simple question: *What unintended effect or consequence might extracting energy from the wind cause to the environment?*

Wind energy companies understand that their business is to extract energy from the natural environment. At HT Blade, we designed airfoils to optimize taking energy out of a windy environment and converting it to mechanical energy for generating electricity. Another picture worth a thousand words makes obvious two environmental effects of taking energy from wind.[4] Taken as dew points and temperatures converge, the photograph of downwind condensation reveals cooling and shows turbulence caused by the wind turbines. Still, wind energy businesses seldom measure the effects of their energy extractions.

It could be that neither of them matter, and wringing energy out of the wind has no meaningful consequences. However, few either know or publish results that address the question. Mark Jacobson, a Stanford University professor of civil and environmental engineering, calculates that 78,000 WTGs in the Gulf Coast could weaken hurricanes' destructive

[4] Rongyong Zhao, Daheng Dong, Cuiling Li, Steven Liu, Hao Zhang, Miyuan Li, and Wenzhong Shen, "An Improved Power Control Approach for Wind Turbine Fatigue Balancing in an Offshore Wind Farm," Appendix A, MDPI, March 26, 2020, https://www.mdpi.com/1996-1073/13/7/1549.

power.[5] (The United States has about 70,000 wind turbines.) Sapping hurricanes' destructive power sounds appealing, but what unintended effects might this cause? Altering the hurricane weather pattern may, for example, reduce rainfall on US farms. The pioneers of electric power may not have anticipated negative consequences of burning fossil fuels, or they may have anticipated them and weighed the effects as worth the benefits derived, such as cooking, cooling, keeping operating room lights running, and other essential functions.

Another phenomenon could further encourage clean energy champions to reconsider their confidence levels. Earth's magnetic north is moving faster than it has in a long time. This has forced several airports across the United States to change designations for runway headings. *Could variations in earth's predominantly iron-nickel outer core cause more climate change than releases of $CO_2$? Could those variations affect the eastward movement of tornado alley and the rainfall predominance line in the United States?*

Remembering the certainty of innocents' injuries from totalitarian strikes, observing that irrationally exuberant renewable energy policies push economic power away from the United States and to the PRC's totalitarian regime, and considering the uncertainties of just two understudied environmental questions, ought to encourage renewable energy advocates to choose protecting life over preserving atmospheric gas balances at all costs irrespective of the interim effects on human life across the world. Helpfully, long-term financial interests encourage a similar evaluation.

Having married a farmer's daughter, I'm keenly aware of climate change and, looking to leave this world better off for my efforts, I appreciate needing to use petroleum products thoughtfully. Still, I recognize that diversifying generation sources balances electricity grids. In turn, this balance creates a more stable energy market, which enables more renewable generation.

---

[5] Mark Fischetti, "Offshore Wind Farms Could Knock Down Hurricanes," *Scientific American*, February 26, 2014. https://www.scientificamerican.com/article/offshore-wind-farms-could-knock-down-hurricanes1.

Upholding a vibrant economy creates similar effects. Populations that enjoy reliably delivered and competitively priced electricity can support energy transitions more dependably and with fewer interruptions to healthy environments. Again, disciplined analysis of environmental priorities improves the financial environment that lifts renewable energy investments. More importantly, it has the greater effect of lifting the quality of life for those at the lower end of our world's wealth spectrum.

Those deeply invested in an environment-only narrative may find this conclusion counterintuitive, but US policy should rank attenuating totalitarians' capabilities ahead of constraining US hydrocarbon production. Raising US oil and gas production, in the long run, protects environments that sustain life. It pushes US pump prices down for the taxpayers whose dollars send weapons and ammunition to Ukraine, and it bolsters the economic power of a democratically governed people. In geopolitical terms, subordinating climate doctrine to compassion for people keeps cash away from totalitarians and returns strategic leverage to the United States.

Some say, if we don't figure out climate change, we're toast, but if we don't figure out how to balance separately noble priorities with humility, thoughtfulness, and respect for each other's perspectives, we're toast anyway. In existential terms, it's the only choice that can make a difference in a time frame that matters to those facing fear, injustice, oppression, indeed annihilation from totalitarians.

# Appendix

July 20, 2015
2015 年 7 月 20 日

Mr. Lin Zuoming
林左鸣先生
Chairman
董事长
Aviation Industry Corporation of China ("AVIC")
中国航空工业集团公司 ("中航工业")

Dear Chairman Lin,
尊敬的林董事长:

We write seeking your assistance to repair Tang Energy Group ("Tang")-AVIC relations and rectify AVIC misconduct materially harming our commercial interests. This includes preventing AVIC Heavy Machinery from taking actions that seem intended to expropriate our investment position in AVIC HT Blade.
我们写信寻求您的帮助来修复美腾能源集团("美腾")与中航工业集团的关系, 纠正中航工业损坏我们商业利益的错误行为. 这包括防止中航重机采取看似意在剥夺我们在中航惠腾投资地位的行动.

Tang has worked with AVIC building globally competitive businesses for 20 years and remains committed to supporting AVIC's commercial objectives. Tang firmly believes that the future of AVIC as a globally competitive corporation depends on elevating its business practices, beginning with those carried out within and among AVIC subordinate units. More broadly, as a state-owned enterprise (SOE), AVIC's actions directly reflect the Chinese government's choices and impacts the perceptions of the US business community when dealing with Chinese investors and firms.
美腾与中航工业合作建造有全球竞争力的业务有 20 年了,并且一直致力于支持中航工业的商业目标. 美腾坚信中航工业将来成为有全球竞争力的公司取决于提升其商业行为, 从中航工业内部和其下属企业之间开始进行. 更广泛地讲,作为一个国有企业(SOE), 中航工业的行为直接反映出中国政府的选择, 并且影响到美国商界与中国投资者和公司进行交往的看法.

In support of elevating AVIC business practices, you should be aware of matters involving AVIC agents violating Party discipline and Chinese law, notably: 1) theft of AVIC HT Blade cash assets by AVIC Huiyang, 2) apparent graft by AVIC HT Blade leadership, 3) illegal fees

Tang Energy Group, Ltd. □ 4925 Greenville Avenue □ Suite 1020 □ Dallas, Texas 75206 USA 1

collected from HT Blade by both AVIC and AVIC Heavy Machinery, and 4) AVIC's breach of its US Soaring Wind joint venture agreement.
要支持提升中航工业的商业行为, 您应该了解关于中航工业代理公司违反党纪和中国法律的事宜, 特别是: 1) 中航惠阳盗窃中航惠腾现金资产, 2) 明显的来自中航惠腾领导层的受贿, 3) 中航工业和中航重机从中航惠腾收取的非法费用, 及 4) 中航工业违反其美国 Soaring Wind 合资公司协议.

**AVIC Huiyang Theft**
**中航惠阳盗窃行为**

In 2010, AVIC Huiyang took cash assets totaling RMB 52,029,820 (US $8.38 million) from AVIC HT Blade bank accounts. AVIC Huiyang argues that it took this action at the direction of AVIC headquarters, demanding profit distribution to AVIC HT Blade shareholders. In fact, AVIC protected AVIC Huiyang's illegal behavior and criticized the victims, HT Blade and its other shareholders, of that illegal behavior. (Copy of AVIC's criticism attached.)
2010年, 中航惠阳从中航惠腾的银行账户提走人民币 52,029,820 元 (838 万美元). 中航惠阳争辩其这样做是在中航工业集团的指导下, 要求分配利润给中航惠腾的股东. 实际上,中航工业保护了中航惠阳的非法行为并且批评了此不法行为的受害者, 惠腾及惠腾其他股东. (附上中航工业批评信的复印件)

- These violations of discipline and law by AVIC management attract alarming attention and erode the competitiveness and reputation of AVIC as a premier Chinese SOE.
  中航工业管理层的这些违纪违法行为引起惊人的关注,并且消弱了中航工业作为中国首屈一指的国有企业的竞争力和声誉.
- This amount far exceeds:
  此金额远远超过:
  - the RMB 20,000,000 (US $3.5 million) that disgraced Party official Bo Xilai improperly received,
    名誉扫地的共产党官员薄熙来非正当收取的人民币 20,000,000 元(350 万美金)
  - the estimated RMB 40,000,000 (US $6.5 million) improper receipts that condemned General Xu Caihou and his family, and
    备受谴责的徐才厚将军及其家人不正当收取的人民币 40,000,000 元(640 美金), 及
  - the RMB 1,117,170 (US $180,000) that ruined former Politburo Standing Committee member Zhou Yongkang.
    毁掉前中共中央政治局常委周永康的人民币 1,117,170 (18 万美金).

**AVIC HT Blade Resin Supplier Cover-up, Corruption**
**包庇树脂供应商, 腐败**

Also in 2010, AVIC HT Blade executives signed contracts with new resin suppliers, leading to the procurement of inferior resin causing at least RMB 500,000,000 (US $80.5 million) in losses to AVIC HT Blade, derailing IPO plans and its superior market position.

也是在 2010 年,中航惠腾高管与新树脂供应商签订了合同, 引发劣质树脂胶的采购造成中航惠腾至少人民币 500,000,000 元(8 千零 5 十万美金)的损失, 使其独立上市(IPO)计划及其优越的市场地位脱离轨道.

- In 2013, AVIC officer Mr. Liu Jinzhong called for an investigation into the AVIC HT Blade contracts with new resin suppliers. No investigation occurred.
  在 2013 年, 中航工业官员刘晋忠先生要求对中航惠腾与新树脂供应商签署的合同进行调查. 没有任何调查发生.
- At this time, Tang Wind Energy does not know the full extent to which Mr. Liu's superiors may have been aware of, participated in this misconduct or thwarted the investigation that Mr. Liu demanded.
  此时,美腾风能不知道刘先生的上级(上司)可能已经意识到,参与到此不正当行为,或阻挠刘先生要求进行的调查的完全程度.

On multiple occasions, Tang has requested investigations and been ignored. More recently, Chairman Liu Zhongwen promised to support an investigation into the matter. This has not been initiated, and AVIC HT Blade is apparently unable to answer simple questions about its resin suppliers, including their names and the amount paid to them, respectively. Oddly, if not irresponsibly, AVIC HT Blade is defending a lawsuit from Sinovel over resin defective blades. A proper investigation could answer why AVIC HT Blade is not pursuing the resin supplier for off-setting damages.
在多个场合下, 美腾要求进行调查,并且都被忽视了. 近期,中航惠腾董事长刘忠文承诺支持对此事情的调查. 此调查还没被启动, 并且很明显中航惠腾对简单的关于树脂供应商的问题,包括他们的名称,分别支付给他们的金额, 都不能回答. 如果不是不负责任,奇怪的是,中航惠腾在辩护华锐对使用劣质树脂的叶片的诉讼案. 一个合适的调查能够回答为什么中航惠腾不去追寻树脂供应商来赔偿损失.

- Tang's independent efforts uncovered that just one resin contract approximated RMB 186,200,000 (US $30 million).
  美腾的独立 努力查出仅一个树脂合同就达约人民币 186,200,000 元(3 千万美金).
- Conclusively, a network of AVIC officers is taking advantage of their positions improperly, misappropriating the People's assets, to gain financially through new resin contracts.
  确凿地讲, 一个中航工业官员的网络不正当地利用他们的地位, 不正当地使用人民资产,通过新树脂合同获得资金.
- Ultimately, understanding who benefitted from these contracts will be vital for recovering AVIC HT Blade's reputation and standing as a champion Chinese enterprise.
  最后,弄清楚谁从这些合同中受益对恢复中航惠腾的名誉和作为一个冠军中国企业而站立起来是至关重要的.

Chairman Lin - 林董事长
July 20, 2015 - 2015 年 7 月 20 日

**Illegal AVIC Coordination Fees and AVIC HM Management Fees**
**不合法的中航工业协调费和中航重机管理费**

In recent years, AVIC HT Blade paid "management fees" to AVIC Heavy Machinery, which AVIC HT Blade management described as "illegal." Despite the illegality, accounting records show that AVIC HT paid these fees, blatantly violating HT Blade's corporate independence.
最近这些年, 中航惠腾支付"管理费用"给中航重机, 中航惠腾管理层(对此费用)描述为"不合法". 尽管不合法,会计记录显示中航惠腾支付了这些费用, 公然违反了惠腾的公司独立性.

- Tang management does not know the purpose of these fees or whether or not they are applied to other AVIC subordinate entities.
  美腾管理层不知道这些费用的用途, 或这些费用是否适用于其它中航工业下属企业.
- AVIC HT Blade's Board of Director never approved these fees, as China's Company Law requires.
  根据中国公司法的要求, 惠腾的董事会从未批准这些费用.

**AVIC's Breach of Contract**
**中航工业违反合同**

After establishing a joint venture with Tang in the US—Soaring Wind Energy, LLC— in 2008, AVIC violated its contractual exclusivity agreements, executing billions of dollars in wind power development projects worldwide. After numerous attempts to resolve this breach with AVIC management, time forced Tang to initiate arbitration proceedings in June 2014.
与美腾在美国成立了一个合资公司—Soaring Wind Energy, LLC 之后—在 2008 年,中航工业违反了其合同的唯一性(独家性)协议, 在全球范围内执行了数以亿计美元的风电开发项目. 在多次试图与中航工业管理层解决此违约(事宜)后,时间迫使美腾于 2014 年 6 月启动仲裁程序.

- AVIC does not dispute its breach of contract. AVIC senior managers in the US attest to this breach and encouraged Tang to seek redress from AVIC headquarters in China.
  中航工业对违反合同没有提出争议.中航工业的高级管理层在美国证明了此违约, 并鼓励美腾从中航工业在中国的总部寻求解决办法.
- AVIC leaders in China remain uncooperative, claiming "non-participation" in these proceedings and forfeiting benefits of direct engagement and resolution.
  中航工业在中国的领导保持不合作, 自称在这些诉讼中 "不参与" 及对直接参与和解决的益处弃权.
- In reaction to these proceedings, AVIC HT Blade is violating Tang's shareholder rights and seeking forfeiture of Tang's HT Blade ownership.
  在对这些诉讼做出反应时,中航惠腾违反了美腾的股东权利, 并寻求没收美腾对惠腾的所有权.

Chairman Lin - 林董事长
July 20, 2015 - 2015 年 7 月 20 日

**Harming US-China Commercial Relations**
**损害中美商业关系**

AVIC's misconduct considerably harms broader China-US commercial relations. Tang energetically supports cooperative China-US relations, which have included advocating for China to receive MFN status and join the WTO. AVIC once considered Tang a "Friend of AVIC," and, in 2009, AVIC senior management awarded that high honor to Tang.
中航工业的错误行为极大损害了更为广泛的中美商业关系. 美腾大力支持合作性的中美关系, 这包括倡导中国获得最惠国待遇并加入世贸组织. 中航工业在把美腾视为"中航工业朋友"的时候,在 2009 年,中航工业高级管理层将此最高荣誉颁发给美腾.

- Tang has remained true to its goal of resolving this dispute privately and discreetly, but AVIC's attorneys have made the disagreement widely public by filing three court cases and appealing its losses to US 5th Circuit Court of Appeals.
  美腾一直坚守着私下和谨慎地解决这一争端的目标, 但是中航工业的律师已通过提起 3 个法庭诉讼,并在败诉后向美国第 5 巡回上诉法庭提请申诉,将此分歧广泛公开化.

- Resolving this arbitration provides an opportunity to demonstrate the maturity of our relationship while avoiding unwanted scrutiny on AVIC activities in the US and harming broader US-China commercial relations.
  解决此仲裁提供了一个机会来展示我们关系的成熟性, 避免了对中航工业在美国活动的不必要的审查及损害更广泛的中美商业关系.

Again, timing challenges us. President Xi Jinping will be visiting the United States in September, on the heels of AVIC-Tang arbitration proceedings. Even as arbitration proceedings are moving forward, Tang stands ready to resolve this dispute in a mutually beneficial manner and seeks your support in this endeavor.
同样,时间向我们提出挑战. 习近平主席将于 9 月份来访美国, 紧跟在中航工业-美腾诉讼之后. 即使仲裁程序正在向前进行, 美腾随时准备以互利的方式解决这一争端，并寻求您对此努力的支持。

Respectfully submitted,
此致,

Tang Energy Group, Ltd.
美腾能源集团

By: ______________________
E. Patrick Jenevein III
CEO 首席执行官

Printed in the USA
CPSIA information can be obtained
at www.ICGtesting.com
LVHW041022210924
R18366600001B/R183666PG790808LVX00001B/1/J

9 781960 865229